PROSECUTING POVERTY, CRIMINALIZING CARE

At the height of the opiate epidemic, Tennessee lawmakers made it a crime for a pregnant woman to transmit narcotics to a fetus. They promised that charging new mothers with this crime would help them receive the treatment and support they often desperately need. In *Prosecuting Poverty, Criminalizing Care*, Wendy Bach describes the law's actual effect through meticulous examination of the cases of 120 women who were prosecuted for this crime. Drawing on quantitative and qualitative data, Bach demonstrates that both prosecuting "fetal assault" and institutionalizing the all-too-common idea that criminalization is a road to care, lead at best to clinically dangerous and corrupt treatment, and at worst, and far more often, to an insidious smokescreen obscuring harsh punishment. Urgent, instructive, and humane, this retelling demands we stop criminalizing care and instead move toward robust and respectful systems that meet the real needs of families in poor communities.

Wendy A. Bach is Professor of Law at the University of Tennessee where she teaches primarily in the clinical program. Over the last twenty-five years, first as a practicing public-interest lawyer, and for the last seventeen years as a law professor, Bach has represented poor clients in the courts and systems highlighted in *Prosecuting Poverty, Criminalizing Care*. She is a nationally recognized scholar in the field of poverty law and has published several law review articles on the relationship between social support and punishment.

T0371442

Prosecuting Poverty, Criminalizing Care

Wendy A. Bach
University of Tennessee College of Law

CAMBRIDGE
UNIVERSITY PRESS

CAMBRIDGE
UNIVERSITY PRESS

University Printing House, Cambridge CB2 8BS, United Kingdom

One Liberty Plaza, 20th Floor, New York, NY 10006, USA

477 Williamstown Road, Port Melbourne, VIC 3207, Australia

314–321, 3rd Floor, Plot 3, Splendor Forum, Jasola District Centre,
New Delhi – 110025, India

103 Penang Road, #05–06/07, Visioncrest Commercial, Singapore 238467

Cambridge University Press is part of the University of Cambridge.

It furthers the University's mission by disseminating knowledge in the pursuit of
education, learning, and research at the highest international levels of excellence.

www.cambridge.org
Information on this title: www.cambridge.org/9781108474832
DOI: 10.1017/9781108693783

First published 2022

A catalogue record for this publication is available from the British Library.

Library of Congress Cataloging-in-Publication Data
Names: Bach, Wendy A., author.
Title: Prosecuting poverty, criminalizing care / Wendy A. Bach, University of
Tennessee School of Law.
Description: Cambridge, United Kingdom ; New York, NY : Cambridge University
Press, 2022. | Includes index.
Identifiers: LCCN 2021060071 (print) | LCCN 2021060072 (ebook) | ISBN
9781108474832 (hardback) | ISBN 9781108465533 (paperback) | ISBN
9781108693783 (ebook)
Subjects: LCSH: Substance abuse in pregnancy – Law and legislation – Tennessee –
Criminal provisions. | Pregnant women – Legal status, laws, etc. – Tennessee. | Fetus –
Legal status, laws, etc. – Tennessee.
Classification: LCC KFT567.C5 B33 2022 (print) | LCC KFT567.C5 (ebook) |
DDC 345.768/05042–dc23/eng/20220110
LC record available at https://lccn.loc.gov/2021060071
LC ebook record available at https://lccn.loc.gov/2021060072

ISBN 978-1-108-47483-2 Hardback
ISBN 978-1-108-46553-3 Paperback

CONTENTS

FIGURES

ACKNOWLEDGMENTS

This book was years in the making. The project was born in the fall of 2015, during a ClassCrits conference hosted at my home institution, the University of Tennessee College of Law. After a plenary session focused on how lawyers and scholars might support mobilization, an organizer from Healthy and Free Tennessee walked up and asked me if I might be able to help figure out what happened in the cases of the women prosecuted in Tennessee for fetal assault. This book and the data it contains originated from that request, and I hope the data I have provided along the way has been helpful to that organization. Thanks go first to the activists on the ground, from Healthy and Free Tennessee and SisterReach and the staff at National Advocates for Pregnant Women, whose collective work to protect and promote Reproductive Justice is an inspiration. Special thanks to SisterReach and in particular to Dr. Orisha Bowers, whose research on the effect of Tennessee's fetal assault law is featured in this book.

Over the six years it took to gather and analyze data and produce this work, I was assisted and supported by both institutions and individuals. My home institution, the University of Tennessee College of Law, has supported me in a myriad of ways that make projects like this possible. First and likely most importantly, the faculty and administration at Tennessee have thought long and hard about what it takes to support faculty as they seek to be both strong clinical teachers and engaged scholars. The job I have reflects this careful thought and dedication, and I know of no other law school that does this as well. I am very lucky in that respect. The University of Tennessee has also provided substantial support to this project in the form of grants for transcription, summer research stipends, salaries for research assistants, travel grants, and a much-needed sabbatical in the spring of 2019. My Tennessee colleagues have also been generous, in everything from summer forums to reading draft chapters to encouragment in the hallways. Outside of the clinic, I am particularly grateful to Teri Baxter, who in her job as associate dean learned Institutional Review Board processes along with me and listened to and challenged my interpretations of stories from the interviews, to Ben Barton, whose constant encouragement was essential, and to Penny White, who generously introduced me to several of the legal professionals in East Tennessee whose voices are heard in this book.

My colleagues in the clinic, Eric Amarante, Sherley Cruz, Brian Krumm, and Joy Radice, have, in our informal scholarship brown bags, read pieces of this book way too many times and the whole thing at least once. They are smart and generous, and I could not be luckier to call them colleagues and friends. Special thanks go to Joy Radice, without whom I can honestly say that this book would not have been finished. Even in the best and most supportive institutions, balancing clinical teaching and lawyering responsibilities with a project of this size and scope is no easy task. Client needs are always urgent and have to come first in ways that can make research and writing hard. Countless times, when the pull of those urgent needs might have slowed down this project, Joy stepped in, structuring semesters in a way that allowed some focus on scholarship even when we taught, and, probably most importantly, body-blocking me from being the one who took the phone call, ran to court, or wrote a brief by doing the work herself.

In the larger University of Tennessee community, I am particularly grateful to Dr. Patrick Grzanka, who was the first person I talked to about qualitative interviewing and who, for years, answered every question I had.

Beyond the University of Tennessee, I am grateful to the many institutions and organizations that supported this work. The two years I spent as a Bellow Scholar were invaluable. I have given talks on this subject at ClassCrits, the University of Baltimore Applied Feminism Conference, at least one Poverty Law Conference, Muhlenberg College, the Law and Society Conference, the Law and Political

Economy Conference, the University of Cincinnati College of Law, and the Association of American Law Schools Clinical Conference. On each occasion, I have been welcomed and supported by friends, have received valuable feedback that pushed the project forward, and have been supported to keep going.

Special thanks to a few colleagues across the country. First to Janet Moore, whose belief in this project has been a bottomless well that I have tapped quite a lot and who read and commented on the entire manuscript at a crucial moment. Next to Maxine Eichner, Clare Huntington, and Jane Spinak who spent hours reading a full draft and workshopping it with me in the summer of 2020 and who have each fielded questions and given crucial guidance. And finally to Lynn Paltrow who has pushed my thinking and deepened my understanding in countless ways; to Amy Bauman, who supported a deep dive into some medical literature; to Nina Martin, who shared research insights as I dove into the daunting project of hunting down case files; to Stephen Patrick and Mishka Terplan, who both took to the time to teach me; to Karen Tani, who pushed me to think more carefully about history; to Grace Howard, whose dissertation and conversation was inspiring; to Michele Goodwin who visited Tennessee and brainstormed with me at a crucial moment; and to Khiara Bridges, whose critical insights have made this project better. While I am grateful for the support and insight of all these colleagues, all mistakes are, of course, my own.

On the research front, I am deeply grateful to everyone who consented to an interview for this book. Most of them are named in the pages that follow. They were generous with their time, their knowledge, and my questions. Several have become colleagues and friends, and I have learned tremendously from them.

This project would also not exist were it not for the labor of student research assistants who worked on the project. Many of them have gone on to amazing careers of their own, and it has been a pleasure to work with and learn from all of them. In the order in which they worked on the project, thanks go to Hannah Hunt, Christine Ball-Blakely, Heather Good, Eboni James, Emma Steele, Daniel Zydiel, Lindsey English, Kelsi Pratt, Della Winters, Cristina Spear, and Samantha Bueller-Young. Collectively these students spent hundreds of hours sending out and following up on record requests, organizing systems, creating annotated bibliographies, analyzing case files, researching doctrine, writing footnotes, editing, and, most importantly, reflecting with me on the story that we were learning and crafting from all of this work. Della Winters, who is a sociology professor in her own right today, spent a summer on the project supporting me as I carried out many of the interviews. Her wisdom, knowledge, and endless curiosity made this book better. Numerous staff members, in sheriff's offices, in District Attorney's offices, and in courts across Tennessee, fielded our questions and hunted down records. Many went above and beyond. Similarly Generosa Kakoti, from the Tennessee Department of Health, was tremendously generous in helping me to obtain and understand birth record and hospital discharge data.

Finally, I am deeply indebted to several members of my large and generous family. My mother, Marilyn Bach, who started a PhD program at MIT when women did not do that sort of thing, has had my back in every way forever. My brother Peter Bach, whose own data-charged muckraking constantly inspires me, has fielded endless questions, lent me his skeptical eye, and provided constant encouragement. My sister Katie Bach is a wonder, in the sheer power of her intellect, in the professional dedication to ensuring economic justice, in her ability to navigate the challenges life has thrown at her, and in her fearsome support of those she loves. I am lucky to be one of those people and could not be more grateful for the brainstorms, the strong opinions, the wry humor, the television and vampire novel recommendations, the willingness to listen, and the constant belief in this project.

Finally, neither this book nor anything else in my life would happen without my partner and my son, Carol O'Donnell and Cayden Bach-O'Donnell. Carol helped me build a life that makes it all possible. Her endless curiosity about the stories of humanity has pushed me to reach deeper as I endeavor to share the stories in this book. Together Carol and Cayden have listened to me talk about this project for years and have tolerated countless weeks and months of losing me to it. They have fended for themselves when I should have been there, and they have met my anxieties with humor, love, and the crucial provision of snacks. I could not be more grateful.

INTRODUCTION

In the spring of 2013, in a hearing room in Tennessee, a group of legislators came together to create a new crime – the crime of fetal assault. A woman would be guilty of this crime if she took illegal narcotics while pregnant and her child was harmed as a result. The maximum punishment for this crime was eleven months and twenty-nine days in jail. Ultimately over the course of two years, about 120 mostly low-income women – rural, urban, Black, and white – would be prosecuted in Tennessee for fetal assault. The law was justified, in large part, by a very strange and deeply disturbing set of ideas: that the only way to help women who used illegal drugs while pregnant was to prosecute them, and that the prosecution itself was not only a road to treatment but was actually a form of treatment in and of itself. Despite these perhaps benevolent seeming ideas, the reality was quite different. Overwhelmingly, those women pled guilty and faced sentencing. Despite the strong assertions by the law's proponents that the prosecution was a road to accessing treatment, it appears that very few women actually got access to treatment through prosecution. Instead, they got what the criminal system almost always delivers: they were placed on probation, they went to jail, and they found themselves owing sometimes thousands of dollars in criminal debt. At the same time, these same women were subject to a child welfare system that equated their substance use during pregnancy with severe abuse and as grounds for rapid termination of their parental rights. Moreover, when we pull the lens out from the individual cases to the legal and social welfare systems in which their cases were embedded – the healthcare system, the child welfare system, and the criminal legal system – we see that for these deeply stigmatized women and others like them, to the extent they do receive any care, that care is corrupted by its location within or near punishment systems. In 2016, though, the Tennessee fetal assault law expired, putting an end to these prosecutions.

It's a fair question, then, to ask why one might want to read (or write) an entire book about these particular prosecutions and the systems in which they took place. The answer, quite simply, is that the ideas that drove the creation of this crime – that criminalization is a road to care, that the care provided at the end of that road is corrupted by its linkage to punishment, and that, for those society deeply stigmatizes, criminalized care is all they deserve – sit firmly at the heart of the US criminal, child welfare, and social welfare systems. The systems at the heart of this book operate on the assumption that poor people and poor communities are not worthy of care in the best sense of that word. In fact, if we look not at what is said but instead at what is done, not at what some in power purport but at the operation of the systems they create, it is clear that the United States has a set of rules and systems that assume that whole categories of deeply stigmatized poor people do not deserve what this book broadly terms care – economic security, housing, healthcare, safety, or support. In poor communities, systems might dole out some meager support, some meager approximation of care, but there is always a high price to pay. That price all too often comes in the form of stigmatization, surveillance, and punishment. Even beyond this, these purported offers of care are often nothing more than a facade behind which we find mostly subordination. A central idea at the heart of these systems is what this book terms *criminalizing care* – the idea and practice of linking the provision of care (in the Tennessee example healthcare and drug treatment) to involvement in systems that punish and the devastating outcomes that result. So, the Tennessee story, and this book, is not only a story about the operation of one law in the lives of 120 women. It is also a book that highlights that story as an extreme and crystal-clear example of criminalizing care, a phenomenon at the heart of US social welfare, child welfare, and criminal system policy.

It's important to note, at the outset, that both the ideas that drive these phenomena and the systems that manifest and carry out these ideas have everything to do with race, gender, and socioeconomic status. Both the ideas and the systems that have resulted were originally built to punish and control poor, Black women and their families. But these systems also draw on and perpetuate a complicated mix of white privilege, when society sees addiction in white communities as a healthcare need rather than a crime wave, and long-existing stigmas around and aggressive efforts to control reproduction by poor women, both white and Black. The book will touch on and attempt to tease out this complicated race, class, and gender story and the way that these stories underpin and support what is termed here criminalized care.

To step back before diving deeper in, it is important to understand how this book uses the words in the title. While prosecuting poverty is relatively straightforward – the criminal system targets, in the fetal assault example and beyond, those in poverty in a way that deepens that poverty – the meaning of the next two words are less immediately clear. Criminalizing, or criminalization, in its most basic form, happens when society uses criminal law and criminal systems (think criminal courts, police, probation, and parole) to address a particular social problem. So, we criminalize conduct like murder, rape, robbery, and assault, and individuals who commit those crimes are subject to the criminal system, with all its punishment and surveillance tools and actors. But criminalization here also refers to three other, broader phenomena: first, criminalization occurs when society makes conduct criminal when a social welfare solution is available (for example making it a crime to sleep outside and then prosecuting homeless people for that crime). Second, criminalization occurs when social welfare programs are built to make its participants feel like criminals, for example by fingerprinting welfare applicants and subjecting them to extensive monitoring that is structured in a way that is eerily similar to probation. Third and finally, criminalization occurs when seeking assistance in a social welfare program puts stigmatized members of society at risk for punishment in the criminal and child welfare system, for example when welfare recipients are drug tested and those drug test results are shared with child welfare and probation staff or here, when seeking care during pregnancy, labor and delivery leads to prosecution.

The next word in the title, care, as used in this book, is intentionally broad and evocative of basic human rights. In its deepest and broadest sense, care is something society owes to its members. It is a set of basic supports – housing, economic security, healthcare, safety, education. But care as it is used here is not only about what society should provide to its members. It is also, crucially, about how it should be provided. Care, as it is used here and in its best form, is inextricable from dignity. Society provides that form of care when it does so in a way that enhances, rather than undermines, the dignity and well-being of the individual, family, or community receiving that care. Throughout this book, because the volume's prime example is about substance use during pregnancy, the forms of care the book talks about the most are obstetrics, gynecology, and addiction treatment, but keep in mind as you read that these forms of healthcare are merely examples of kinds of care that society sometimes provides and that should be provided in a form that enhances the dignity and well-being of those who require it.

When it comes to care, one of the central arguments of this book is that there is a wide gulf between both the substance and the form of care available in the United States and that this gulf breaks down on race and class lines. When it comes to those in poverty, many of whom society deeply stigmatizes, what society provides falls far short of a robust form of care. Instead, when it comes to women like those prosecuted for fetal assault in Tennessee, care is all too often criminalized. Offers of care are often nothing more than a smokescreen for punishment; care comes at the risk of severe punishment, and, even when care is provided, its proximity to punishment systems degrades the quality of care itself. This book highlights the prosecution of 120 women for fetal assault as a way to understand criminalizing care: the ideas that drive criminalized care, the means by which criminalized care comes into existence in society's systems, and what actually happens, both to people and to care, when criminalized care dominates parts of the healthcare, child welfare, and criminal systems. Finally, this book asks what the United States might do to shrink our systems of punishment, build better systems of care outside of and away from punishment, and, in the meantime, erect firm walls between systems that can punish and systems that deliver support.

To tell the fetal assault story as an example of criminalized care, the book draws on several bodies of data.[1] The criminal court case files are central to the story. These files, which the research team gathered over nearly a year from court clerks, prosecutors, and sheriffs across the state, lay out, in tellingly bureaucratic form, who was prosecuted and what happened in the prosecutions. Through them, we learn about the charges that were brought, how much jail time a woman served, whether she pled guilty, what sentence was imposed, what she was required to do, whether there is any indication that treatment was offered as a part of the case, and what fees and other costs were assessed. In addition, the story relies on the birth records of infants who were born with neonatal abstinence syndrome (the condition that those who supported the law said they were targeting) when the law was in effect. Those files enable us to learn more demographic information about the women who were prosecuted and, crucially, to assess how effective the criminal system was at targeting women who gave birth to infants diagnosed with neonatal abstinence syndrome, the syndrome purportedly targeted by the fetal assault law.

The bulk of the remaining data comes from in-depth interviews of professionals in the healthcare, child welfare, and criminal legal systems in Tennessee. Over the course of about two years, I interviewed over forty professionals in those systems both about their particular views and experiences in the fetal assault cases and about their views and practices about providing care close to and inside punishment systems. In addition, I interviewed several medical experts, both in Tennessee and nationally, about best practices for women who are pregnant and struggling with substance use disorder. Finally, although the qualitative research for this book focused primarily on the systems and the views of system actors, the voices of the women who were prosecuted are also heard here. These voices come from public records, from moments in which women who were subject to prosecution testified or spoke publicly, and, crucially, from qualitative research on the implementation of the fetal assault law conducted by SisterReach, a nonprofit based in Memphis, Tennessee "that supports the reproductive autonomy of women and teens of color, poor and rural women, LGBTQIA+ people and their families through the framework of Reproductive Justice" and whose mission is to "empower our base to lead healthy lives, raise healthy families and live in healthy and sustainable communities."[2]

Ultimately, *Prosecuting Poverty, Criminalizing Care* seeks to use the example of the fetal assault law to convince you of several interconnected ideas. First, the United States targets criminalized care not at all people who engage in particular stigmatized conduct (in this case taking illegal drugs while pregnant) but only at poor people, who are racialized in very specific ways. Second, when those in power put forward the idea of offering care in the criminal system, often that's just a smokescreen. Instead, for this group of stigmatized poor people, they are prosecuted. Prosecution in turn leads not only to deepened poverty but goes hand-in-hand with a deeply degraded form of justice. Third, in poor communities in Tennessee and well beyond, care is linked to punishment: to the extent that society is willing to provide care in poor communities, it has increasingly offered that care in ways that are closely linked to systems that punish. And locating care within punitive systems fundamentally corrupts the structure and quality of that care. That corruption plays out in public assistance and healthcare, in child welfare, and in the criminal legal system itself. And finally, the book seeks to convince you that there is a better way, that we can and must shrink our punishment systems, erect firm legal walls between systems that support and systems that punish, and invest substantial resources in creating systems of care that promote the dignity and well-being of individuals, families and communities.

The argument is laid out in four sections. Part I, "A Problem, a Solution, and a Quick Dive into History and Theory," provides much-needed context. Chapter 1, *Creating a Crime to Create Care*, begins to delve into the case study, describing the basic structure of the fetal assault law. It also draws on the law's legislative history to describe the thesis about both the problem and the solution presented by those who supported the creation of the fetal assault law. The law's proponents argued both that, for the women they were targeting, care is better provided inside rather than outside punishment systems and that criminal system processes in and of themselves are a form of care. Both these ideas are central to the criminalization of care. Chapter 2, *Defining the Problem*, delves more deeply into how we think about the "problem" that this law was supposed to solve. It presents both the framing of the problem as described by those who supported the law and then, drawing on medical research, the research of SisterReach, as well as the qualitative interviews of several experts, reframes the serious needs of poor pregnant women struggling with substance use disorder, to start to introduce a different notion of what "problem" might exist and what kinds of solutions and support might actually help. Finally, Chapter 3, *Historical and Theoretical Roots*, turns briefly to history and theory, contextualizing the Tennessee law as an example of a far broader history of prosecuting pregnant women for substance use during pregnancy, the location of care resources within courts, and the criminalization of social welfare programs.

Part II, "Care As a Smokescreen" returns to the case study. Chapter 4, *Prosecuting Poverty*, presents evidence that the prosecutions targeted not fetal harm in general and by all classes of women but instead drug use by poor women, predominantly white in Appalachia and both Black and white in Memphis. Moreover, in the majority of cases, the files bear no evidence that women were offered care as part of their criminal cases. Instead, the women faced what every poor person faces when charged with a misdemeanor: bail, jail, probation, fines and fees, and sometimes more jail. While we tend to focus on felonies when we talk about the injustices at the heart of the criminal legal system, these cases add data to the scholarship describing the crushing nature of our misdemeanor system. Chapter 5, *Deepening Poverty and Degrading Justice*, demonstrates that the punishment women received was just that – punishment, and that punishment came in forms characteristic of the misdemeanor system. So, rather than addressing the poverty or healthcare needs of these women, prosecution deepened their poverty through the imposition of high levels of criminal debt. In addition, again as is characteristic of cases at the low end of the criminal system, little justice was available. Instead, women faced extraordinary pressure to plead guilty and subject themselves to the risk of additional punishment, even in those cases in which their files indicated a strong possibility of a defense to the charge. In all these ways the rhetorical focus on care in the legislation turned out, in the majority of cases, to be nothing more than a smokescreen for deepening poverty and degrading justice.

Part III, "Criminalized Care" presents the books' second primary argument. This Part lays out the series of mechanisms that enable the criminalization of care for women like the fetal assault defendants and then argues that when you link care to punishment defendants face not only a tremendous set of risks of additional punishment as a cost of care, but they receive a degraded form of care. Chapter 6, *The Path In: From Healthcare to Child Welfare to Criminal Systems*, begins the Part by laying out the legal, regulatory, and practice mechanisms by which information about women, and ultimately the women themselves, traveled from the moment when they sought healthcare, through the child welfare system, and to the moment of prosecution and punishment. Chapter 7, *Criminalization As a Road to Care and the Price You Pay*, takes on a different part of the structural puzzle, describing the ways in which opportunities for care are located proximate to or inside punishment systems, effectively drawing individuals who need care into those systems. In addition that Chapter explores the price of that care, in terms of the risk of punishment. Chapter 8, *Corrupting Care*, takes up the issue of care itself, demonstrating that, in the case highlighted in this book, the form of care itself is corrupted by its proximity to or location inside punishment systems. This corruption of care takes three distinct forms: First, treatment providers, whose clients are referred predominantly from the child welfare and criminal systems, inevitably find themselves accountable not just to their patients but to actors in those systems who have the power to punish their patients. These connections inevitably undermine the trust essential to the provision of health care. Second, and related to the first, as a result of these risks, women engage strategically, taking the risk of punishment into consideration as they decided what information to share with their health care providers. The effect of this, of course, is that health care providers may not have the information they need to provide the best care for their patients. Third, decisions about the course of treatment itself are deeply affected not only by data about the medical risks and benefits of particular treatment decisions but also by the implications of those decisions in the child welfare and criminal systems, leading, in this books' terminology, to corrupted care.

Part IV, "Rejecting Criminalization and Reconceptualizing the Relationship between Punishment and Care," concludes with Chapter 9, *A Path Forward*. That chapter recenters the focus on the ways in which bias and subordination enable and reinforce the criminalization of care. It highlights the many dangers of reform in these systems and presents a framework for evaluating possible reforms that might minimize those risks. It then offers a series of possible reforms, in the health care, child welfare, and criminal settings, that are designed to build stronger walls between care systems and punishment systems, shrink punishment systems, and build systems that provide care in the best and broadest sense of that term.

NOTES

1. This book does not contain a separate methodology section. However, as conclusions from various data sources are introduced, the text and endnotes contain a brief description of the data and methods employed.
2. SisterReach, *Who We Are* (2021), https://www.sisterreach.org/who-we-are.html [https://perma.cc/42KA-P6UX].

PART I

A Problem, a Solution, and a Quick Dive into History and Theory

In the spring of 2013, a group of criminal system professionals and Tennessee state legislators came together. They articulated their understanding of a crisis in their state and crafted a solution that they said would meet that crisis. The problem as they framed it was the rise in the number of infants being born manifesting symptoms of neonatal abstinence syndrome, or NAS, a phenomenon many of these actors described as infants "born addicted." The problem as they framed it was also about the pregnant women giving birth to those infants. They were, depending on who you listen to in those hearing rooms "bad mothers," "not even mothers," and "the worst of the worst." Ever so slightly more beneficently, they were also mothers for whom drugs had taken away their ability to be mothers. The solution they turned to was one deep inside the operation and logic of today's criminal system. They decided to create a crime to get these mothers the care they needed and to use the mechanisms of the criminal system itself to provide that care. If it worked, terrific. If it did not, that was fine as well. If these bad mothers did not take advantage of the opportunities offered within the criminal system, not only would they lose their children to the child welfare system, but they would also get the punishment they deserved in the criminal system. This book posits that the decision to create this crime was deeply informed by stigma-ridden beliefs about poor women who use drugs and a specific and deeply embedded conceptualization of the relationship between punishment and care. More specifically, it was driven and made possible by a specific set of beliefs and practices about the women they targeted and how the criminal system does and should function. Both the beliefs and the practices, in turn, were deeply grounded in history.

The combination of that particular framing of the problem and the reliance on the criminal system as the source of a solution led directly to the stories told in this book. This Part dives deeply into the rationales articulated in the legislature, the framing of the "problem" that underpinned the fetal assault law, and the historical, structural, and theoretical roots of that framing. It also suggests a shift in perspective, reconceptualizing the "problem" in a way that might lead to another set of solutions. The next three chapters tell this part of the story.

1 CREATING A CRIME TO CREATE CARE

Drugs tend to take your right mind away ... [but the] discipline ... [of the] court system, along with the medical attention and the counseling, allows them to go back to being the nurturing, caring parents that they would want to be.[1]

Representative G. A. Hardaway, Memphis, Tennessee, 2013

Tennessee's fetal assault law was originally proposed in the spring of 2013. It became law about a year later, in the spring of 2014. It remained in effect until June 30, 2016. The law was proposed again in the spring of 2019, but that proposal did not make it out of committee. Although the United States has a long history of prosecuting women for this conduct, Tennessee's law was the first and, as of this writing, the only state law of its kind in the United States.[2] Before moving on to how the law was justified by those who supported it, we first need to understand some information about how the law was structured. This chapter begins with that information and then moves into the hearing rooms where the fetal assault law was debated.

First the structure of this particular law: Technically speaking, the legislature created this crime, not by creating an entirely new crime but by enacting a law expanding the scope of an existing criminal statute. This is how it worked: Like every other state, Tennessee makes assault a crime. It is a misdemeanor, which means that if you violate the statute, you can be incarcerated for no more than eleven months and twenty-nine days. Assault is defined, in Tennessee, as "[i]ntentionally, knowingly or recklessly caus[ing] bodily injury to another."[3] You will notice, when you read this, that this particular language says nothing about pregnancy or a fetus. For prosecutors who might want to charge a woman with assault because of her drug use during pregnancy, the absence of specific language about pregnancy or the fetus in the statute

13

could cause legal problems. She could argue, in that case, that taking drugs while pregnant is not what the legislators meant by assault.

Despite this possible legal problem, across the nation, and in Tennessee, women have been prosecuted for drug use during pregnancy for violating statutes that were not initially designed to criminalize this particular conduct. For example, women have been charged with assault, chemical endangerment of a minor, or child abuse, and the prosecutors in those cases have argued that in utero drug exposure was included in the definitions of those crimes. In many states, however, these charges led to legal disputes. The disputes in these cases often came down to the question of whether or not in utero drug exposure was the kind of conduct that the legislature intended to make criminal when they wrote the law. These legal disputes highlighted a tremendously important principle in criminal law. Prosecuting someone for a crime is a serious act. It can lead to prison as well as a whole host of other consequences. Thus, courts are generally very careful to make sure that the conduct being charged is actually what the legislature intended to criminalize. To figure that out, the court is supposed to look first to the language of the criminal statute. If the conduct being charged does not fit squarely into the words of the statute, that can be a serious problem for the prosecution. Here the argument was that exposing a fetus in utero is not assault, or chemical endangerment, or child abuse because when those legislatures were writing those laws they were not thinking about a fetus as a victim of those crimes. With two exceptions, in South Carolina[4] and Alabama,[5] prosecutors lost those cases on appeal for exactly these reasons.[6] In general, courts were coming to the conclusion that the victim contemplated in those criminal statutes did not include a fetus.

If you take another look at the Tennessee assault statute with these legal concepts in mind, the problem is pretty clear. The legal question facing prosecutors was whether a court would conclude that the word "another" in Tennessee's definition of assault included a fetus in utero. In fact, on February 1, 2013, the Tennessee Attorney General issued a memo making clear that the answer was no. According to the Attorney General, Tennessee law at the time "exempt[ed] from criminal liability any act or omission by a pregnant woman with respect to an embryo or fetus with which she is pregnant."[7] This was, however, an interpretation of a then-existing state law. If the legislature passed a new law creating a new crime, this would no longer be the case. And that is precisely what happened. The fetal assault law that was in effect from 2014 to 2016 stated that:

> [N]othing in this section shall preclude prosecution of a woman for assault . . . for the illegal use of a narcotic drug . . . while pregnant, if her child is born addicted to or harmed by the narcotic drug and the addiction or harm is a result of her illegal use of a narcotic drug taken while pregnant.[8]

The enactment of this law set the legal ground for the prosecutions. As Part II of this book lays out in great detail, the vast majority of women prosecuted for this crime were poor. Their race varied. In the eastern, Appalachian regions of the state, the prosecutions were targeted almost exclusively at poor white women. In Memphis, in the far west of the state, both poor Black and poor white women were prosecuted.

Now that we have a basic sense of how the law worked, we can move on to how it was justified. This moves us into the hearing rooms. As we will see, those that supported the fetal assault law put forward, in addition to standard justifications for a criminal law, a seemingly strange set of arguments. They argued that it made sense to create a crime for the purpose of creating opportunities for women to receive care. To know just how strange that is, you have to know a little bit about how crimes are traditionally justified and about the conceptual difference between government systems that punish and government systems that provide support.

First, punishment: As every student who has completed the first year of law school could tell you, there are two fundamental schools of thought about the purpose of punishment in the criminal system. The first is retribution. As John Rawls explains, "the retributive view is that punishment is justified on the ground that wrongdoing merits punishment. It is morally fitting that a person who does wrong should suffer in proportion to his wrongdoing."[9] The second school of thought, utilitarianism, sees the purpose of punishment differently. The purpose of the criminal system, in a utilitarian view, is forward-looking. As stated in a criminal casebook that a typical first-year law student might read "[u]tilitarian thought held that punishment's sole aim was to prevent crime and that it could do so by deterring, reforming and incapacitating offenders."[10] Therefore, the criminal system is either about retribution (getting even) or about some practical view of what we might do to those who commit a crime to try to make sure it does not happen again.

Utilitarianism splits into two basic ideas: incapacitation and rehabilitation. Incapacitation suggests that the purpose of the criminal system is just that – to separate the criminal from the society so that they cannot commit crimes. Rehabilitation suggests something different – that society might provide individuals in the criminal system with some level of support as a means to transform them from someone who is likely to commit crimes to someone who is less likely to commit crimes. For example, a person in prison might get the equivalent of high school classes, anger management, or drug treatment on the theory that these might make it less likely that the person will commit crime (or recidivate) afterwards. As one prominent legal theorist explains, the concept of rehabilitation is tied inextricably to our belief in prisons. "Convicted felons are separated from their former life, confined in a secure facility and subjected to some regiment that will change their attitude and enable them to be productive, law-abiding citizens once they are released."[11] Thus, prisoners receive services (drug treatment, anger management) and education (high school and college classes, vocational training) in the hope that they will leave prison and no longer commit crimes. The enormous attention we pay to the recidivism rates of those who participate in these programs is a sure tell that the goal of rehabilitation is precisely that – to provide services designed to make sure that those convicted of crimes no longer commit crimes. When it comes to rehabilitation, we have not only traditional "programs" that are located in prisons and included as a part of community-based sentences, but as Chapter 3 lays out, problem-solving courts, providing treatment inside the court process itself. While they are take a slightly different form, problem-solving courts are, for the most part, designed to accomplish the same goal that rehabilitation has always focused on: "customizing punishment . . . thereby reducing the likelihood of repeat offending and increasing the likelihood that the offender can become a productive member of society."[12]

In addition, in punishment systems (our jails and prisons), we also have to provide some basic level of care (food, shelter, health care) for those who are incarcerated because their incarceration bars them from providing that care for themselves. That is, however, a by-product of our basic punishment purpose, not the purpose of the system itself.

Second, social welfare: In contrast to our criminal system, programs designed to provide social welfare support are, at least in theory, designed to do something very different than criminal systems. For a sense of what society claims these programs are for, we can take a look at the preamble to the first Social Security Act, the legislative source of much of the United States' social welfare system. According to that 1935 Congress, the Social Security Act was:

> An act to provide for the general welfare by establishing a system of Federal old-age benefits, and by enabling the several States to make more adequate provision for aged persons, blind persons, dependent and crippled children, maternal and child welfare, public health, and the administration of their unemployment compensation laws; to establish a Social Security Board; to raise revenue; and for other purposes.[13]

To take another example, Congress has told us that the purpose of Medicaid, the health care program that provides medical care to more than seventy million low-income children and adults,[14] is to enable states to "furnish (1) medical assistance on behalf of families with dependent children and of aged, blind, or disabled individuals, whose income and resources are insufficient to meet the costs of necessary medical services, and (2) rehabilitation and other services to help such families and individuals attain or retain capability for independence or self-care."[15] This sounds like care and not like punishment. What you will notice, though, in the legislative record in Tennessee, is that these distinctions, between punishment and care, start to blur.

This takes us into the hearing rooms. Fetal assault was the subject of hearings twice, in 2013, in advance of the original passage, and in 2016, as advocates tried, and ultimately failed, to lift the sunset date and keep the law on the books. While, as explained later in this chapter, there was an enormous emphasis on the relationship between the crime and care in those hearings, to be fair, it is true that this record also contains a hefty dose of traditional rationales for criminal laws. Take for example Representative Lamberth who repeatedly justifies the law as targeted at conduct meriting punishment. As he questions witnesses during the hearings, he continually asks one question:

> Do you agree that a woman should be charged with child abuse for putting cocaine in her newborn baby's bottle? And if you do, what is the difference between that act and taking cocaine in the days before birth?[16]

For him both are equal and should be crimes and should be punished simply because we as a society should target this conduct for condemnation. He is not looking to provide care here, he is condemning the conduct as morally wrong and worthy of punishment, plain and simple. This sounds exactly like retribution.

Similarly, Amy Weirich, the District Attorney for Shelby County, called the mothers the "worst of the worst."[17] Representative Teri Lynn Weaver, who was the primary sponsor of the bill in the house, offered a slightly different set of rationales – rationales that sound more like deterrence and incapacitation. She described the women targeted by the law as women who "don't want help; they don't even recognize there's life in there."[18] In the 2013 hearing, Weaver is clear about her intent: "Let's just focus on the children."[19] Although both Wyrick and Weaver temper their remarks at different points, clearly for them and for others, there is a piece of what was happening that was about some mixture of separating the women from society and getting that proverbial eye for an eye.

In addition, a good deal of what was said in the hearings sounds like rehabilitation. As we listen, though, something strange starts to happen. Instead of thinking about rehabilitation as something society does as a part of punishing bad conduct and rehabilitating those who commit crimes, voices supporting the bill talk about the rehabilitation that prosecution can provide as so inherently valuable that it makes sense to create a crime just to get women access to that care. In their words we find two hypotheses. First, that creating a crime will lead to prosecution that will, in turn, lead to opportunities to access care, and second, and even more strange, that creating a crime will lead to prosecution, which, in and of itself, is a form of care.

We can begin with the first hypothesis – that prosecution is a road to accessing care. In both the hearings on initial enactment and the hearings on reauthorization, there are multiple statements suggesting that the women who would be subject to prosecution could not access treatment without being prosecuted. Perhaps most striking was the statement of Barry Staubus, the Sullivan County District Attorney. Staubus characterized the crisis in dramatic terms: "We are drowning in east Tennessee ... with these babies and we feel powerless."[20] For him the fetal assault law was the solution:

> I think when we see this statute ... we are going to be able to bring lots and lots of women into a program we're creating specifically for drug addicted mothers and so I think that with this statute, what we'll see is that there will be a vacuum for that and we'll see a lot of programs and we'll see a lot of judges and we'll see a lot of prosecutors wanting to do this and recommending this and the judges I think will find the resources to do it.[21]

This is a really remarkable statement. He is saying that his community has an overwhelming need for health care for pregnant women struggling with substance use disorder, but the only way that that care need would be met is if the legislature creates a crime. Staubus was not alone. In 2016, District Attorney General Amy Weirich spoke in favor of reauthorization and offered the same rationale: "What was happening before we had this legislation is that those babies were being taken from their mothers and their mothers were left helpless without any chance of getting the help they need."[22] The way she said this, emphasizing that treatment was not available "before we had this legislation," clearly indicates that, in Weirich's view, it was the creation of the crime that led to women being able to access help.

Weirich suggests that prosecution is a road to accessing care, and Staubus suggests that we need prosecutions to convince those in power to provide care opportunities. Others posit however that that prosecution plays another role – that prosecution itself is a form of care. Listen, for example, to Representative G. A. Hardaway, a representative from Shelby County. He characterized the legislation as serving as a benevolent force in the mothers' lives: "[while] drugs tend to take your right mind away ... [with the] discipline ... [of the] court system ... [the mothers can] go back to being the nurturing caring parents that they would want to be."[23] Here, prosecuting does not just provide opportunities to access care; it is framed as a form of care in and of itself.

Admittedly, characterizing criminal sanctions as incentivizing defendants to cease engaging in illegal behavior and choose more positive paths is not unusual. Nor is it particularly unusual to characterize courts as able to use their coercive authority to compel behavioral changes in criminal defendants as well as others subject to the jurisdiction of various courts. What is unusual in this legislative record is the way that prosecutors and representatives begin to frame the creation of the crime, not just as creating an incentive for women to seek treatment but as the precondition to and provider of treatment itself. In the rhetoric of the supporters, it is the creation of the crime and the ability to prosecute that both makes treatment possible and is a form of treatment in and of itself. Repeatedly, legislators and prosecutors characterize prosecution itself as that which will provide access to treatment that is not otherwise available to the women. This point bears emphasis. In the rhetoric of the hearings justifying the passage of the statute, the "treatment" available only through the courts is contemplated as so beneficial that it justifies the criminalization of previously noncriminal conduct.

As we will learn in more detail in Chapter 3 these ideas are, in fact, closely linked to the growth, beginning in the late 1980s, of a new generation of problem-solving courts. At that time, as a result of the war on drugs, criminal courts found themselves with courtrooms filled with individuals with extensive needs that led to their criminal conduct, which led in turn to a new generation of courts that would attempt to address this problem. And in fact, the care rationale of the fetal assault law was largely born of the close linkage between this particular legislation and the Memphis drug court. For example, Senator Tate explained that "this bill what it does is gives the DA or a judge the right or authority if you will to send a mother of a child to a drug court."[24] Similarly, Representative Lamberth, looking back in 2016, argued that the law succeeded because it provided access to a drug court: "one hundred percent of the women that were seeking drug court assistance right ... now would not be aware of it."[25]

Quite explicitly in the view of these proponents, if the problem is the lack of resources for women needing help, the solution is the creation of the crime. One proponent described the law as "offering their mothers the help they so desperately need but cannot obtain on their own."[26] As Senator Kelsey explained:

> The other issue that this committee also needs to consider is that these women are usually not being sent to jail at all but in fact the beginning of the prosecution is what the court [is] able to do to send them to drug treatment. That's another very important and positive aspect for the bill.[27]

This view is not restricted to legislators. Instead, for those women who desperately need treatment, it is descriptive of the searing reality in their communities. In one of the most revealing moments in the hearings, Nikki Brown,[28] an African American woman from Memphis who was prosecuted under the statute, and graduated from the Memphis Drug Court, testified in favor of making the fetal assault law permanent.[29] During the hearing, Representative William Lamberth asked Ms. Brown if "[w]ithout a statute on the books … would you have gotten the help that you are getting right now?"[30] She responded, "No, I am very thankful for the program."[31] Clearly for Ms. Brown, no help was available to her before she was prosecuted.

Finally, revealing what some imply was the real justification for the statute – namely filling the seats of drug courts throughout the state – Senator Finney, from Jackson, Tennessee, talked about how his district might benefit from the creation of this crime: "we have a great drug court in Jackson … and I'm sure it would benefit from something like this."[32] In Senator Finney's view, his drug court is so valuable that we should create crimes in order to create clients for that program.

At this point it should be clear that the central rationales for the creation of this crime included the idea that prosecution is a mechanism to create and help women access treatment resources and that accessing a drug court was a valuable form of treatment in and of itself. The defeat of the attempt to renew the crime and its ultimate demise, it turns out, had everything to do with those ideas. Nowhere among the statements of proponents of the legislation is there any suggestion that this state of affairs – the seemingly overwhelming lack of resources available to support pregnant women struggling with addiction – might call not for the creation of a new crime but instead for the augmentation of community-based social support. Instead, in their statements, criminalization and treatment are inextricably intertwined.

When the last hearings on the issue of making the fetal assault permanent were held, the bill was in the Tennessee House of Representatives Criminal Justice Subcommittee. That committee had six members, and the bill needed four votes to move out of committee. Ultimately it got three. Representative Andrew Farmer, of Sevierville Tennessee, cast the deciding vote. Although one can never know precisely what motivates someone to cast a vote, he did make some statements that give us a window into his thinking. Here is what he said:

> If we are going to put these ladies in a situation that they can potentially be prosecuted ... let's fund the treatment ... Once they're prosecuted, we've all lost ... The goal is to have these mothers off these opioids well before birth ... Once we are to the prosecutorial stage, we've lost.. Let's ask this state to give $10, $20 million for rehabilitative funding for these ladies that are addicted to opioids ... In a situation like that I may be able to support the bill but right now, to put the burden on these ladies the way we do and then leave them just hung out to dry, I just can't do that.[33]

Now it is possible that Representative Farmer was just being polite, or politically careful, when he stated that he might support the bill if treatment was available, but let us assume for a minute either this was his actual position, or, even if we do not think that, that he believed this to be a reasonable position. Representative Farmer was fine with criminalization. He just was not fine with criminalization without care.

As this chapter has laid out, care linked to punishment was a primary solution posited by those who supported the fetal assault law. The next chapter steps back from that "solution" to the question of what problem those legislators were trying to solve.

NOTES

1. *Hearing on S.B. 1295 Before the H. Crim. Just. Sub-Comm.*, 108th Gen. Assemb., 0:48:43 (Tenn. April 9, 2013) [hereinafter *Hearing on 1295 Before the H. Crim Just. Subcomm. (II)*], http://tnga.granicus.com/MediaPlayer.php?view_id=269&clip_id=7751 [https://perma.cc/5BB6-XGNK] at 0:28:25.

2. Although no other US state has passed a law that explicitly targets this conduct, Rewire News has reported that the Assiniboine and Sioux Tribes in Montana have similar crimes on the books. Rewire. *The Breach: Investigating Big Horn County* (2018), https://the-breach.simplecast.com/epi sodes/a789ffaa-a789ffaa [https://perma.cc/GT5D-Z4MM].

3. TENN. CODE ANN. § 39–13–101(a)(1)–(2) (2018).

4. Whitner v. State, 492 S.E.2d 777 (S.C. 1997).

5. In Re. Ankrom, 152 So.3d 397 (Al. 2013).

6. *See, e.g.*, State v. Aiwohi, 123 P.3d 1210, 1223 (Haw. 2005) (holding that definition of "person" in a manslaughter statute did not include a fetus); Cochran v. Commonwealth, 315 S.W.3d 325, 330 (Ky. 2010) (*following* Commonwealth v. Welch, 864 S.W.2d 280, 285 (Ky. 1993) holding that wanton endangerment does not extend to mother's use of drugs while pregnant); State v. Mondragon, 145 145 P.3d 574, 579 (N.M. Ct. App. 2008) (*following* State v. Martinez, 137 P.3d 1195, 1198 (N.M. Ct. App. 2006) holding that the ordinary meaning of "child" in a child abuse statute did not include a fetus in a case where the mother used cocaine during pregnancy); State v. Bales, 2013-Ohio-4957 (Ohio Ct. App. Knox County 2013) (*following* State v. Gray, 584 N.E.2d 710, 711 (Ohio 1992) holding that criminal child endangerment does not apply to a fetus). *But see* Hicks v. State, 153 So.3d 53, 54 (Ala. 2014) (interpreting "child" in a criminal chemical-endangerment statute to include unborn); State v. McKnight, 352 S.C. 635, 576 S.E.2d 168 (2003) (*following* Whitner v. State, 492 S.E.2d 777, 778 (S.C. 1997) interpreting "person" in a criminal statute to include viable fetus).

7. Liability for Infants Born with Narcotic Drug Dependency, Op. Tenn. Att'y Gen. No. 13–01 (Revised) (February 1, 2013).

8. TENN. CODE ANN. § 39–13–107(c)(2) (2014) (expired July 1, 2016).

9. John Rawls, Two Concepts of Rules, 44 The Philosophical Rev. 3, 5 (1955).

10. J. Kaplan, R. Weisberg, & G. Binder, *Criminal Law Cases and Materials* 32 (2008).

11. Edward L. Rubin, The Inevitability of Rehabilitation, 19 Law & Ineq. J. 343, 347 (2001).

12. Robert V. Wolf, *Ctr. for Ct. Innovation, Principles of Problem-Solving Justice* 1, 7 (2007), www.courtinnovation.org/sites/default/files/Principles.pdf [https:// perma.cc/2VE7-959D].

13. Social Security Act, H.R. 7260, 74th Cong. (1935).

14. Medicaid.gov *September 2020 Medicaid and CHIP Enrollment* (2021), www .medicaid.gov/medicaid/program-information/medicaid-and-chip-enrollment-data/report-highlights/index.html.

15. Social Security Act § 1901, 42 U.S.C. § 1396 (1994).

16. *See Debate on H.B. 1660 Before the H. Crim. Just. Sub-Comm.*, 109th Gen. Assemb. (Tenn. March 15, 2016) (statement of Rep. William Lamberth,

Chair, H. Crim. Just. Subcomm.), http://tnga.granicus.com/MediaPlayer .php?view_id=341&clip_id=12002 # [https://perma.cc/EE24-56F2] at 1:48.

17. *See id.* at 1:25:40.

18. *See Hearing on S.B. 1295 Before the H. Crim. Just. Sub-Comm.*, 108th Gen. Assemb., 0:56:06 (Tenn. March 13, 2013) [hereinafter *Hearing on 1295 Before the H. Crim Just. Subcomm. (I)*], http://tnga.granicus.com/MediaPlayer.php? view_id=269&clip_id=7499&meta_id=140901 [https://perma.cc/A2C6-LS8A].

19. *See id.* at 1:03:23.

20. *Hearing on S.B. 1391 Before the S. Judiciary Comm.*, 108th Gen. Assemb., 59th Sess. 2:04:00 (Tenn. March 18, 2014) [hereinafter *Hearing on S.B. 1391 Before the S. Judiciary Comm. (I)*], http://tnga.granicus.com/MediaPlayer.php ?view_id=269&clip_id =9050 # [https://perma.cc/86M6-KQDV] (testimony of Barry Staubus, District Attorney of Sullivan County) at 2:14:05.

21. *See id.* at 2:15:09.

22. *See supra* note 16 at 1:30:00; *Hearing on S.B. 1391 Before the S. Judiciary Comm. (I), supra* note 20; *Hearing on S.B. 1391 Before the S. Judiciary Comm.*, 108th Gen. Assemb. (Tenn. April 9, 2013) [hereinafter *Hearing on S.B. 1391 Before the S. Judiciary Comm. (II)*], http://tnga.granicus.com/MediaPlayer .php?view_id=262&clip_id=7746 # [https://perma.cc/8QA6-R2CP] (statement Dist. Attorney Gen. Amy Weirich).

23. *See Hearing on 1295 Before the H. Crim Just. Subcomm. (II) supra* note 1 at 0:28:25.

24. *See supra* note 22 at 2:27:57.

25. *See supra* note 16 at 2:20:45.

26. *See id.* at 1:04:03.

27. *Id.* (statement of Sen. Brian Kelsey, Chair, S. Judiciary Comm.) at 2:29:24.

28. Although this individual chose to testify publicly and used her real name in her testimony, the name used here is a pseudonym assigned by the research team. The pseudonym is used in the main text as well as in the notes that follow. Despite the public nature of many of the records cited in this book, to protect from unwanted additional disclosures, pseudonyms were assigned for each of the women whose cases are discussed in this book.

29. *See supra* note 16 at 1:12:50.

30. *See id.* at 1:15:00; *Hearing on S.B. 1391 Before the S. Judiciary Comm. (I), supra* note 20; *Hearing on S.B. 1391 Before the S. Judiciary Comm. (II), supra* note 22.

31. *See supra* note 16 at 1:15:10; *Hearing on S.B. 1391 Before the S. Judiciary Comm. (I), supra* note 20; *Hearing on S.B. 1391 Before the S. Judiciary Comm. (II), supra* note 22 (statement of Nikki Brown).

32. *Hearing on S.B. 1391 Before the S. Judiciary Comm. (I), supra* note 16 (statement of Sen. Lowe Finney) at 2:20:50.

33. *See supra* note 16 (statement of Rep. Andrew Farmer, Chair, H. Crim. Just. Subcomm.) at 2:27:17.

2   DEFINING THE PROBLEM

A Baby's Life Shouldn't Begin With Detox.

Roadside Sign, East Tennessee

Fox News called them *The Tiniest Addicts.*[1] Living in East Tennessee, the billboards and posters are everywhere – in the courthouse, along the highway, and in the grocery store. The image you see is a close-up of two tiny white feet, held stiffly flexed. Around the arch of the right foot is a grey, rubber-looking strap connected to thin tubes that travel beyond the border of the photo. On the left ankle is a blue hospital band, folded over itself several times to accommodate the tiny limb. In bold, centered text: *A Baby's Life Shouldn't Begin with Detox.* Other images you see in press coverage: overwhelmed neonatal intensive care nurses and white infants abandoned into the arms of beneficent elderly volunteer cuddlers. The sounds too are front and center: shrill, persistent cries that nurses say are a sure tell that the infant is withdrawing. It was these images and those sounds that drove the conversation about Tennessee's fetal assault law, both in the popular press and in the Tennessee House and Senate hearing rooms. As we heard in the last chapter, mothers who let this happen to their children were "the worst of the worst." Tennessee should, in their eyes, "just focus on the children." As we will see, the focus on the effect of in utero transmission of opiates to a fetus not only justified the fetal assault law, but it supported a whole host of interventionist child welfare policies – from rules that labeled in utero exposure even to prescribed medication as "severe abuse" and a set of practices that sped families toward separation and termination of parental rights. Given the centrality of NAS to this story, understanding what it really is and what it really tells us about a particular woman and child, is fundamental.

The Tennessee Department of Health provides this definition of NAS:

> Neonatal Abstinence Syndrome (NAS) is a condition in which an infant undergoes withdrawal from a substance to which he or she was exposed in-utero. Different classes of substances, including opioids, antidepressants and barbiturates, may cause NAS when used during pregnancy. The most common substances causing NAS are opioids. This can include legally prescribed opioids (such as pain relievers like morphine and medication assisted treatment opioids such as buprenorphine and methadone) or illegally obtained opioids, e.g., heroin. In addition, a pregnant woman may obtain a substance through drug diversion, i.e. transfer of legally prescribed controlled substance from the individual for whom it was prescribed to another person for any illicit use.[2]

There is no question that, in Tennessee, at the time the fetal assault law was in effect, recorded NAS rates had been rising.

As the Tennessee Department of Health noted in becoming the first state in the nation to require data reporting on NAS from providers, "[s]ince the early 2000s, the incidence of NAS in Tennessee has increased by 10-fold, far exceeding the national 3-fold increase over the same time period."[3]

Places like Sullivan County, Tennessee, where Barry Staubus, who testified at the legislative hearings lives and works, were at the epicenter of this trend. Given larger trends, there's nothing surprising about this. The rise in NAS rates go hand in hand with dramatic increases in the use and abuse of opiates in the region.[4] As widespread reporting has taught us, the problem stems, to a large degree, from a dramatic increase in opioid prescriptions.[5] "From 1991 to 2011, there was a near tripling of opioid prescriptions dispensed by U.S. pharmacies: from 76 million to 219 million prescriptions."[6] Nationally, rates of prescription opiates rose steadily from 2006 to 2012, and then began falling.[7] At the height of prescription rates in 2012, there were over 255 million opiate prescriptions written.[8] This meant that for every 100 people, doctors wrote 81.3 prescriptions.[9] Although national rates began to fall after 2012, to just under 155 million prescriptions, or a rate of 46.7 prescriptions per 100 people in 2019, these falling national figures hide significant regional and state variations.[10] Rates remain highest in the southeast.[11] In 2019, in Alabama there were 85.8

prescriptions written for every 100 people, and in Kentucky, Tennessee, Mississippi, Louisiana, Arkansas, and Oklahoma, rates were between 66 and 80.9 prescriptions per 100 people.[12]

Not only are these prescription rates concentrated in particular regions, but they are evident at disproportionate rates among those with lower incomes.[13] "[T]he Medicaid patient population is more likely to receive prescriptions for opioid pain medications and to have opioids prescribed at higher doses and for longer periods of time than the non-Medicaid patient population."[14] In addition, "[r]acial-ethnic disparities in opioid prescription have been documented nationally, with minorities being less likely to receive opioids."[15] White women are in fact significantly more likely than African-American women to use and abuse opiates and to die of an opiate overdose.[16] This confluence of factors leads to a concentration of addiction in several white, poor, rural, and geographically concentrated regions in the states.[17]

Along with this rise in the rate of opiate prescriptions is a dramatic rise in the number of overdose deaths due to opiates.[18] As reported by the Centers for Disease Control, "[o]pioids were involved in 46,802 overdose deaths in 2018, and opioid overdose deaths were five times higher in 2016 than 1999."[19]

Neither women as a whole nor pregnant women are exempt from these statistics.[20] Between 1999 and 2010, "yearly prescription opioid overdose deaths among women increased from 1,287 to 6,631. These numbers represent a 400 percent increase over 10 years."[21] Like the overall trends, these trends manifest disproportionately among low-income women.[22] One study, "using data from Medicaid-enrolled pregnant women from 47 states in the United States reported that 21.6% of the women filled at least one opioid prescription during their pregnancy."[23] In Tennessee, "[f]rom 1995–2009, pregnancy-related use of opioid analgesics nearly doubled among [Medicaid] participants."[24] While rates are higher among poor women, women who use commercial health plans and are therefore less likely to be low income "also showed high rates (14.4%) of prescription opioid dispensing between 2005 and 2011."[25]

These trends lead to an increase in cases of both opiate use disorder among mothers and NAS among infants both nationally and in Tennessee.[26]

> Between 2006 and 2012, the rate of infant and maternal hospital-
> izations related to substance use increased substantially, from 5.1 to
> 8.7 per 1,000 infant hospitalizations and from 13.4 to 17.9 per
> 1,000 maternal hospitalizations . . .. In 2012, among the neonatal
> stays with a substance-related condition, approximately 60% were
> related to neonatal drug withdrawal . . . or NAS. Among maternal
> stays related to substance abuse, almost one-fourth involved
> opioids.[27]

In addition, the infants of low-income women are more likely to be
diagnosed with NAS than their higher-income peers. During the
course of conducting the study for this book I obtained birth record
data for every infant born in Tennessee, while the fetal assault law was
in effect, who was diagnosed with NAS. In those records, covering just
over two years between 2014 and 2016, 82 percent of the families
reported an income level below $25,000 per year.[28] In addition, 95 per-
cent of these women were white.

So yes, NAS was on the rise, and it was deeply tied to the opiate
epidemic and the particular manifestation of that epidemic among
poor, predominantly white women. What's important though is that
the policies and practices at the heart of this book – criminalization and
intervention – were justified as a means to respond to NAS. The ideas
were twofold – both that an NAS diagnosis was cause for concern
about the family and, maybe more importantly, that the right reaction
for society was to intervene, separate mothers and children, and use
separation and punishment as a means to coerce women into treatment. But was this punitive and interventionist reaction justified?
There are moments that perhaps intervention makes sense, but the
more I learned about NAS, addiction, pregnancy, treatment, trauma,
and community health, the more I came to believe that Tennessee had
misdiagnosed the problem.

2.1 NAS REVISITED

First, a couple of facts about NAS. While the billboard imagery suggests that all infants who are diagnosed with NAS receive medications
in the process of detoxification, that is not the case. As the Tennessee

Department of Health states in its definition of NAS, "[l]ess commonly, very sick babies may receive medications after birth to help control pain or agitation." In addition, contrary to the stigma associating NAS with illegal drug use, one thing that is certainly true is that the women who are giving birth to infants with NAS are very likely following their doctor's advice when they took the opiates.[29] This is because the long-standing medical consensus is that pregnant women who are addicted to opiates should be treated throughout their pregnancies with medication-assisted therapy or MAT.[30] A possible, but certainly not inevitable, result of that use is the development of NAS in the infant. While there are some small and early studies that seem to suggest that women can detoxify during pregnancy, and therefore limit the exposure of the fetus to opiates,[31] that research has been subject to challenge.[32] This means that pregnant women who suffer from substance-use disorder often take prescribed medications during their pregnancies.[33] The majority of infants who are born with NAS manifest these symptoms because of in utero exposure to MAT.[34] In addition, while it is true that some infants develop NAS as a result of exposure to illicit substances, comparatively few NAS cases arise from exposure to only illicit substances.[35] The Tennessee Department of Health, relying on mandated reporting data,[36] breaks exposure down into three major categories: prescription only, illicit only, and both prescription and illicit use.[37] According to this data, the largest portion of NAS cases (49.4 percent in 2019) result from prescription use of opiates, predominantly the use of MAT.[38] Less than 30 percent (29.1 percent in 2019) results from purely illicit exposure, and finally the remaining cases (20.5 percent) result from a combination of illicit and legal exposure.[39] In Tennessee in particular, illegal (as opposed to legal but diverted) opiates play a very small role.[40] For example, in 2019 only 8.2 percent of NAS cases resulted in whole or in part from the use of heroin.[41]

Finally, some information about what we know about long-term effects. While some short-term effects of NAS are well documented, and the medical community is making substantial progress in the treatment of NAS in infants,[42] the evidence about long-term effects is inconsistent at best.[43] In 2016 a group of experts convened at a workshop jointly organized by the Eunice Kennedy Shriver

National Institute of Child Health and Human Development, American Congress of Obstetricians and Gynecologists, American Academy of Pediatrics, Society for Maternal-Fetal Medicine, Centers for Disease Control and Prevention, and the March of Dimes Foundation. The executive summary from that convening sums up the state of the literature on long-term effects: "[t]here is a lack of evidence on the long-term effects of prenatal opioid exposure." The authors identified a series of problems with the literature to date, including that "most studies were conducted prior to the start of the current opioid epidemic and have not included addiction related to prescription drug use." More concerning, though, when it comes to framing problems and solutions, is the failure of the literature to distinguish between opiate exposure or NAS, and a variety of other factors that might be affecting women and children. As these authors stated, "in [some] studies, a number of cognitive, motor, and behavioral deficits were identified, such as lower IQ scores and poor social skills." However, "[s]ample sizes were small and thus could not account for multiple confounding factors, such as polydrug use, environmental exposures, and poverty." In addition, they noted that "earlier studies have not found significant differences in cognitive development between children exposed to methadone in utero when followed to 5 years of age compared to control groups matched for age, race, and socioeconomic status. *However, scores were often lower in both groups compared with data from the general population.*"[44] Since that convening, there have been some additional studies,[45] but again the literature is inconclusive, and the debate and research continue.

While those who were testifying during the hearing framed the "problem" in one way, as one about bad mothers, NAS, and the necessity of preventing it through separation, coercion, and punishment, many of the experts I spoke to, as well as a good deal of research, define the "problem" or need quite differently. To reimagine the care needs, if any, of the women targeted by prosecution, you have to challenge a few more assumptions at the heart of Tennessee's framing of the problem and then look again at need from the perspective of the infant, the mother–infant pair, the family and, ultimately, the community. First, a few assumptions to challenge.

2.2 THE SAFETY OF CHILDREN AND THE DANGERS OF INTERVENTION AND REMOVAL

A fundamental premise of much of the rhetoric that drove the fetal assault law is the firm belief that these infants are in danger and that the communication of information about their drug exposure out of the health care setting and into, at the very least, child welfare, is essential to their safety. Clearly, referral is appropriate in some circumstances. But this book ultimately argues that there are several reasons to think that designing a system that makes referral and removal much rarer and that is structured with the assumption that comprehensive and robust forms care should be provided as the first line of defense, in the community and in the healthcare system, will in fact promote the health, safety, and well-being of all members of that family. Understanding this involves weighing any risk of leaving the mother and child together against the risks associated with intervention and removal.

First, in both the specific context of substance-exposed newborns and in the general context of child abuse and neglect, there's a good deal of evidence that keeping parents and children together is often better for children and that the contrary, removal, brings with it a whole host of harms that we do not take seriously enough.

As to the specific circumstances at the center of this story, two medical practices, rooming mother and infant together ("rooming in") and breastfeeding,[46] lessen the symptoms of NAS and can lower the chance that a particular infant needs medication to treat their NAS. For this reason, any policy that interferes with either requires a good deal of scrutiny. More generally, we know that both removal and foster care stays bring with them additional risks of harm to children. As Professor Shanta Trivedi has argued, the damage caused by removal from one's parent "may be 'more damaging to the child than doing nothing at all.'"[47] Removal disrupts the possibility of secure attachment with a parent, and foster care itself brings with it significant risks of "later problems such as aggression and depression."[48] And contrary to what one might assume, these risks apply even to children who are subject to shorter-term removals.[49] Children are more likely to face abuse in the foster care system than in the general population, and foster care is characterized by significant abuse and neglect. Foster care can involve multiple placements, and children in foster care have higher rates of physical and mental health conditions than the general population. While it is certainly true that some of this might be the result of the original abuse and neglect, Joseph Doyle, an MIT economist, has found that for children on the margin, children for whom professionals disagreed about whether removal was appropriate, children who were left at home, had better outcomes than those who were removed.[50] All of this suggests that intervention and removal should be the exception and the last step rather than the rule and the first.

2.3 THE WILLINGNESS TO VOLUNTARILY SEEK CARE

In the legislative hearing room, the hypothesis about treatment was clear: women needed both the carrot of treatment and the stick of family separation and criminal punishment. This rationale not only justified the law, but it implicitly justifies the societal decision to allocate scarce treatment resources away from the community and toward the punitive systems described in this book. This set of assumptions proves untrue both generally, in terms of how individuals access treatment in the United States, and in the specific circumstances of pregnant women engaging in substance misuse.

Generally, despite a perception that it takes the hammer of punishment to force individuals into treatment, the data simply does not bear that out. For example, the Substance Abuse and Mental Health Services Administration maintains something called the Treatment Episode Data Set or TEDS. TEDS contains detailed information on every admission to publicly funded substance abuse treatment in the United States. Among other data points, TEDS details the referral source for each instance in which treatment is provided. In 2017, the majority of admissions to treatment were the result of self-referral (42.7 percent), referral by another substance abuse or healthcare provider (16.1 percent), or some other community provider (10.8 percent). Only 28.3 percent of referrals came from criminal legal system-related entities.[51] So although courts and criminal system entities do play a significant role in referring individuals to treatment, the vast majority of individuals reach treatment through other paths.

In addition, with respect to pregnant women in particular, there is significant data indicating that, despite their fears about child welfare involvement, and despite the struggles that go along with substance-use disorder, women who become pregnant do make substantial efforts to curtail their drug use and obtain prenatal care. For example, in 2002 a group of researchers published the Maternal Lifestyle Study, which was based on data from 19,079 mother–infant pairs at four clinical centers across the country.[52] The researchers were looking at the short-term effects of substance use during pregnancy with a focus on cocaine, opiates, and polysubstance use. The researchers gathered data at the time of and shortly after delivery. They found an impressive level of engagement with prenatal care. Seventy-six percent of women who used cocaine only and 94 percent of those who used opiates (in contrast to the 97 percent of the women whose infants were not exposed) reported receiving prenatal care during their pregnancies.[53] Qualitative studies suggest similar results. For example, in 2003 Martha A. Jessup and colleagues published a qualitative study designed to identify barriers to treatment. Based on qualitative interviews of thirty-six women, they concluded that, although women feared puni-tive responses, overwhelmingly they sought care. "Most participants (n = 34) sought prenatal care. Many (n = 28) spoke of the importance of prenatal care for themselves and their infants, and 21 sought care independent of a mandate from substance abuse treatment or jail."[54]

Moreover, engagement in voluntary treatment during pregnancy appears to lead to more prenatal engagement. For example, in a study conducted in the late 1990s in California, a group of researchers examined the outcomes for substance-using women and infants for whom voluntary outpatient, onsite care, in the form of counseling, and, when appropriate, access to chemical dependence treatment programs was available.[55] Women in that study who engaged in treatment had significantly higher rates of prenatal care than those who used sub-stances during pregnancy but did not engage in treatment.[56]

So, there is no question that pregnancy creates an opportunity. Despite the barriers and complications in the lives of women with substance-use disorder, pregnancy and impending parenthood is a time when women are motivated to seek care. What matters in that moment though, is what opportunity society creates to capitalize on that motivation. Dr. Andy Hsi, whose comprehensive practice focused on treating pregnant and parenting women struggling with substance-use disorder and trauma is discussed in more detail in Chapter 9, explained his experience of women's desire to get better. His answer centered on the responsibility of medical systems to create responsive care.

> No matter who it is, our job is to make it so easy to get care for themselves and their babies that it makes sense. All the women I've ever talked to [have said] the reasons that I come to clinic is I want a better life for my kid. So, we know that that's tremendous love and we have to just quite honestly be willing to create systems that allow people to act on their best intentions.[57]

Not only that, but our understanding has to move beyond addiction to the broader circumstances that so many women who use opiates find themselves facing.

2.4 POVERTY, TRAUMA, ADVERSE CHILDHOOD EXPERIENCES, AND SUBSTANCE-USE DISORDER

I met Dr. Nzinga Harrison at an event at SisterReach in the spring of 2019. Dr. Harrison is a psychiatrist whose practice focuses on the care of those who suffer from serious persistent mental illness including severe substance-use disorders. From 2011 to 2019 she was the Chief Medical Officer for Anka Behavioral Health, a nonprofit behavioral health care organization operating in California and Michigan. She has recently moved to Eleanor Health, a new organization trying to rethink addiction treatment. Dr. Harrison is very serious about creating models of community health and has a deep and compassionate understanding of the needs of her patient community. During our conversation, I asked her how she would think about framing and addressing the problem that was the focus of the Tennessee legislation. She answered the question by focusing on the ways in which it makes no sense, in terms of children's health, to separate mothers and children. As

Dr. Harrison framed it, you have to think of the harm to the infant more globally:

> If what we are trying to prevent is harm to the baby, then we have to start with a solution that keeps the baby attached to mom because detaching babies from moms also causes harm. So, if we look at NAS, that's a short-term consequence, that medically we know how to manage which does carry some risk for the infant but does not carry life-long risks for the infant like detachment and placement in a child welfare system does, for example. I also think that we can actually focus on protecting the baby and focus on protecting the mom at the same time. Those two things are not mutually exclusive and so the best way to prevent NAS is to get mom in treatment earlier in pregnancy. And so, I would move those efforts upstream and that has to include creating access outside the legal system because as soon as you put the legal system in it then you scare people away.[58]

Dr. Harrison's starts with the knowledge that to protect babies you have to care for mothers. As she explained, and as the data discussed above substantiates,

> overwhelmingly, mothers want to take care of their babies. And so, if a woman has a substance use disorder and she gets pregnant, you want to create the environment and the community that 1. She automatically knows where she can go, and 2. That when she gets there she's going to be received with compassion and open arms and following throughout her pregnancy with increased access to the resources that she does not have. We have to get them into treatment in a voluntary way as much as possible before you get to the delivery window.[59]

And if that does not happen and, "she delivers a baby with NAS, that really should be the trigger that this mom needs an increased set of supports."[60]

Our conversation went further, into the ways in which poverty and trauma increase the risk of substance-use disorder and the support we need in place to care for families. Dr. Harrison explained that the word trauma has both a lay meaning and a particular diagnostic meaning. In the conversation below she used it in both senses. As she explained,

Trauma, and poverty and substance abuse are inextricably linked. Poverty increases the chance that you will experience a [clinically defined] trauma ... but it also increases cumulative traumatic experiences every day ... the instability of food and security, of housing and stability, of violence in the surrounding neighborhood, of being marginalized, of being denigrated, of being discriminated against, of not having access to [what you need to meet] your basic needs ... And so all of that actually compounds, changes brain development, and makes these individuals more susceptible, so the environment increases the chance that they will experience a clinically-defined trauma. [At that point] their brain in not equipped to integrate that trauma or heal from that trauma. [All this] feeds depression, anxiety, substance-use disorder, psycho-social difficulties.[61]

Furthermore, all of this ups the chance that a particular person will suffer from substance-use disorder. In order to heal, you have to address the trauma. As Dr. Harrison put it, "yes, you can get a person to stop using drugs, but if you don't address the trauma and all the consequences for the trauma that will pull a person back into drug use. One of the most effective relapse predictors is untreated trauma."[62]

Dr. Harrison's words certainly rang true based on what we know about the women who were targeted by Tennessee's law. As I mentioned in the introduction, at the same time that I was researching this book, Dr. Orisha Bowers and a team of researchers at SisterReach, a nonprofit reproductive justice organization based in Memphis, Tennessee, were interviewing women affected by the Fetal Assault law. They spoke both to women who were prosecuted and to women who were not prosecuted but who were using and pregnant during the time the law was in effect. Both groups described a tremendously high level of trauma in their pasts. As the authors reported,

Eighty percent of the women in [the SisterReach] listening sessions were raised in households where substance use was common. More than two-thirds of the women were unemployed at the time of the discussion and reported having had sex in exchange for money, drugs, or other basic needs over the course of their life. The stress of limited finances was compounded by a history of domestic and sexual abuse for almost all participants – highlighting the impact of adverse childhood and adult life experiences and the vulnerability of substance using women.[63]

This data was reinforced in my conversations with care providers. What was clear, in these conversations, was that, in a profound sense, NAS, particularly in cases where women were not receiving treatment, was not so much the center of the problem but was instead often an indication of the existence of trauma and the sign of a need for comprehensive, trauma-informed care. Certainly, all these care providers believed that the infant involved should receive high quality care for the short-term symptoms of NAS, but providing care to that family involved a much deeper understanding of how the histories of trauma, so searingly described in the SisterReach report, impact family health.

As I traveled and researched, I heard some version of these facts, over and over again. Dr. Stephen Lloyd, who ran one of the only practices for pregnant women struggling with substance-use disorder in East Tennessee, described his own learning about the extraordinary trauma often associated with substance-use disorder in his patients:

> When I started taking histories, I would get these young women. They would come in, and I would be going through my history. I would get to the abuse part, and ... I couldn't believe the [amount] of sexual abuse, and I couldn't believe the severity of it. I couldn't believe the number that happened inside their own house. In one afternoon, in Greenville, Tennessee, I got four women, brand new, pregnant, in one afternoon, that were all victims of incest and not by an uncle who was living in the house, but by dad.[64]

Dr. Lloyd's stories were not unusual. Rebecca Fetzer is the Executive Director of Susannah's House, an intensive outpatient program in Knoxville, Tennessee, for mothers in recovery. Ms. Fetzer is a Methodist Pastor who decided, many years ago, to create a way to address the epidemic of addiction in her community. The result was, among other things, the founding of Susannah's House in 2014. Susannah's House provides services to pregnant and parenting mothers and their children. The program is intensive and evidence-based and provides services entirely free of charge. The organization chose, early on, to accept only donations and foundation support and not to accept insurance. They wanted to serve the mothers and children who could not get help elsewhere and did not want insurance rules controlling the treatment they provided or the length of time a woman spent in the program. The import of that decision was quickly clear. At the point I interviewed Ms. Fetzer I had learned a lot about the structure of treatment at most programs. If one thing was clear from those interviews it was that insurance rules control what providers can offer. When I asked Ms. Fetzer about how long her program is, her response was simple: "It's as long as it needs to be." She went on to explain that their program is structured into four phases that the women need to complete. For some a phase can take ninety days, and for others it can take much longer, but what's important to Ms. Fetzer is that she provides a program that allows the mothers to go at their own pace. Susannah's House has an extensive wait-list and is known in the community for providing high quality intensive and effective support. I learned a tremendous amount talking to Ms. Fetzer but the piece that stuck with me the most was our conversation about NAS.

At the end of our interview, I brought up the topic of NAS. She responded by describing the extraordinary trauma her clients have experienced:

> Ninety-nine percent of our moms have been raped. Maybe one hundred percent ... so many of them have been abused in every possible way as children. We have a number of mothers who have been ... prostituted by their parents ... And you have a father who's incarcerated. You have a mother who prostitutes you when you were 16 and started using with you when you were 16 and you have children who are in DCS custody. In that circumstance, NAS is serious, but it doesn't come close to defining the challenge that these women and children face, nor does it do much to help define what form of care might help them heal.

So, many of the women who spoke to SisterReach, and who receive care by providers such as Dr. Lloyd, Dr. Harrison, and Susannah's House, are likely to have suffered enormous trauma. Understanding and addressing individual trauma histories and their effects is key. But you cannot stop there.

2.5 POVERTY, COMMUNITY, AND HEALTH

To understand the full scope of need, society cannot stop at the boundaries of any particular family. We have to look further, at poverty and structural disadvantages that correlate with poverty. In the next chapter of this book, I talk about an earlier moment in our history when the USA similarly misdiagnosed a problem in a way that led to punishment. That story is rooted in the crack epidemic of the late 1980s and 1990s. At that time, prosecutors targeted predominantly poor Black women for taking crack while pregnant. Although the highly stigmatized idea of the crack baby, like the oxytot, led to and justified punishment rather than care, as it turns out this was based on some dangerously wrong ideas about the medical significance of in utero cocaine exposure. Dr. Hallam Hurt is a researcher who led a twenty-five-year longitudinal study of infants exposed in utero to crack cocaine. After watching these children for twenty-five years and comparing their outcomes to the outcomes of their socioeconomic and racially similar peers, she stated her conclusions in stark term: "Poverty is a more powerful influence on the outcome of inner-city children than gestational exposure to cocaine."[65] This is a problem both at the individual family level and at the community level. Communities characterized by a lack of safety and supportive resources can also undermine family health.[66] The exposure of young children to violence noted in Dr. Hurt's work is emblematic of these enormous community-based harms.[67] In short, place matters. "Place-based research and analysis has shown that poorer neighborhoods are characterized by much less physical, economic, educational, and social capital than more affluent ones."[68] As the field of pediatrics is coming to understand,

> [t]he more distressed a neighborhood, the more the daily toll of seeking to get by and stay safe produces stress ... At some point, there must not only be a focus upon individually based services and supports for young children and their families, but for community-building activities to support and strengthen the community's overall capacity to support its children.[69]

This is absolutely not to say that everyone in poor communities is an addict or parents badly. To the contrary, we know that the vast majority of parents, poor or not, succeed in raising healthy children in healthy families. It is, however, to say that structural conditions, a lack of resources, a lack of employment opportunities, safety, over- and under-policing, underfunded schools, racism, and violence, just to name a few, make everything much harder. Living in those conditions significantly increases the chance of experiencing trauma. So, if we really want to design a system of care, we have to frame the need as one based in the individual, family, and community effects of racism, poverty and trauma. We need a system that rejects the stigma so strongly attached to low-income women suffering from substance-use disorder, that respects their privacy and their autonomy, and that offers them an on-demand, comprehensive, integrated system of care, within the medical and social welfare systems, to address the needs of that family.

One place to turn, in understanding what this might look like, is reproductive justice. The concept of reproductive justice was born in 1994 in a conversation among twelve African American women attending a national pro-choice conference.[70] These women centered their conversations on the needs of black women and "challenged how liberal ideology misused the concept of rights and justice to situate responsibility for health and wellness in individual choices, while ignoring the institutionalized barriers that constrict individual choices."[71] Reproductive justice is steeped in intersectionality theory and demands three interlocked human rights: "the right *not to have children* using safe birth control, abortion, or abstinence; the right *to have children* under the conditions we choose; and the right *to parent the children we have* in safe and healthy environments."[72] Crucially, the framework is based not only on the right "to make personal decisions about one's life" but also "the obligations of government and society to ensure that the conditions are suitable for implementing one's decisions."[73] In addition, "although reproductive justice was created by African American women and popularized by women of color, it does not apply only to women of color. Everyone deserves the same human rights, and our intersectional identities inform how to honor them in specific ways based on our experiences and circumstances."[74]

Chapter 9 of this book returns to this reframing to ask what it might mean to frame the need at the heart of these cases in this way and how we might begin to reform institutions and reallocate resources in order to address those needs. But before that, and even before returning to the Tennessee story and the mechanisms of criminalized care, we have to understand a bit of history about criminal systems, social welfare systems, and stigma. That much longer story reveals the roots of what would happen in Tennessee.

NOTES

1. Stephen Davis & Meghan Dwyer, *The Tiniest Drug Addicts: More Babies Born Dependent on Drugs*, FOX 6 Now MILWAUKEE (November 27, 2013, 9:00 PM), https://fox6now.com/2013/11/27/the-tiniest-addicts-more-babies-born-addicted-to-drugs/ [https://perma.cc/ZGC5-R55C]. The practice of referring to infants diagnosed with NAS as "addicted" or "addicts" has been widely condemned by experts in the field. Addiction is a very specific mental health diagnosis that has biochemical as well as behavioral criteria. While a newborn can be born having been exposed to various substances in utero, by definition or she is not addicted.

2. *Neonatal Abstinence Syndrome (NAS)*, TENN. DEP'T OF HEALTH, https://www.tn.gov/health/nas/ [https://perma.cc/AE5U-VXWF].

3. *Id.*

4. Matthew R. Grossman et al., *Neonatal Abstinence Syndrome: Time for a Reappraisal*, 7 HOSP. PEDIATRICS 115 (2017) (alleging that reliance on the traditional method of diagnosis and treatment of NAS could be outdated and hindering health care providers' ability to assess the effectiveness of non-pharmacological interventions recommended by the American Academy of Pediatrics).

5. *Increased Drug Availability Is Associated with Increased Use and Overdose*, NAT'L INST. ON DRUG ABUSE (January 2018), https://www.drugabuse.gov/publica tions/research-reports/relationship-between-prescription-drug-abuse-heroin-use/increased-drug-availability-associated-increased-use-overdose [https://perma.cc/8NQ7-V46Z].

6. *Id.*

7. *Id.*

8. *U.S. Prescribing Rate Maps*, CTRS. FOR DISEASE CONTROL & PREVENTION (July 31, 2017), https://www.cdc.gov/drugoverdose/maps/rxrate-maps.html [https://perma.cc/7VCU-PW5E].

9. *Id.*

10. *Id.*

11. *U.S. State Prescribing Rates, 2019*, CTRS. FOR DISEASE CONTROL & PREVENTION, https://www.cdc.gov/drugoverdose/maps/rxstate2019.html [https://perma.cc/7VCU-PW5E].

12. *Id.*

13. *See* U.S. Dep't of Health & Human Servs., Pub No. (SMA) 16–4978, A Collaborative Approach to the Treatment of Pregnant Women with Opioid Use Disorders 6 (2016), https://store.samhsa.gov/product/A-Collaborative-Approach-to-the-Treatment-of-Pregnant-Women-with-Opioid-Use-Disorders/SMA16-4978 [https://perma.cc/527K-HJBX].
14. *Id.*
15. Astha Singhal et al., *Racial-Ethnic Disparities in Opioid Prescriptions at Emergency Department Visits for Conditions Commonly Associated with Prescription Drug Abuse*, 11 PLOS One 1, 2 (2016) (citing M. J. Pletcher et al., *Trends in Opioid Prescribing by Race/Ethnicity for Patients Seeking Care in US Emergency Departments*, 299 JAMA 70 (2008)).
16. *See* Michele Goodwin, *Fetal Protection Laws: Moral Panic and the New Constitutional Battlefront*, 102 Calif. L. Rev. 781, 793–94 (2014) (citing Committee on Health Care for Underserved Women, American College of Obstetricians and Gynecologists, Committee Opinion No. 538: Nonmedical Use of Prescription Drugs 2 (2012), https://www.ncbi.nlm.nih.gov/pubmed/22996128 [https://perma.cc/K55U-3TKF]); Allen A. Mitchell et al., *Medication Use During Pregnancy, with Particular Focus on Prescription Drugs: 1976–2008*, 205 Am. J. Obstetrics & Gynecology 51.e1, 51.e5 (2011); Leonard J. Paulozzi et al., *Vital Signs: Overdoses of Prescription Opioid Pain Relievers: United States, 1999–2008*, 60 Morbidity & Mortality Wkly. Rep. 1487, 1488 (2011) https://www.cdc.gov/mmwr/preview/mmwrhtml/mm6043a4.htm (reporting that non-Hispanic white women have a higher drug overdose death rate than women of other races).
17. Paulozzi et al., *supra* note 16 (reporting that non-Hispanic white women have a higher drug overdose death rate than women of other races).
18. *Drug Overdose Death Data*, Ctrs. for Disease Control & Prevention (December 19, 2017), https://www.cdc.gov/drugoverdose/data/statedeaths.html [https://perma.cc/RF2J-KDSG].
19. *Id.*
20. *See* U.S. Dep't of Health & Human Servs., Pub No. (SMA) 16-4978, A Collaborative Approach to the Treatment of Pregnant Women with Opioid Use Disorders 6 (2016), https://store.samhsa.gov/product/A-Collaborative-Approach-to-the-Treatment-of-Pregnant-Women-with-Opioid-Use-Disorders/SMA16-4978 [https://perma.cc/527K-HJBX].
21. *Id.* at 3 (citations omitted).
22. *See* Mahsa M. Yazdy et al., *Prescription Opioids in Pregnancy and Birth Outcomes: A Review of the Literature*, 4 J. Pediatric Genetics 56, 57 (2015).
23. *Id.*
24. Peter R. Martin & A. J. Reid Finlayson, *Opioid Use Disorder During Pregnancy in Tennessee: Expediency vs. Science*, 41 Am. J. Drug & Alcohol Abuse 367, 367 (2015).

25. *See* Mahsa M. Yazdy et al., *Prescription Opioids in Pregnancy and Birth Outcomes: A Review of the Literature*, 4 J. PEDIATRIC GENETICS 56, 57 (2015).

26. *See* U.S. DEP'T OF HEALTH & HUMAN SERVS., PUB NO. (SMA) 16–4978, A COLLABORATIVE APPROACH TO THE TREATMENT OF PREGNANT WOMEN WITH OPIOID USE DISORDERS 6 (2016), https://store.samhsa.gov/product/A-Collaborative-Approach-to-the-Treatment-of-Pregnant-Women-with-Opioid-Use-Disorders/SMA16-4978 [https://perma.cc/527K-HJBX].

27. *Id.* (citations omitted).

28. The entire data set consisted of 2,952 separate entries during the just over two-year period. 2049 individuals, or about 70 percent provided income data. The per-year reported income level data broke down as follows:

Below $10K:	45.24%
10K–14.9K:	20.11%
15K–24.9K:	16.45 %
25K–34.9K:	8.54%
35K–49.9K:	4.93%
50K–74.9K:	2.54%
75K–99.9K:	1.27%
Over 100K:	.93%

29. AM. C. OBSTETRICIANS & GYNECOLOGISTS, COMM. ON OBSTETRIC PRAC., ACOG COMMITTEE OPINION NO. 711: OPIOID USE AND OPIOID USE DISORDER IN PREGNANCY 6 (2017), https://www.acog.org/Clinical-Guidance-and-Publications/Committee-Opinions/Committee-on-Obstetric-Practice/Opioid-Use-and-Opioid-Use-Disorder-in-Pregnancy [https://perma.cc/MY9V-MPH3].

30. *Id.*

31. *See, e.g.*, Robert D. Stewart et al., *The Obstetrical and Neonatal Impact of Maternal Opioid Detoxification in Pregnancy*, 209 AM. J. OBSTETRICS & GYNECOLOGY 267 (2013); Jennifer Bell et al., *Detoxification from Opiate Drugs During Pregnancy*, 215 AM. J. OBSTETRICS & GYNECOLOGY 374, 374 (2016).

32. *See* John J. McCarthy & Mishka Terplan, *Detoxification from Opiates During Pregnancy: Stressing the Fetal Brain*, 215 AM. J. OBSTETRICS & GYNECOLOGY 670, 670 (2016). *But see* Craig V. Towers & Mark D. Hennessy, *Reply*, 215 AM. J. OBSTETRICS & GYNECOLOGY 670, 671 (2016).

33. Stewart, *supra* note 31 at 267.

34. *Id.*

35. ALICE M. NYAKERIGA & MORGAN MCDONALD, TENN. DEP'T HEALTH, NEONATAL ABSTINENCE SYNDROME SURVEILLANCE ANNUAL REPORT, at 5 (2019), https://www.tn.gov/content/dam/tn/health/documents/nas/2019-NAS-Annual-Update.pdf. [https://perma.cc/WRV6-T5HJ].

36. In 2013, in an effort to understand the scope and nature of the problem, the Tennessee Department of Health began requiring hospitals to report the

numbers of infants diagnosed with NAS. Michael D. Warren et al., *Implementation of a Statewide Surveillance System for Neonatal Abstinence Syndrome – Tennessee, 2013*, 64 MORBIDITY & MORTALITY WKLY. RPT. 125, (2015), https://www.cdc.gov/mmwr/preview/mmwrhtml/mm6405a4.html.

37. NYAKERIGA & MCDONALD, *supra* note 35, at 7, tbl. 1.

38. *Id.*

39. *Id.*, at 8, fig. 3. There are also a very small number of cases where the source of exposure is unknown.

40. *Id.*, at 6, tbl. 1.

41. *Id.*, at 6, fig. 2.

42. For a discussion of the state of the literature as of 2016 *see, e.g.*, Uma M. Reddy, et al., *Opioid Use in Pregnancy, Neonatal Abstinence Syndrome, and Childhood Outcomes: Executive Summary of a Joint Workshop by the Eunice Kennedy Shriver National Institute of Child Health and Human Development, American Congress of Obstetricians and Gynecologists, American Academy of Pediatrics, Society for Maternal-Fetal Medicine, Centers for Disease Control and Prevention, and the March of Dimes Foundation*, 130(1) OBSTETRICS & GYNECOLOGY 10 (July 2017), doi:10.1097/AOG.0000000000002054.

43. Emmalee S. Bandstra et al., *Prenatal Drug Exposure: Infant and Toddler Outcomes*, 29 J. ADDICTIVE DISEASES 245, 247, 249 (2010).

44. Reddy, *supra* note 42, at 23.

45. *See, e.g.*, Mary-Margaret A. Fill et al., *Educational Disabilities Among Children Born with Neonatal Abstinence Syndrome*, 142 PEDIATRICS 1, 1 (2018) (matching birth record data and special education outcomes for children born with NAS between 2008 and 2011 and finding that "children with NAS were significantly more likely to be referred for a disability evaluation, to meet criteria for a disability, and to require classroom therapies or services."); Marian P. Jarlenski et al., *Five-Year Outcomes Among Medicaid-Enrolled Children with In Utero Opioid Exposure*, 39:2 HEALTH AFFAIRS 247 (2020) ("Examined well-child visit use and diagnoses of pediatric complex chronic conditions in first five years of life among children with opioid exposure, tobacco exposure or neither exposure in utero. Children with in utero opioid exposure had a lower predicted probability of recommended well-child visit use at age fifteen months (42.1 percent) compared to those with tobacco exposure (54.1 percent) and those with neither exposure (55.7 percent). Children with in utero opioid exposure had a predicted probability of being diagnosed with a pediatric complex chronic condition similar to that among children with tobacco exposure and those with neither exposure (20.4 percent, 18.7 percent, and 20.2 percent, respectively). Our findings were consistent when we examined a subgroup of opioid-exposed children identified as having neonatal opioid withdrawal symptoms."); Romuladus E. Azuine, et al., *Prenatal Risk Factors and Perinatal and Postnatal Outcomes Associated with Maternal Opioid Exposure in an Urban, Low-Income, Multiethnic US*

Population, 2:6 PEDIATRICS 1, 1 (June 2019) ("This cohort study analyzed data from the Boston Birth Cohort, an urban, low-income, multiethnic cohort that enrolled mother-newborn pairs at birth at Boston Medical Center (Boston, Massachusetts) starting in 1998, and a subset of children were prospectively observed at Boston Medical Center pediatric primary care and subspecialty clinics from birth to age 21 years. Data analysis began in June 2018 and was completed in May 2019 ... At birth, opioid exposure was associated with higher risks of fetal growth restriction (odds ratio [OR], 1.87; 95%CI, 1.41-2.47) and preterm birth (OR, 1.49; 95%CI, 1.19-1.86). Opioid exposure was associated with increased risks of lack of expected physiological development (OR, 1.80; 95%CI, 1.17-2.79) and conduct disorder/emotional disturbance (OR, 2.13; 95%CI, 1.20-3.77) among preschool-aged children. In school aged children, opioid exposure was associated with a higher risk of attention deficit/hyperactivity disorder.").

46. United States Government Accountability Office, *Newborn Health, Federal Action Needed to Address Neonatal Abstinence Syndrome* 24 (2017); Kathryn Dee L. MacMillan & Alison Volpe Holmes, *Neonatal Abstinence Syndrome and the Pediatric Hospitalist: 5 Years Later,* 8 HOSP. PEDIATRICS 51, 52 (2018).

47. Shanta Trivedi, *The Harm of Child Removal,* 43 N.Y.U. REV. L. & SOC. CHANGE 523, 528 (2019) (citing Lynn F. Beller, *When in Doubt, Take Them out: Removal of Children from Victims of Domestic Violence Ten Years After Nicholson v. Williams,* 22 DUKE J. GENDER L. & POL'Y 205, 216 (2015)).

48. *Id.*

49. Christopher Church and Vivek S. Sankaran, *Easy Come, Easy Go: The Plight of Children Who Spend Less Than Thirty Days in Foster Care,* 19 U. PA. J. L. & SOC. CHANGE 207 (2016).

50. *Id.* at 212 (citing Joseph J. Doyle Jr., *Child Protection and Child Outcomes: Measuring the Effects of Foster Care,* 97 AM. ECON. REV. 1583, 1583 (2007)); *see also* Josh Gupta-Kagan, *Toward a Public Health Legal Structure for Child Welfare,* 92 NEB. L. REV. 897 (2014).

51. TREATMENT EPISODE DATA SET (TEDS) 2017: ADMISSIONS TO AND DISCHARGES FROM PUBLICLY-FUNDED SUBSTANCE USE TREATMENT, DEP'T HEALTH & HUMAN SERVS., 58, https://www.samhsa.gov/data/report/treatment-episode-data-set-teds-2017-admissions-and-discharges-publicly-funded-substance-use [https://perma.cc/X8ZE-4Q5J].

52. Charles R. Bauer et al., *The Maternal Lifestyle Study: Drug Exposure during Pregnancy and Short-Term Maternal Outcomes.,* 2002 AM. J. OBSTETRICS & GYNECOLOGY 487(2002).

53. *Id.* at. 493.

54. Martha A. Jessup et al., *Extrinsic. Barrier to Substance Abuse Treatment Among Pregnant Drug Dependent Women,* 2003 J. DRUG ISSUES 285, 292 (2003).

55. Mary Anne Armstrong et. al., *Perinatal Substance Abuse Intervention in Obstetric Clinics Decrease Adverse Neonatal Outcomes,* 233–39 J. PERINATOLOGY 3 (2003).

56. *Id.* at. 5.
57. R. D. Stewart, D. B. Nelson, E. H. Adhikari et al., *The Obstetrical and Neonatal Impact of Maternal Opioid Detoxification in Pregnancy*, 209 Am J Obstet Gynecol 267.e1-5 (2013). Telephone interview with Dr. Andy Hsi, Professor, Department of Pediatrics, University of New Mexico School of Medicine (February 12, 2019).
58. Interview with Dr. Nzinga Harrison, Chief Medical Officer and Cofounder Eleanor Health (June 25, 2018).
59. *Id.*
60. *Id.*
61. *Id.*
62. *Id.*
63. Orisha A. Bowers et al., *Tennessee's Fetal Assault Law: Understanding Its Impact on Marginalized Women* at 4 (2019) https://www.sisterreach.org/uploads/1/3/3/2/133261658/full_fetal_assault_rpt_1.pdf [https://perma.cc/8BKC-VYTE].
64. Interview with Dr. Stephen Lloyd, Chief Medical Officer Journey Pure (August 9, 2018).
65. Susan FitzGerald, *"Crack Baby" Study Ends with Unexpected but Clear Result*, Phila. Inquirer (June 21, 2017), http://www.philly.com/philly/health/20130721__Crack_baby__study_ends_with_unexpected_but_clear_result.html?arc404=true [https://perma.cc/MQW4-P2MF].
66. *See* Charles Bruner, *ACE, Place, Race, and Poverty: Building Hope for Children*, 17 Acad. Pediatrics 123 (2017).
67. FitzGerald, *supra* note 65.
68. Bruner, *supra* note 66 at 124.
69. *Id.* at 125.
70. Loretta J. Ross, et al., *Introduction to* Radical Reproductive Justice: Foundations, Theory, Practice, Critique, at 16 (Loretta J. Ross et al. eds., 2017).
71. *Id.* at 18–19.
72. *Id.* at 14.
73. *Id.*
74. *Id.* at 23.

3 HISTORICAL AND THEORETICAL ROOTS

Tennessee's fetal assault statute, and the systems in which it was embedded, did not appear out of thin air. To the contrary, both the statute and the systems in which it operated are deeply rooted in the history and practices of US punishment and social support systems and in the stigmas about race, sex, and socioeconomic status that undergird and inform those systems. Similarly, this book does not stand alone. It is rooted in, and in conversation with, the work of many other scholars writing in the fields it touches. This chapter lays the historical ground and locates this book in these larger academic conversations. There are two main pieces to this story: first the long and deeply racialized history of using criminal prosecution to punish poor women who use drugs during pregnancy, and second the neoliberal and again deeply racialized turn away from social support and toward criminalization, resulting in the location of residual care provision for poor communities, proximate to or inside punishment systems.

3.1 PROSECUTING WOMEN WHO USE DRUGS DURING PREGNANCY: USING THE CRIMINAL LEGAL SYSTEM TO PUNISH AND CONTROL BLACK (AND THEN WHITE) WOMEN'S DRUG USE

While Tennessee was the first U.S. state to enact a statute explicitly criminalizing in utero drug transmission, it was by no means the first state, or the last, to prosecute women in these circumstances. For decades prosecutors across the country have brought these prosecutions using other legal theories. Prosecutors across the nation have brought these cases since at least the 1970s, by charging women with violating statutes originally intended to target crimes against living persons, not fetuses. For example, between 1973 and 2005, the majority of prosecutions charged women who allegedly transmitted drugs to their fetus in utero with child abuse or child endangerment. Similarly, between 2006 and 2015, at least 479 women were prosecuted in Alabama for "chemical endangerment," a crime originally created to target the harm to children who were living in houses where methamphetamine was being produced.[1]

Lynn Paltrow and Jeanne Flavin documented prosecutions and/or other forced interventions against pregnant women in forty-four states between 1973 and 2005.[2] Since 2005, the point at which Paltrow and Flavin's data ends, researchers have documented hundreds of additional prosecutions. At this point it is fair to estimate that over 1,000 women have been prosecuted in the US for in utero drug transmission.[3]

One can trace these prosecutions back to the 1970s and the prosecution of women for giving birth to what were then termed "heroin babies." While these early prosecutions mark the start of this phenomena, the majority of prosecutions have come in two large waves. The first began in earnest in 1989 and targeted poor, disproportionately African American women, predominantly in the South, who were accused of ingesting crack cocaine while pregnant. The second, in more recent years, targeted both white and Black poor women, also predominantly in the South, for using methamphetamine and opiates, as well as other illegal drugs. The first wave of prosecutions spiked between 1989 and 1991 and continued at a steady pace through the mid-2000s. Those prosecutions were strongly associated with the crack cocaine epidemic and were targeted, both as a matter of empirical fact and as a matter of rhetoric, at poor African American women giving birth to what were then termed "crack babies." The second wave began in the mid-2000s with the rise of methamphetamine and opiates. In this second wave the prosecutions shifted, again both empirically and as a matter of rhetoric, to "meth babies" and "oxy-tots."

During the second wave of prosecutions, beginning roughly in the early 2010s, prosecutions appear to have remained focused in the South and in poor communities, but the overall racial makeup of those prosecutions began to shift from Black to white. As Grace Howard revealed in her study of prosecutions in South Carolina and Alabama, as the targeted substances shifted from cocaine to methamphetamine and opiates, the racial makeup of defendants shifted overall from Black to white.[4] This is not to say that prosecutions against women for cocaine or heroin exposure or prosecutions against low-income African American women ceased. Those prosecutions continue to this day. Nor is it to say that women of other races were not prosecuted. But it is to say that as drug use patterns have shifted, so too have the prevalence of particular drugs, and particular drug users, in these prosecutions.

This result is confirmed both through the data underlying this study of the Tennessee prosecutions as well as the work of other scholars. Tennessee's prosecutions sit squarely within what I am calling the second wave of these prosecutions.

In response to the first wave of prosecutions, a wide variety of scholars demonstrated that these prosecutions were a means to control the reproductive conduct of poor, African American women. Most importantly, in 1991 Dorothy Roberts published an article in the Harvard Law Review entitled *Punishing Drug Addicts Who Have Babies: Women of Color, Equality and the Right of Privacy*.[5] Before her article, other scholars had certainly been writing about the wave of prosecutions against women for using crack cocaine during pregnancy and had been framing it as a growing contest between reproductive freedom and fetal rights.[6] But these prosecutions did not target *all* women who used drugs during pregnancy. Instead, the first wave focused, nearly exclusively, on poor Black women who used crack cocaine during their pregnancies. Professor Roberts was the first to center an analysis of the prosecution on that fact. As she described it, we could understand the prosecutions as a new chapter in the "systematic, institutional denial of reproductive freedom [that] has marked Black women's history in America, [and] the devaluation of Black women as mothers."[7] She demonstrated that "these women are the primary targets of prosecutors, not because they are more likely to be guilty of fetal abuse, but because they are Black and poor."[8] Professor Roberts, and the many scholars who built upon her work, helps us understand why that particular group of women was targeted.

Her analysis also laid bare the ways in which stigma and stereotype led to the dangerous notion of the "crack baby" and the subsequent targeting of their mothers for prosecution and punishment. That story begins during the War on Drugs and, more particularly, with a doctor named Ira Chasnoff.

Dr. Chasnoff was at the Department of Pediatrics at the Northwestern Medical Center in Chicago. He noticed what he thought was a pattern among infants born to mothers who had taken cocaine during their pregnancies. The infants seemed more likely to be born prematurely, and it seemed like they were struggling in similar ways. Chasnoff, working with a few colleagues, conducted an initial study involving twenty-three women, the results of which were published in the New England Journal of Medicine in 1985.[9] The researchers compared the pregnancies of these twenty-three women to the pregnancies of women who were drug-free but were otherwise similar in terms of maternal age, socioeconomic status, number of pregnancies and cigarette, marijuana, and alcohol use. The findings were limited and were framed as preliminary:

> Neonatal gestational age, birth weight, length, and head circumference were not affected by cocaine use. However the Brazelton Neonatal Behavioral Assessment Scale revealed that infants exposed to cocaine had significant depression of interactive behavior and poor organizational response to environmental stimuli. These preliminary observations suggest that cocaine influences the outcome of pregnancy as well as the neurologic behavior of the newborn, but a full assessment will require a larger number of pregnancies and longer follow up.[10]

Despite these preliminary and sometimes contrary findings and hypothesis, what happened next stunned the researchers, although given the racial politics around crack cocaine and Black motherhood, it should not have. Within days of the publication of the study, Chasnoff's phones were ringing. The press stories were dramatic and overblown. The term *crack baby* soon took hold in the popular press, and the predictions were dire. The term suggested, in the most sensational terms, that there was something tremendously wrong with these particular children, that they were destined to be different than any group we had seen before. In 1988, ABC proclaimed the existence of "an entirely new underclass of children, unable to care for themselves." In 1990, Peter Jennings of ABC News proclaimed: "In the United States this year, at least 100,000 crack babies will be born. Today the government said it will cost $5 billion dollars a year to care for such babies and money doesn't begin to tell the whole story."

In 1991 Time Magazine ran a cover story with the title *Crack Kids: Their Mothers Used Drugs, and Now It's the Children Who Suffer.* The cover depicted a young, Black boy in tears. The prediction for the children's future was dire. In 1989, John Silber, the president of Boston University, spoke of "crack babies who won't ever achieve the intellectual development to have consciousness of God. Theirs will be a life of certain suffering, of probable deviance, of permanent inferiority."[11] The panic and hysteria traveled to education circles. According to a report written at the time in the American School Board Journal, "The arrival of those first afflicted youngsters will mark the beginning of a struggle that will leave your resources depleted and your compassion tested."[12]

And it wasn't just the popular media and the nonmedical establishment that was on this speeding stigma train. The scientific and medical community overall was entirely complicit. Dr. Chasnoff for example, was quoted in an ABC new segment as stating that "These children are not normal in the sense that they are going to be able to enter the classic schoolroom and function in large groups of children."[13]

While the popular media was telling this sensational and deeply racist story about both the mothers and the children, others were asking different questions and coming to different conclusions. From the very beginning, Dr. Claire Coles at Emory University had her doubts. She and her graduate students were observing drug-exposed infants and they simply were not seeing the same effects: "You could not distinguish the cocaine-exposed babies from the other babies."[14] Moreover,

> The effects [other researchers were describing] didn't seem consistent with the action of the drug itself . . . Many of the children who were the so-called, classic cocaine babies were premature babies and the symptoms that were seen on the videos, on television – the tremoring arms and all that was prematurity. You could have taken any premature baby and gotten the same image.[15]

Today our understanding of the children exposed to crack cocaine in utero during that period is far more nuanced. Although in utero cocaine exposure has been shown to have some moderate effects on various developmental and behavioral outcomes[16] and to cause clear short-term effects in pregnancy, the effect of in utero exposure to other substances, such as alcohol and cigarettes, is far more damaging.[17]

Equally importantly, we now know that we were largely misframing the problem. The intellectual journey of Dr. Hallam Hurt, then chair of Neonatology at the Albert Einstein Medical Center, makes this clear.[18] Dr. Hurt and her team conducted a twenty-five-year longitudinal study comparing the development of infants exposed to crack cocaine to similarly situated infants who were not exposed.[19] Dr. Hurt and her team followed 224 babies born between 1989 and 1992.[20] Half had been exposed to cocaine in utero and the other half had not.[21] All the infants were born near or at full term and were from low-income, predominantly African American families.[22] At the initiation of this study, Philadelphia was in the midst of the crack epidemic. "[N]early one in six newborns at city hospitals had mothers who tested positive for cocaine."[23] What Hurt and her team found was that, as the infants aged, there were "no significant differences between the cocaine-exposed children and the controls."[24] What they did find, however, was that both groups of poor children, those who had been exposed to cocaine and those who had not, "lagged on developmental and intellectual measures compared to the norm."[25] Similar results have been echoed in other long-term and rigorous studies.[26] These consistent results throughout the many years of the study led Hurt and her team to look at other factors that might be harming the development of these children.[27] They looked at a variety of environmental factors and found that although "being raised in a nurturing home" led to better outcomes, substantial proportions of the children, by age seven, had been exposed to significant violence including hearing gunshots, witnessing a shooting, and seeing a dead body.[28] That exposure correlated with increased signs of depression and anxiety.[29] These findings echo similar research that has firmly established that exposure to what are termed "adverse childhood experiences" (or ACEs) has harmful long-term physical and mental effects on children.[30] At the end of the nearly quarter of a century study of these children, Hurt framed her conclusions succinctly: "Poverty is a more powerful influence on the outcome of inner-city children than gestational exposure to cocaine."[31] Ultimately, Hurt and her team turned their focus to the effects of poverty on developmental growth and Hurt has since gone on to focus her research on these crucial and complex issues.[32] And the mainstream press, far after the fact, issued a series of retractions and apologies, all of which acknowledged their role in hyping what Lynn Paltrow, the executive Director of National Advocates for Pregnant Women, has called "the epidemic that wasn't."[33]

The epidemic that wasn't led to some extraordinarily harsh consequences for the poor, predominantly Black women who were the target of these prosecutions. Perhaps the most notorious set of prosecutions took place in Charleston, South Carolina. These prosecutions were the subject of a lawsuit, *Ferguson* v. *City of Charleston*, that made it all the way to the Supreme Court. As the Supreme Court tells the story, "in the fall of 1988, staff members at the public hospital operating in the city of Charleston by the Medical University of South Carolina (MUSC) became concerned about an apparent increase in the use of cocaine by patients who were receiving prenatal treatment." After initial attempts at referring women to treatment, the medical staff concluded that the hospital needed a different strategy. Shirley Brown, who was a nurse and the case manager of the MUSC obstetrics department, heard a radio broadcast about prosecutions, by the local District Attorney, for using cocaine during pregnancy. She reached out to the hospital's lawyer, and they ultimately reached out to the local prosecutor in that jurisdiction. The prosecutor assembled a task force which included "representatives of MUSC, the police, the County Substance Abuse Commission and the Department of Social Services"[34] and they ultimately developed a protocol for these cases. Women were drug screened, without their knowledge or consent, during prenatal visits, if they met one of nine criteria. Hospital staff were instructed to follow a protocol for collecting and maintaining evidence from these drug tests, specifically so that the results would be admissible in any future prosecution. Women who tested positive were told that if they did not agree to enter treatment they would be prosecuted. Initially, if a woman used during labor, "the police were to be notified without delay and the patient promptly arrested." If she tested positive during pregnancy, she was referred to treatment but would be arrested "if she tested positive for cocaine a second time or if she missed an appointment with a substance abuse counselor." Later the policy surrounding drug tests during labor was amended to conform to the policy concerning cocaine use during pregnancy.[35] The City of Charleston and the hospital "repeatedly insisted [that] their motive was benign rather than punitive." They also maintained that the policy was justified to respond to the extraordinary "social and economic costs of the epidemic" of babies exposed to crack cocaine.

Ten women brought suit against the City, arguing that the policy and practices violated their rights, under the Fourth Amendment to the US Constitution, to be free from unwarranted search. The search in question was the collection of urine without their consent. All ten women had been subject to arrest and prosecution under these protocols, and, in every case, the medical evidence collected by hospital staff was used against them in the criminal case. The Court concluded that these searches did in fact violate the Fourth Amendment, but what I want to focus on, for the purposes of this chapter, is the extraordinarily punitive nature of the program and the way in which it was targeted. As explained by Professor Michele Goodwin,

> Medical staff at MUSC along with police and prosecutors "disproportionately targeted indigent, African American women for search and arrest." In their search program, of the thirty women arrested, twenty-nine were African American. Special dispensation was sought for at least one white woman who met the criteria for arrest but remained free. Racial profiling may have contributed to the arrest of another white woman because a nurse and member of the interagency task force made a point of notating the patient's chart with the following information: "Patient live[s] with her boyfriend who is a Negro." This particular nurse admitted at trial that she believed interracial relationships violated "God's way," and "raised

the option of sterilization for black women testing positive for cocaine, but not for white women."[36]

Women in Charleston were arrested from their hospital bed, in their hospital gowns. Police arrested women, "'while still bleeding, weak and in pain from having just given birth.' Some were handcuffed and shackled, with chains circling their abdomen."[37] In some cases, women were transported in leg irons. All in response to an epidemic that wasn't.

All of this, however, begs the question: How did this happen? How did a series of fairly tentative and, ultimately, largely disproven scientific findings explode into a cultural hysteria over crack babies and aggressive targeting of their mothers? To this question, Roberts provides a compelling and definitive answer:

> Focusing on Black crack addicts rather than on other perpetrators of fetal harms serves two broader social purposes. First, prosecution of these pregnant women serves to degrade women whom society views as undeserving to be mothers and to discourage them from having children . . .
>
> [T]he prosecution of crack-addicted mothers diverts public attention from social ills such as poverty, racism, and a misguided national health policy and implies instead that shamefully high Black infant death rates are caused by the bad acts of individual mothers. Poor Black mothers thus become the scapegoats for the causes of the Black community's ill health . . . Making criminals of Black mothers apparently helps to relieve the nation of the burden of creating a health care system that ensures healthy babies for all its citizens.[38]

To say the least, this history counsels caution. We are being told that we face another epidemic of drug use during pregnancy that is harming infants. Tennessee's fetal assault law was justified by its supporters almost entirely as a logical response to that epidemic. This led, as we will see, to punishment reminiscent of the punishment meted out in the late 1980s in Charleston, South Carolina. It led, as this book will lay out in detail, not only to the prosecution of at least 120 women but, as a result, to extensive punishment in the form of jailing and fines, and to either no treatment at all or treatment at a high punitive price. As was the case in South Carolina, although some averred that all of this was intended to help women and protect babies, what resulted, as was in the case in the late 1980s, was punishment.

3.1.1 Race, Whiteness, Privilege, and Need

The Tennessee prosecutions continued this story but, as this book details, in contrast to the earlier prosecutions, the Tennessee prosecutions focused in particular on Appalachia and on poor white women. Scholars have turned their attention to this trend and have asked important questions about how we should understand the relationship between racism, gender, white privilege, and the shift to the prosecution of poor white women. On the issues of race and white privilege for example, Khiara Bridges has argued that the fetal assault data coming out of Tennessee, and specifically the fact that the majority of women prosecuted for fetal assault were low-income white women, raises questions and adds complexity to our understanding of white privilege, white disadvantage, and the mechanisms of intersectional subordination.[39] To begin, there is no question that overall the national response to the opiate epidemic is far more compassionate and treatment-focused than our prior response to the crack cocaine epidemic. It is clear that this focus on treatment over punishment has everything to do with the whiteness of its victims and their attendant privilege.

At the same time, as this book demonstrates, the predominantly white women who were prosecuted experienced a great deal of punishment and at best a degraded and risky form of care, treatment that is far more similar to the treatment of Black women at the height of the crack epidemic than not. If these women had privilege, the Tennessee story indicates that that privilege was severely attenuated. In the end, their whiteness did not protect the women in East Tennessee from either punishment or deprivation of care. In fact, as we will see, the paucity of resources in rural, largely white, Appalachia in comparison to urban, majority-Black Memphis ultimately meant that the African American women in the case study gained more access to "treatment," admittedly through drug court, than did white women. But that access, as discussed in detail in Chapter 7, came at extraordinary risk and cost. Women who were prosecuted in Memphis faced higher financial costs and higher terms of incarceration, both as they participated in the program and in particular if they failed to complete the drug court program.

Confronting the questions of race and privilege directly, Professor Bridges, drawing in part on Christopher Wray's[40] work and focusing specifically on the prosecution of poor white women for drug use during pregnancy, begins to answer a crucial question: How are we to understand the prevalence of current forms of white disadvantage, in particular in the punishment of poor white women for opiate use during pregnancy, in the context of our clear understanding of the existence and strength of white privilege? Some might ask, on this topic, whether the fact that poor white women, who are at the center of the story told in this book, were severely punished, somehow means that white privilege does not exist. Certainly, the women subject to subordination and punishment in Tennessee could not possibly have been feeling privileged as they lost their children and faced prosecution and punishment. And indeed, as one reads these stories and looks at the economic devastation in poor white communities in the United States, it is politically essential to acknowledge and understand the real suffering and subordination in poor white communities and to ask directly how that might inform the idea of white privilege.

Bridges provides a crucial response to these questions. For example, we might understand the prosecutions of white women here as a kind of racist path dependency or an attenuation of white privilege by the existence of a racist precedent. In short, in response to the use of crack cocaine by poor African American women in the 1980s and 1990s we laid down a response – degradation and criminalization – and that is the path and the system we have. Had we responded differently and more compassionately at the time, perhaps we would have a better system. However, we did not and now, for stigmatized white women, we continue on the path.

In addition, these prosecutions support a nuanced understanding of white privilege. White privilege, understood as a system that subordinates people of color, is a double-edged sword. It is constituted by, and in fact relies on, the existence of white disadvantage. One cannot exist without the other. As Matt Wray has detailed, to preserve the purity of the idea of whiteness as superior, some white people and some white behavior has to be excluded from the racist ideal.[41] So, poor white women who use opiates during pregnancy are, in Wray's terms, *not quite white.*

Racialized gender and motherhood too play a particular role. As Roberts demonstrated, during the crack cocaine era the racist trope of degraded Black motherhood and the prosecutions justified diverting focus from the failure to provide the care that women, families, and communities desperately needed. Here white motherhood is wielded differently, not as a stigmatized identity, but as an elevated and idealized white category from which "bad [white] mothers" are excluded. The result is the same. The racist trope is used to lay blame and to divert society's focus from real need.

For example, in Chapter 1 we saw those who supported the fetal assault law labeled the mothers "bad mothers" who can, through discipline, be transformed into "nurturing, caring" mothers. While the fetal assault law did not explicitly label the race of the mothers, given the strong association between the opiate epidemic and poor, white communities, it is clear that the racial imagery here is white. Telling another part of the race narrative, in Chapter 2 we saw the strategic use of images of innocent white babies as a further means to justify a framing of the "problem" as NAS and bad motherhood. We also saw, in Chapter 2, that the focus on NAS and drug use during pregnancy diverts focus away from taking on the hard issues of poverty, trauma, and community need. So here, idealized tropes of white motherhood and innocent white babies are wielded to exclude poor white women from the idealized category of white motherhood. These "bad mothers" are quite literally excluded from motherhood, through child welfare intervention and prosecution, purportedly in the name of saving their white babies from harm. Like the stigmatized images that justified prosecution of poor Black women at the end of the twentieth century, here too the wielding of stigma results in a system that, as we will see, punishes stigmatized mothers and either fails to provide care or provides a risk-filled and degraded form of care. In addition, again as was the case before, the stigma, separation and prosecution diverts society's attention from a richer, more compassionate, and more responsive view of need.

3.2 US SOCIAL WELFARE HISTORY AND THE MERGING
OF PUNISHMENT WITH SUPPORT

This book's focus is certainly on the operation of intersectional race, class, and gender stigma, but it is also on systems: on how systems like those making up the health care, child welfare, and criminal legal institutions are complicit in and the instruments of stigmatization, control, and punishment in poor communities. These systems operate in a very particular social and historical context. This context is broad and deep and there is not nearly enough space in this chapter to provide it all. Having said that, there are a few crucial pieces to the story. It is to this particular set of stories that this chapter now turns, beginning with a very brief history of systems that support and systems that punish and then tracing several different aspects underlying what this book terms criminalizing care.

3.2.1 A Very Brief Dive into History

First, an extremely truncated version of US social welfare history: one could certainly start earlier and tell the story differently, but one important thread of modern US social welfare history starts in the 1930s, during the New Deal, grows through the Great Society in the 1960s, and ebbs into an era of retrenchment and disinvestment in social support, culminating in 1996, with the abolition of Aid to Families with Dependent Children. This story has been well-told elsewhere[42] and encapsulates the arc of key national social welfare programs including Social Security, Medicaid, Medicare, Unemployment Insurance, Food Stamps (now Supplementary Nutrition Assistance), public housing, Section 8, Temporary Assistance to Needy Families, Head Start, and countless other programs. That story, like so many, has a story of racial subordination embedded within it.[43] New Deal benefits were specifically constructed to exclude African American people. For example, unemployment benefits specifically excluded domestic and agricultural workers.[44] In the 1960s, as African American women organized to access benefits like Aid to Families with Dependent Children (AFDC), and the program began to transform from a small one serving predominantly white widows to one that, while never ceasing to serve more white than Black families, became associated with the racist trope of the welfare queen.[45] This trope, first introduced nationally by Ronald Reagan, would come to epitomize the right's campaign against welfare.[46] Between the Reagan years and 1996, the year when the Clinton administration ended the guarantee of minimal support to poor families embodied in the Aid to Families with Dependent Children, the United States retreated from its prior commitment to provide basic aid to families.[47] The focus on "workfare" as well as a whole host of strategies to push families off of assistance, resulted in dramatically reducing the number of families receiving basic aid.[48]

In addition, during the early twentieth century, the United States made what would turn out to be a crucial decision that would lay groundwork for the integration of punishment and support targeted at poor communities. While other nations were establishing universal systems of support,[49] the US made a different choice, bifurcating the system in two: one system for those in poverty and another system for those who work. So, benefits like welfare, Food Stamps, and public housing are means-tested and target those in poverty, whereas benefits like social security and Medicare are reserved for those who "paid into the system."[50] The basic structure was left in place in the 1960s, during the Great Society, with the creation of programs such as Medicaid, Food Stamps, and various housing supports. This bifurcation set the conditions necessary to maintain social insurance largely separate from the punitive institutions of the state.

On the criminal system side, for the last several years, scholars and activists have brought much-needed attention to what many refer to as the carceral state.[51] That's an academic's word for sure, but it's helpful because it includes not just what some refer to as the criminal legal system, but a far wider range of punitive institutions and policies in poor communities. Thanks to the work of scholars like Michelle Alexander[52] and James Forman,[53] among many others,[54] what used to be known only by those touched by or working in the criminal legal system has become more common knowledge. The US incarcerates a far higher percentage of its population than any other nation.[55] We not only incarcerate, but we impose punitive consequences far beyond the prison walls. Post-release conditions severely limit those subject to them[56] and the presence of a conviction often severely restricts employment and housing opportunities, as well as voting rights.[57] We ensnare poor people in a web of fines and fees from which escape is extremely difficult, resulting in a whole host of tangible harms.[58] The burdens of this larger carceral state are borne disproportionately by poor African American people and the geographic concentration of these effects harms whole families and communities.[59]

While these two broad systems – social support on the one hand and criminal legal on the other – are separate, their histories intersect. First, beginning in earnest in the mid-1980s, we saw an era of significant retrenchment in parts of the social welfare space at the same time as we saw astronomical growth in the criminal system. In what many scholars identify as a hallmark of neoliberal governance, as social welfare support for poor families shrank, carceral systems directed at the same communities grew exponentially. As Professor Loic Wacquant observed, the US transitioned from a "social welfare state" to a "penal state" and in the process became increasingly reliant on criminal legal systems to regulate poor communities.[60] Not only did these two systems (social welfare and criminal legal) shrink and grow together, but they intertwined in a few ways crucial to understanding what happened in Tennessee.

3.2.2 Criminalizing Social Welfare

Social welfare programs targeting poor families are deeply stigmatizing and humiliating. Beginning in the late twentieth century, in a phenomena Jonathan Simon labeled a part of *governing through crime*,[61] social welfare institutions took up criminal system techniques. As one of the leading scholars in the field, Professor Kaaryn Gustafason once observed, because of the use of practices like finger imaging and drug testing, "applying for welfare mirrors the experience of being booked for a crime."[62] Drawing another piece of the picture, Khiara Bridges' work provides a stunning picture, in the area of public benefits and beyond, of how any notion of privacy rights is nonexistent for poor women seeking help.[63] Bridges' ethnographic work tells a story of women seeking prenatal care. The women are subject to extraordinary scrutiny as a price of that support, facing a wide range of inquiry about deeply personal and clearly unrelated aspects of their lives. From this work it is clear that for poor women seeking support from the state, intervention, coercion, and regulation are the norm.

Not only is the experience of accessing support deeply stigmatizing and invasive, but it is clear that the two systems – poverty-focused social welfare and criminal – have merged in ways that have brought surveillance and punishment into the mechanisms of social welfare provision. In the last several decades, scholars have been focused on these interactions. For example, as Elizabeth Hinton demonstrates, beginning in the late 1960s, federal policymakers began integrating the policing and surveillance of low income urban communities into the very fabric of US urban social welfare programs.[64] "By the mid-1970s, social welfare agencies in urban centers had little choice but to incorporate crime control measures in their basic programming in order to receive funding."[65] Over time, basic and vital social supports, like public housing and schools, became sites for surveillance, policing, and criminalization.[66] Take, for example, the Carter-era Urban Initiatives Anti-Crime Program, which "establish-[ed] stronger partnerships between social and law enforcement institutions and devot[ed] the majority of funds to surveillance and security needs."[67] In so doing, the program "vastly enhanced the scope and power of punitive authorities in the most deteriorated and segregated public housing sites in the country."[68] By that time, "law enforcement and criminal justice institutions could involve themselves in virtually any community-based effort."[69]

Not only are criminal systems actors integrated into social welfare programs, but they function together to heighten punishment. Dorothy Roberts, for example, describes the way that prisons and foster care agencies work in tandem to heighten the punishment of Black women and their children.[70] Similarly Victor Rios's *Punished* paints a vivid picture of the way that social welfare institutions in highly policed areas are deeply intertwined with police and probation staff to stigmatize and criminalize young Black and Latino men.[71]

3.2.3 The Criminal System As a Locus of Care

In an era in which social support for poor families has shrunk and carceral institutions have grown, carceral institutions have increasingly become the location where members of poor communities can access residual forms of care. As we have already seen, this relationship between care and punishment provided the ideological justification for the fetal assault law. On the ground nationally, one can see the location of care within punishment system most clearly in jails and problem-solving courts. In the fetal assault story, we will see both jails and courts play an important role.

As to jails, Carolyn Sufrin's *Jailcare: Finding the Safety Net Behind Bars* provides a devastating window into this reality.[72] Sufrin is a physician and anthropologist who worked for many years in a women's jail in San Francisco.[73] Starting with the strange fact that the incarcerated are the only population in the United States with a constitutional right to health care,[74] Sufrin provides a rich and nuanced description of how care is provided in that setting.[75] She argues, starkly, that, "[j]ail is the new safety net."[76] Throughout her narrative, we meet women who choose to be incarcerated in order to receive care and who come to count on jail as a place where they can receive that care.[77] Sufrin provides not only a nuanced look into these realities but a sharp and clear indictment of the structures that lead to women viewing jail as a respite and a source of care.[78] As she frames it,

> [j]ailcare is a symptom of social failure, of abandonment of a group of people that includes poor, predominantly black women, whose reproduction has been vilified in policies and broader cultural narratives. Jailcare illustrates how mass incarceration and the frayed safety net are matters of reproductive justice, for they impair women's abilities to parent their children in stable and safe environments. The safety net's shortcomings are not simply a matter of quantity or funding, although shortages of public mental health care, housing, and addiction treatment absolutely play a role. Safety net inadequacies also emerge from the ways services are delivered, from ... the nature of the interpersonal relationships and how people are made to feel when accessing services ... Jailcare reflects the failure of society to provide an adequate safety net and the failure of our social imagination to consider that these women have contributions to make to society.[79]

In Sufrin's analysis, then, jails are not only the locus of care, but locating it there affects the quality and nature of care. In Chapter 8 of this book, we will see both those phenomena too – using jails as a locus of care, and the corruption of care that results when care is located proximate to or within punishment systems.

On the court side, since at least the Progressive Era, American legal systems have created courts that purport to solve social problems by providing assistance to those who come before the court.[80] In the late 1980s, as the War on Crime continued to escalate, the prison population grew exponentially.[81] At the same time, in this era of retrenchment, the social safety net remained profoundly inadequate to meet the needs of those struggling in poor communities. Resources for mental health treatment deteriorated.[82] As a result, judges saw before them an increasingly devastated and systemically failed population.[83] In what in retrospect seems an inevitable development, the modern version of the problem-solving court movement was born.[84] Since the founding of the Miami Drug Court in 1989, this movement, posited as a direct response to the War on Drugs and the presence, in courts, of individuals with enormous need, has exploded.[85] Instead of focusing efforts on shrinking the feeder systems that led to the criminalization of wide swaths of poor communities and growing social support,[86] the problem-solving court movement took the fact of prosecution and criminalization as a given.[87] In the face of this, they sought a way to respond for those individuals who found themselves subject to prosecution and potential incarceration.[88]

Today there are over 3000 problem-solving courts found throughout every state in the nation.[89] They include not only the traditional drug courts, but a wide range of specialized courts, including domestic violence courts, mental health courts, veterans courts, and community courts, just to name a few.[90] They are supported by significant federal, state, and local funding streams, a series of well-funded national organizations, and a robust research agenda evaluating their effectiveness along several metrics.[91]

Largely echoing their progressive predecessors, problem-solving courts embrace rather than reject the central role of courts and judges in solving social problems. Problem-solving courts purport to accomplish this objective by "customizing punishment . . . thereby reducing the likelihood of repeat offending and increasing the likelihood that the offender can become a productive member of society."[92] While it is certainly true that these courts are newer versions of courts that existed during the progressive era, it is also true that they exist in a very different historical moment. As Professor Kerwin Kaye has observed,

> While drug courts share a number of features of Progressive Era courts ... [t]he transition from what Wacquant terms a "social state" to a "penal state" gives "problem-solving justice" a very different function. The dramatic reduction in welfarist benefits offered to those who have *not* suffered from a criminal conviction, combined with the significant growth in imprisonment ... [r]esult in a situation in which the criminal justice system plays a growing role in the management of welfare services. Drug court ... creates a new role for criminal justice in the administration of welfare services, expanding the state's surveillance capacities in the process.[93]

Problem-solving courts have been a key focus of scholarship exploring a central topic in this book: the interaction between punishment and care. These courts have been the subject of a large body of social science research. The studies are, by and large, "designed to provide information that is useful to the professionals and managers running the courts."[94] While this literature certainly adds significantly to developing best practices for problem-solving courts, as Kaye notes, "basic propositions are left unexamined and investigations seek only to answer questions within a previously established frame."[95] So, for example, while the studies pay enormous attention to the recidivism rate and length of treatment participation, they tend to leave unexamined "the extent to which lowered recidivism corresponds with changes in peoples' lives that they themselves consider positive."[96] As Kaye argues,

> the narrowed scope of administrative research not only ignores the lives of participants, it similarly ignores the larger structural shifts that drug courts initiate within the neoliberal state as a whole. Far from simply marking a straightforward revival of the rehabilitative ideal within criminal justice, the rise of drug courts and other problem-solving courts represents a restructuring of what Loic Wacquant refers to as the "carceral-assistential net" the series of criminal justice and welfare-oriented programs that together manage the (racialized) poor.[97]

In addition, and of particular interest for this study, the literature pays little attention to the effect of problem-solving courts on the larger communities and structures in which they are embedded and the effect on the form of care individuals receive in these programs. Other scholars have picked up those threads and have waged a broader critique. This critique takes several forms.

First, these courts have been critiqued for what scholars call net-widening. This critique argues that individuals who might otherwise have been either diverted out of the system entirely or would have received very minimal punishment, are instead brought within far more invasive and long-term monitoring by the courts.[98] This is true both in drug courts[99] and in community courts – those courts established specifically to use community-based courts to solve intractable "problems" in poor communities. For example, the first community court, established in New York City, was part and parcel of the "broken windows" theory of policing, and was "designed to handle a wide range of low-level misdemeanor offenses that generally were not prosecuted at all prior to … the establishment of these courts."[100] So the net gets wider. Individuals who would not be subject to the criminal system at all are drawn in. The net is wider not only in widening who is drawn into the system but in widening what kind of conduct can be monitored and controlled by the Judge.

On another front, critics argue that problem-solving courts, although framed in the language of rehabilitation, turn out to mete out quite a lot of punishment, a phenomenon I refer to in Chapter 7 as *care at a cost*. Study after study has revealed that approximately half of all participants in problem-solving courts fail to complete the program.[101] And when they do fail, they face "terms in prison that are significantly longer than they would have received had they not undergone court-supervised treatment in the first place."[102] As explained by the National Association of Criminal Defense Lawyers, "For example, a simple crack possession case will usually net a 10-to-20 day jail sentence in Manhattan. A defendant may wait 20 to 30 days for placement in a [drug court] program. If defenders enter a treatment program and fail, they may be sentenced to six months in jail."[103]

Moreover, while it is true that problem-solving courts do often confer opportunities for treatment, these benefits tend to be distributed in discriminatory ways. For example, several studies have concluded that the admission criteria of these courts systematically favor white defendants.[104] Second, the 50 percent on average who fail are "disproportionately black and poor (with white graduation rates approximately twice as high as non-white [rates])."[105]

In addition, some studies indicate that success in drug court is strongly associated with what researchers have called "stakeholder values."[106] The problem here is that drug courts then, in effect, privilege already privileged actors, by removing them from the harshest parts of the criminal system. As Professor Kaye argues, in this way, "drug courts act as a structure of *stratified penalization*, significantly intensifying the war on drugs for the nonwhite poor, even while lessening its burden for the moderately poor and working-class whites who are increasingly caught within a widening net of criminal justice."[107]

All of these critiques come together in an assessment that, while participation in problem-solving courts sometimes correlates with reduced recidivism and they certainly do provide access to treatment for some, these successes can come at the cost of bringing more individuals into the system, elevating the risk and severity of punishment for those who participate, increasingly linking the provision of care to the mechanisms of punishment, and distributing the benefits of these courts in discriminatory ways.

In the fetal assault study, problem-solving courts play several roles. First, a small minority of the cases were actually heard and processed within the Shelby County Drug Court, with effects quite similar to those describe above. Second, the fetal assault law is a quite startling and unique example of the net-widening that we saw in Chapter 1. The legislators went beyond using existing crimes to draw more people into the system to actually justifying the creation of a new crime because of the purported care value of prosecution. Third, and perhaps most importantly, the idea of problem-solving justice justified net-widening far beyond the rarified context of problem-solving courts. The majority of fetal assault prosecutions were not heard in problem-solving courts. They were heard in regular lower-level criminal courts. The result is what Part II of this book labels *care as a smokescreen*. In the vast majority of those cases, there is no mention of any form of treatment in the criminal court files. Instead, the focus is on what it is always on in misdemeanor courts – very little justice, punishment, and an unrelenting focus on the collection of criminal debt. The idea of criminalized care here has the effect, mostly, of obfuscating the harsh effects of the criminal system with the rhetoric of care.

3.2.4 The Broader Risks of Criminalized Care

The risks of linking punishment and care are not limited to jails and problem-solving courts. As scholars have looked more closely at the relationship between social support and punishment, one area of focus has been the risks associated with accessing care and support both in highly stigmatizing social welfare institutions and inside courts. I've been thinking about these ideas for many years, and a few years ago, I wrote a paper called *The Hyperregulatory State*. In it I described something I called *regulatory intersectionality*, which at the time I thought of as the mechanisms used by social welfare systems to collect and transmit evidence about recipients from social welfare systems to child welfare and criminal systems. Now this sounds pretty theoretical, but the on-the-ground consequences are nothing but real. To get a sense of what this looks like picture a home inspection. In some states, when you apply for benefits, a caseworker will come to your house to perform an inspection. They are looking for evidence that what you said in your application for benefits is true, things like who lives in your home. But along the way, they might see something that disturbs them – very little food in the refrigerator, scales and baggies in your kitchen, a heating system that does not work. Now you might be applying for assistance to try to help pay for heat and food, and let's assume that if you get the assistance it will be easier to pay for those things. The scales and baggies could be for perfectly legal activity, but it's certainly true that in any household, low- or high-income, it could be a sign of illegal activity. But there are two big differences between the low-income home and the higher-income home. First, we tend as a society to assume the worst about those who are poor, and even more so when someone is both poor and Black or Brown. We tend to assume that something bad about the person or the family is what keeps them poor, so we might be more likely to assume that someone in the family is engaging in illegal activity and that the mother is not feeding her children out of bad judgment rather than lack of funds. Also, and importantly, the inspector is in the home of the poor family. Even though higher-income families get plenty of benefits from the government, for example through tax deductions, we do not send inspectors to rich people's homes in order to make sure they qualify for a tax deduction.[108] So, upon seeing all of this, the inspector calls child welfare. That initial inspection can, as we will see in this book, lead to both child welfare intervention and prosecution. So the three systems (public benefits, child welfare, criminal) *intersect*, leading to escalating harm. And these harms play out in poor communities, and often disproportionately in Black and Brown poor communities, in a way that simply does not occur in more economically and racially privileged communities. So poor communities, in particular, are subject to criminalization of their poverty, leading to intervention and often to devastating harm.

In another striking example of the risks of these intersections, in *The New Racially Restrictive Covenant: Race, Welfare, and the Policing of Black Women in Subsidized Housing*, Priscilla Ocen described the targeting of African American Section 8 voucher holders by an astounding and devastating set of collaborations between social welfare, juvenile, and criminal system actors in three California cities, including two suburban communities outside of Los Angeles.[109] Ocen traces the risks and harm these families faced, all as a condition of support.

In Chapter 6, we see these phenomena playing out in the systems in which the fetal assault prosecutions took place. Legal and regulatory systems facilitate the flow of presumptively private health care information from the health care system, through the child welfare system, and into the criminal system, where that information is the evidence for prosecution with its resulting harms.

3.2.5 Addiction Treatment and Criminalized Care

Another group of scholars has begun to focus on these issues in the specific context of courts and addiction treatment. These scholars are asking crucial questions: How is treatment functioning when it is tied to punishment systems? What does addiction treatment actually look like when it is access through punishment systems? Is it the same treatment accessed through a different path, or does the form of treatment differ depending on the path you access it? This scholarship makes at least two key contributions.

First, these scholars examine how the idea of addiction, and the ubiquitous presence of that diagnosis, has justified what Teresa Gowan and Sarah Whetstone term a "'fuzzy edge' of the criminal justice system."[110] Gowan and Whitestone's study focused on the operation of a local rehabilitation center for men associated with a county drug court. The vast majority of men in that program were mandated to be there either through the drug court or as a condition of a criminal case being processed in a regular criminal court. They begin with the observation that, "[t]he large-scale mandatory, state-subsidized treatment opened up by drug courts and other jail and prison diversion programs has expanded the numbers of the nation's poor and working class who are labeled addicts and sent to rehab."[111] The analysis focuses on the use of what they term "strong arm rehab." The goal of this model is not merely sobriety. Instead it is wholesale "habilitation" – a full construction of the individual from the "criminal addict" to what staff define as the goal – becoming "Joe Taxpayer."[112] In this analysis, while "whiter and richer drug offenders are filtered out to non-custodial community care, the 'criminal addict' is held to strict accountability within the quasi-incarceration of the strong-arm rehab."[113] In their analysis the form of treatment varies by both race and class, with less coercion being targeted at those who are "whiter and richer" and more coercion targeted at others.

Similarly sociologist Alison McKim[114] looked carefully at the way treatment operates in programs that are associated with criminal courts. McKim's study looked deeply at the structural differences between two treatment programs – Women's Treatment Services (WTS), a program "funded by the state's criminal justice system,"[115] and Gladstone Lodge, a program with "no relationship to the criminal justice system."[116] She found that the structure of treatment in these two programs differed significantly. In short, "Women at the Lodge were customers, from higher class backgrounds, and were not criminalized. In contrast WTS was fundamentally more punitive. The threat of prison backed the program's power and this showed in its therapeutic and disciplinary methods."

In her assessment then, the location of the treatment deeply affected the form of care. In Chapter 8, in a phenomena labeled *corruption of care*, we see manifestations of a related phenomenon, in which the realities of punishment systems weigh in strongly on particular treatment decisions, corrupting decision-making that should take place within the context of the doctor–patient relationship.

3.2.6 Negotiating Criminalized Care

In a focus group conducted by SisterReach researchers, a woman affected by the fetal assault law commented that, "[w]hen I was pregnant, I was scared to death to have that open relationship with my doctor because the laws in effect prevented me from it being a care issue. It became a law, a liability issue ... I was freaking terrified."[117] That comment, that for her being a "liability issue" meant it could not be a "care issue," takes us to another body of scholarship that asks how individuals subject to these systems negotiate the risks and opportunities posed by the integration of punishment with care. A few pieces of scholarship in this area are particularly relevant for the Tennessee story – first some work around the ways in which Black mothers negotiate their relationship to the police and second some work around women's negotiation of child welfare agencies. When institutions that provide care and support are proximate to or located within agencies that can punish, either by removing children or by meting out criminal punishments, those who need that care and support face an impossible set of decisions: Does it make sense to access the support and take the risk? Should one avoid these programs even if help is needed? Is there a way to negotiate need and risk that mitigates the risk? Might one face risks by avoiding help? Monica Bell's work on what she calls "situsituational trust" give us a window into some of these decisions.[118] Bell's work is based in rich interviews of fifty low-income African American women with children living in Washington, DC in 2012 and 2013. The interviews focused on how women negotiate their relationship to police. While there is extensive literature demonstrating the long-standing cynicism about the police that exists in African American and low-income communities, it is also clear that members of those communities often engage the police. Bell sought to understand how African American women with children negotiated their decisions around whether and when to engage police. She found that the women she interviewed employed several strategies, two of which are relevant here. First, women engaged police when they believed there would be positive therapeutic consequences for the target of the call, "such as getting into social service programs or interrupting destructive patterns."[119] So the women in her study engaged or disengaged depending on the risks and benefits of both.

Similarly, Kelley Fong's work is centered in the child welfare system and asks what happens when society couples "assistance with coercive authority."[120] On the issue of trust and engagement, Fong challenges the prevailing understanding that women engage in system avoidance and finds instead that, in her study, that

> CPS concerns rarely prompted mothers to avoid systems wholesale, but within their participation in healthcare, educational, and social service systems, they engaged in a selective visibility, presenting themselves but not their full selves to authorities. Worried that others would interpret their disclosures or behaviors as abuse or neglect and notify CPS, mothers sought to shield areas of perceived vulnerability from view.[121]

Fong describes the women in her study, eighty-three low-income mothers in Providence, Rhode Island, as "caught in the social safety net,"[122] needing the services offered by supportive agencies but fully aware of what this book terms care at a cost. As Fong describes it, "Mothers want and need to connect their children with doctors, schools, and other services, yet must do so in ways that do not expose them to CPS intervention, prompting a selective or reluctant participation. Ultimately, poor children's needs become less visible to these systems and they may not benefit fully from available supports."[123] These women were navigating dilemmas similar to the dilemmas faced by poor women who use drugs while pregnant, sometimes needing and wanting the care they can access, facing the compromised form of care offered proximate to or inside punishment systems, while being all too aware of the risks of both engagement and disengagement. The women Fong interviewed acted strategically, weighing the costs of engagement and avoidance and were, as a result, likely unable to benefit as much as they might have been able to had they not faced the risks associated with care at a cost. The women prosecuted in Tennessee as well as all those who were struggling with substance use during pregnancy in the shadow of the fetal assault law and the punitive policies that remain were negotiating similar territory.

When Tennessee decided, in the spring of 2014, to enact the fetal assault law, it was standing on all this history – a long history of prosecuting first poor Black and more recently poor women across race for drug use during pregnancy and a structurally embedded history of merging punishment with support in poor communities. With this history and context in hand, it is to the fetal assault prosecutions themselves that the next several chapters turn.

NOTES

1. *See* Nina Martin, *Take a Valium, Lose Your Kid, Go to Jail*, PROPUBLICA (September 23, 2015), https://www.propublica.org/article/when-the-womb-is-a-crime-scene. [https://perma.cc/29F5-S5JF].

2. Lynn M. Paltrow & Jeanne Flavin, *Arrests of and Forced Interventions on Pregnant Women in the United States, 1973–2005: Implications for Women's Legal Status and Public Health*, 38 J. HEALTH POLS., POL'Y & L. 299 (2013).

3. I arrive at this number by pulling data from a variety of sources. First, Paltrow and Flavin document 413 cases of forced intervention, 354 of which involved criminal prosecution. *Id.* at 309. As to the post-2005 prosecutions, I am including data gathered in this study documenting at least 121 prosecutions for fetal assault in Tennessee, and prosecutions documented by Grace Howard in two additional Southern states (182 in South Carolina and 501 in Alabama). Grace Elizabeth Howard, *The Criminalization of Pregnancy: Rights, Discretion, and the Law* (October 2017) (unpublished Ph.D. dissertation, Rutgers University), https://rucore.libraries.rutgers.edu/rutgers-lib/55493/PDF/1/play/ [https://perma.cc/8AHX-4ATW]. The number is likely a substantial undercount, however, because, at the time of this writing, there is no post-2005 published data available for states other than Tennessee, Alabama, and South Carolina. Equally importantly, every researcher who has attempted to gather this data has noted the significant difficulties in finding complete data due in large part to the ways criminal court records are kept.

4. *See* Howard, *supra* note 3.

5. Dorothy E. Roberts, *Punishing Drug Addicts Who Have Babies: Women of Color, Equality, and the Right of Privacy*, 104 HARV. L. REV 1419 (1991).

6. *See generally* Doretta Massardo McGinnis, *The Prosecution of Mothers of Drug-Exposed Babies: Constitutional and Criminal Theory*, 139 U. PA.

L. Rev. 505 (1990) (connecting prosecutions to larger national debate over women's reproductive freedom and concluding that the criminal legal system is ill-equipped to intervene in the area of drug use during pregnancy); Jacqueline Berrien, *Pregnancy and Drug Use: The Dangerous and Unequal Use of Punitive Measures*, 2 Yale J.L. & Feminism 239 (1990) (connecting the punitive treatment of some pregnant drug users to the history of reproductive control as an economic practice within chattel slavery); John E. B. Myers, *A Limited Role for the Legal System in Responding to Maternal Substance Abuse During Pregnancy*, 5 Notre Dame J.L. Ethics & Pub. Pol'y 747 (1991) (rejecting criminal prosecution as an appropriate response to drug use during pregnancy, instead arguing that juvenile courts play a revitalized role more similar to what they did at the start of the twentieth century); Joyce Lind Terres, *Prenatal Cocaine Exposure: How Should the Government Intervene?* 18 Am. J. Crim. L. 61 (1990) (examining the struggle between reproductive freedom and the government's interest in fetal well-being and concluding that government intervention is warranted, but ought to be limited to the child protection system, as opposed to the criminal legal system); Paul A. Logli, *Drugs in the Womb: The Newest Battlefield in the War on Drugs*, 9 Crim. Just. Ethics 23 (1990) (exploring the constitutional issues around prosecutions for drug use during pregnancy, as well as the legislative drafting efforts around the issue); Stephanie Ridder & Lisa Woll, *Transforming the Grounds: Autonomy and Reproductive Freedom*, 2 Yale J.L. & Feminism 75 (1989) (examining how privacy rights and equal protection intersect with reproductive freedom and acknowledging criminal and civil liability for harm to fetuses as one area where women's autonomy is under assault).

7. Roberts, *supra* note 5, at 1436.
8. Roberts, *supra* note 5, at 1432.
9. Ira J. Chasnoff et al., *Cocaine Use in Pregnancy: Perinatal Morbidity and Mortality*, 9 Neurotoxicology & Teratology 291(1987).
10. *Id.*
11. Theresa Vargas, *Once Written Off, "Crack Babies" Have Grown into Success Stories*, Washington Post (April 18, 2010), http://www.washingtonpost.com/wp-dyn/content/article/2010/04/15/AR2010041502434.html [http://perma.cc/H8L8-BTRE].
12. Katharine Greider, *Crackpot Ideas*, Mother Jones (July/August 1995), https://www.motherjones.com/politics/1995/07/crackpot-ideas/.
13. Sarah Weiser, *From Crack Babies to Oxytots: Lessons Not Learned*, Retro Rep. (July 22, 2015), https://www.retroreport.org/transcript/from-crack-babies-to-oxytots-lessons-not-learned/ [http://perma.cc/YLV6-Z9UP].
14. Greider, *supra* note 12.
15. Weiser, *supra* note 13.

16. *See* Barry M. Lester & Linda L. Lagasse, *Children of Addicted Women,* 29 J. ADDICTIVE DISEASES 259, 264 (2010).

17. Michele Goodwin, *Fetal Protection Laws: Moral Panic and the New Constitutional Battlefront,* 102 CAL. L. REV.781, 849–52 (2014).

18. Susan FitzGerald, *"Crack Baby" Study Ends with Unexpected but Clear Result,* PHILA. INQUIRER (June 21, 2017), http://www.philly.com/philly/health/ 20130721__Crack_baby__study_ends_with_unexpected_but_clear_result .html?arc404=true [http://perma.cc/K8NF-BCVU].

19. *See id.*

20. *See id.*

21. *See id.*

22. *See id.*

23. *See id.*

24. *See id.* For the research underlying these claims see, for example, Laura M. Betancourt et al., *Adolescents with and Without Gestational Cocaine Exposure: Longitudinal Analysis of Inhibitory Control, Memory and Receptive Language,* 33 NEUROTOXICOLOGY & TERATOLOGY 36 (2011) (finding no significant developmental differences between cocaine-exposed children and controls); Hallam Hurt et al., *Functional Magnetic Resonance Imaging and Working Memory in Adolescents with Gestational Cocaine Exposure,* 152 J. PEDIATRICS 371 (2008); Hallam Hurt et al., *A Prospective Evalution of Early Language Development in Children with in Utero Cocaine Exposure and in Control Subjects,* 130 J. PEDIATRICS 310 (1997); Hallam Hurt et al., *Children with In Utero Cocaine Exposure Do Not Differ From Control Subjects on Intelligence Testing,* 151 ARCHIVES PEDIATRICS & ADOLESCENT MED. 1237 (1997).

25. FitzGerald, *supra* note 18.

26. *See, e.g.,* Deborah A. Frank et al., *Level of Prenatal Cocaine Exposure and Scores on the Bayley Scales of Infant Development: Modifying Effects of Caregiver, Early Intervention, and Birth Weight,* 110 PEDIATRICS 1143 (2002); Deborah A. Frank et al., *Problematic Substance Use in Urban Adolescents: Role of Intrauterine Exposures to Cocaine and Marijuana and Post-Natal Environment,* 142 DRUG & ALCOHOL DEPENDENCE 181 (2014); Josephine V. Brown et al., *Prenatal Cocaine Exposure: A Comparison of 2-Year-Old Children in Parental and Nonparental Care,* 75 CHILD DEV. 1282 (2004); Rina D. Eiden et al., *Externalizing Behavior Problems Among Polydrug Cocaine-Exposed Children: Indirect Pathways via Maternal Harshness and Self-Regulation in Early Childhood,* 28 PSYCHOL. ADDICTIVE BEHAV. 139 (2014).

27. *See* FitzGerald, *supra* note 18.

28. *See* FitzGerald, *supra* note 18.

29. *See* FitzGerald, *supra* note 18.

30. Anthony Biglan et al., *Evolving a More Nurturing Society to Prevent Adverse Childhood Experiences*, 17 ACAD. PEDIATRICS 150, ix–xi (2017).

31. FitzGerald, *supra* note 18.

32. FitzGerald, *supra* note 18.

33. *See, e.g.*, Michael Winerip, *Revisiting the "Crack Babies" Epidemic That Was Not*, NY TIMES (May 20, 2013), https://www.nytimes.com/2013/05/20/booming/revisiting-the-crack-babies-epidemic-that-was-not.html [http://perma.cc/3Z7C-LHZP].

34. Ferguson v. City of Charleston, 532 U.S. 67, 71 (2001).

35. *Id.*, 71–72.

36. Goodwin, *supra* note 17, at 824.

37. Goodwin, *supra* note 17, at 824.

38. Roberts, *supra* note 5, at 1435–36.

39. Khiara M. Bridges, *Race, Pregnancy, and the Opiod Epidemic: White Privilege and the Criminalization of Opiod Use During Pregnancy*, 133 HARV. L. REV. 770 (2020). This article is focused on the Tennessee fetal assault prosecutions, as well as prosecutions documented by Grace Howard, and relies on data on these prosecutions that I published previously in Wendy A. Bach, *Prosecuting Poverty, Criminalizing Care*, 60 WILLIAM AND MARY L. REV. 809 (2019).

40. MATT WRAY, NOT QUITE WHITE: WHITE TRASH AND THE BOUNDARIES OF WHITENESS (2006).

41. *Id.*

42. For books focusing on the earlier period, *see, e.g.*, MICHAEL B. KATZ, IN THE SHADOW OF THE POORHOUSE (1986); LINDA GORDON, PITIED BUT NOT ENTITLED: SINGLE MOTHERS AND THE HISTORY OF WELFARE 1890–1935 5 (1994); FELICIA KORNBLUH, THE BATTLE FOR WELFARE RIGHTS: POLITICS AND POVERTY IN MODERN AMERICA (2007); MICHAEL B. KATZ, THE UNDESERVING POOR, FROM THE WAR ON POVERTY TO THE WAR ON WELFARE (1989). For books focusing on welfare reform, *see, e.g.*, MARISA CHAPPELL, THE WAR ON WELFARE: FAMILY, POVERTY. AND POLITICS IN MODERN AMERICA (2010); SHARON HAYS, FLAT BROKE WITH CHILDREN: WOMEN IN THE AGE OF WELFARE REFORM (2003); MICHAEL B. KATZ, THE PRICE OF CITIZENSHIP: REDEFINING THE AMERICAN WELFARE STATE 4–5 (2008).

43. *See, e.g.*, JILL QUADAGNO, THE COLOR OF WELFARE (1996).

44. *Id.* at 21–22.

45. GWENDOLYN MINK, WELFARE'S END 22–23 (1998). *See, also*, Michele Estrin Gilman, *The Return of the Welfare Queen*, 22 AM. U. J. GENDER SOC. POL'Y & L. 247 at 256–67 (2014).

46. *Id.* at 259.

47. *See generally* MINK, *supra* note 45; R. KENT WEAVER, ENDING WELFARE AS WE KNOW IT (2000).

48. WEAVER, *supra* note 47, at 343–44.

49. For a detailed history of the impact on families of the USA's failures see MAXINE EICHNER, THE FREE MARKET FAMILY: HOW THE MARKET CRUSHED THE AMERICAN DREAM (AND HOW IT CAN BE RESTORED) (2020).
50. LINDA GORDON, PITIED BUT NOT ENTITLED: SINGLE MOTHERS AND THE HISTORY OF WELFARE 1890–1935, 253–54 (1994); KATZ, THE PRICE OF CITIZENSHIP, *supra* note 42, at 4–5.
51. The term "carceral state" describes "the sprawling, dynamic network of policies, institutions, personnel, and apparatuses through which federal, state, local, and tribal governments exercise power to police, prosecute, and punish." Janet Moore, *Isonomy, Austerity, and the Right to Choose Counsel*, 51 IND. L. REV. 167, 177 (2018) (citing MARIE GOTTSCHALK, CAUGHT: THE PRISON STATE AND THE LOCKDOWN OF AMERICAN POLITICS (2015)).
52. *See generally* MICHELLE ALEXANDER, THE NEW JIM CROW: MASS INCARCERATION IN THE AGE OF COLORBLINDNESS (2010).
53. *See generally* JAMES FORMAN JR., LOCKING UP OUR OWN: CRIME AND PUNISHMENT IN BLACK AMERICA (2017).
54. *See, e.g.*, NICOLE GONZALEZ VAN CLEVE, CROOK COUNTY: RACISM AND INJUSTICE IN AMERICA'S LARGEST CRIMINAL COURT (2016); GOTTSCHALK, *supra* note 51.
55. *See* ALEXANDER, *supra* note 52, at 6.
56. *See* GOTTSCHALK, *supra* note 51, at 241–57.
57. For an extensive discussion of the many consequences of a criminal conviction see generally Joy Radice, *The Reintegrative State*, 66 EMORY L.J. 1315 (2017).
58. For an extensive recent discussion of this problem see PETER EDELMAN, NOT A CRIME TO BE POOR 8–15, 26 (2017).
59. *See* ALEXANDER, *supra* note 52, at 121–24.
60. *See generally* LOIC WACQUANT, PUNISHING THE POOR: THE NEOLIBERAL GOVERNMENT OF SOCIAL INSECURITY (2009).
61. JONATHAN SIMON, GOVERNING THROUGH CRIME; HOW THE WAR ON CRIME TRANSFORMED AMERICAN DEMOCRACY AND CREATED A CULTURE OF FEAR (2007).
62. KAARYN GUSTAFSON, CHEATING WELFARE: PUBLIC ASSISTANCE AND THE CRIMINALIZATION OF POVERTY 57 (2011).
63. KHIARA BRIDGES, THE POVERTY OF PRIVACY RIGHTS (2017).
64. ELIZABETH HINTON, FROM THE WAR ON POVERTY TO THE WAR ON CRIME: THE MAKING OF MASS INCARCERATION IN AMERICA 61–62 (2016).
65. *Id.* at 236.
66. *See id.*
67. *Id.* at 288.
68. *Id.*
69. *Id.* at 293.

70. Dorothy E. Roberts, *Prison, Foster Care, and the Systemic Punishment of Black Mothers*, 59 UCLA L. REV. 1474, 1476 (2012).

71. VICTOR M. RIOS, PUNISHED: POLICING THE LIVES OF BLACK AND LATINO BOYS 38, 91–93 (2011).

72. CAROLYN SUFRIN, JAILCARE: FINDING THE SAFETY NET FOR WOMEN BEHIND BARS (2017).

73. *Id.* at ix–xi.

74. *See id.* at 7 (citing Estelle v. Gamble, 429 U.S. 97 (1976)).

75. *See id.* at 6–7.

76. *Id.* at 5.

77. *See id.* at 208–26.

78. *See id.* at 215–17.

79. *Id.* at 236.

80. Michael Willrich's *City of Courts* provides one stunning window into this history as it was born and played out in Progressive Era Chicago. MICHAEL WILLRICH, CITY OF COURTS: SOCIALIZING JUSTICE IN PROGRESSIVE ERA CHICAGO (2003).

81. HINTON, *supra* note 64, at 314.

82. HINTON, *supra* note 64, at 314–16.

83. *See* Jane M. Spinak, *Romancing the Court*, 46 FAM. CT. REV. 258, 270 (2008).

84. While the modern problem-solving court movement can be traced to the founding of the Miami Drug Court in 1989, the idea of courts as problem-solvers finds older roots in the history of juvenile and family courts. *See* Spinak, *supra* note 83, at 259–60; *see also* Eric J. Miller, *Drugs, Courts, and the New Penology*, 20 STAN L. & POL'Y REV. 417, 420 (2009).

85. *See generally* Miller, *supra* note 84.

86. *See* Joe Soss & Vesla Weaver, *Police Are Our Government: Politics, Political Science, and the Policing of Race-Class Subjugated Communities*, 20 ANN. REV. POL. SCI. 565, 567 (2017).

87. *See* Miller, *supra* note 84, at 432.

88. *See* Miller, *supra* note 84, at 436–37.

89. *About NADCP*, NAT'L ASSOC'N DRUG CT. PROFS., www.nadcp.org/about [https://perma.cc/S49M-F3JA].

90. *See* ROBERT V. WOLF, CTR. FOR CT. INNOVATION, PRINCIPLES OF PROBLEM-SOLVING JUSTICE 1 (2007), https://www.courtinnovation.org/sites/default/files/Principles.pdf [https://perma.cc/VJ37-JJ2A].

91. *See* Suzanne M. Strong et al., *Census of Problem-Solving Courts, 2012*, BUREAU JUST. STATS. (October 12, 2016), https://www.bjs.gov/content/pub/pdf/cpsc12.pdf [https://perma.cc/9ZGM-8796]; *Statewide Coordination of Problem-Solving Courts: A Snapshot of Five States*, CTR. FOR CT. INNOVATION, https://www.bja.gov/Publications/CCI_ProblemSolvingCoord.pdf [https://perma.cc/5KQE-WVMS].

92. WOLF, *supra* note 90, at 7.

93. KERWIN KAYE, ENFORCING FREEDOM: DRUG COURTS, THERAPEUTIC COMMUNITIES AND THE INTIMACIES OF THE STATE 15 (2019) and REBECCA TIGER, JUDGING ADDICTS: DRUG COURTS AND COERCION IN THE JUSTICE SYSTEM (2012).

94. KAYE, *id.* at 13.

95. *Id.*

96. *Id.* at 14.

97. *Id.*

98. Eric J. Miller, *Embracing Addiction, Drug Courts and the False Promise of Judicial Interventionism,* 65 OHIO ST. L.J. 1479, 1551–61 (2004). *See also* Richard Boldt, *A Circumspect Look at Problem-Solving Courts, in* PROBLEM-SOLVING COURTS: JUSTICE FOR THE TWENTY-FIRST CENTURY, at 17 (Paul Higgins and Mitchell B Mackinem eds., 2009) ("drug treatment courts and many other problem-solving courts serve to extend the reach of the criminal system, by retaining in the system defendants who otherwise might not be subject to criminal justice control or by failing to diversity a significant number of other offenders – often those facing more serious charges – into alternative treatment-based dispositions. Drug treatment courts thus may produce a 'net-widening' effect by channeling into the system defendants who would otherwise have avoided a criminal justice disposition."); *see also* Jane M. Spinak, *A Conversation About Problem-Solving Courts: Take 2,* 10 U. MD. L.J. RACE RELIG. GENDER & CLASS 113, 118 (2010) ("the creation of problem-solving courts may result in more families being drawn into the court system – often referred to as 'net widening' – because the lack of community resources leaves the court as the only place to secure help" (citations omitted)).

99. Miller, *supra* note 98, at 1551–61.

100. Boldt, *supra* note 98, at 18 (2009).

101. *See, e.g.,* Josh Bowers, *Contraindicated Drug Courts,* PUBLIC L. & LEGAL THEORY, Working Paper no. 180, 9 (2007) (citing a study of NYC drug courts clearly indicating more punishment than traditional court dispositions, even when including graduates).

102. KAYE, *supra* note 93, at 10.

103. NAT'L ASS'N OF CRIM. DEF. LAWS., AMERICA'S PROBLEM-SOLVING COURTS: THE CRIMINAL COSTS OF TREATMENT AND THE CASE FOR REFORM (2009) https://www.nacdl.org/drugcourts/.

104. *See, e.g.,* Jimmy Steyee, *Program Performance Report: Implementation Grantees of the Adult Drug Court Discretionary Grant Program,* Table 6 (2013) https://bja.ojp.gov/library/publications/program-performance-report-implementation-grantees-adult-drug-court (providing evaluation of adult drug court program funded by the Bureau of Justice Assistance in 2012 and 2013 and finding that "the data show that at screening, about 60 percent of drug court candidates are white . . . At admission, the percentage of white participants increases to over 70 percent. On the other hand,

the percentage of Black of African American candidates at screening is about 30 percent, decreasing to only 10 percent at admission.").

105.   KAYE, *supra* note 93, at 10.

106.   KAYE, *supra* note 93, at 11.

107.   KAYE, *supra* note 93, at 11. In addition to the critiques described above, Professor Kaye in particular, concentrates on the highly punitive nature of treatment in the treatment facilities that drug court participants attend.

108.   Wendy A. Bach, *Poor Support/Rich Support: (Re)Viewing the American Social Welfare State*, 20 FLORIDA TAX. REV. 495 (2017). *See also* CLARE HUNTINGTON, FAILURE TO FLOURISH: HOW LAW UNDERMINES FAMILY RELATIONSHIPS (2014).

109.   Priscilla A. Ocen, *The New Racially Restrictive Covenant: Race, Welfare, and the Policing of Black Women in Subsidized Housing*, 59 UCLA L. REV. 1540 (2012). These trends have been noted not only by legal scholars but also by historians and political scientists. For example, in 2017, noted political scientists Joe Soss and Vesla Weaver published a piece in the *Annual Review of Political Science* pointing out that the field of political science's focus on the devastation of democratic participation in what they term "race-class subjugated communities" has left political scientists unable to adequately respond to the building up of policing in those communities. Central among their observations is that:

> In [race-class subjugated] communities today, police, courts, and welfare agencies work alongside one another as interconnected authorities and instruments of governance. The densely woven fabric of social control encompasses a host of "collaborative practices and shared information systems between welfare offices and various branches of the criminal justice system." Core functions of social provision – such as housing, employment, physical and mental health, and education – are carried out on a large scale by agencies of the carceral state; in fact, prisons are now the largest public providers of mental health services in the United States. In agencies such as Child Protective Services, the pursuit of child welfare goals blends seamlessly into the policing and prosecution of criminal negligence and abuse. In traditional means-tested welfare programs, officials employ criminal logics of "penalty for violation" to discipline clients and aggressively investigate and prosecute cases of welfare fraud as felonies.

> Joe Soss & Vesla Weaver, *Police Are Our Government: Politics, Political Science, and the Policing of Race-Class Subjugated Communities*, 20 ANN. REV. POL. SCI. 565, 565–68 (2017).

110.   Terea Gowan and Sarah Whitestone, *Making the Criminal Addict: Subjectivity and Social Control in a Strong-arm Rehab*, 14(1) PUNISHMENT & SOCIETY 69 (2012).

111.   *Id.* at 70.

112. *Id.* at 80.

113. *Id.* at 87.

114. ALLISON MCKIM, ADDICTED TO REHAB: RACE, GENDER AND DRUGS IN THE ERA OF MASS INCARCERATION (2017).

115. *Id.*, at 1.

116. *Id.*, at 2.

117. SISTERREACH: DR. ORISHA A. BOWERS, ET. AL., TENNESSEE'S FETAL ASSAULT LAW: UNDERSTANDING ITS IMPACT ON MARGINAL WOMEN 22, https://www .sisterreach.org/uploads/1/2/9/0/129019671/full_report.pdf [https://perma .cc/U9T5-NAA3].

118. Monica Bell, *Situational Trust: How Disadvantaged Mothers Reconceive Legal Cynicism*, 50 LAW AND SOCIETY REV, 314 (2016).

119. *Id.*, at 332.

120. Kelley Fong, *Getting Eyes in the Home: Child Protective Services Investigations and State Surveillance of Family Life*, 85(4) AMERICAN SOCIOLOGICAL REV. 610 (2020); Kelley Fong, *Concealment and Constraint: Child Protective Services Fears and Poor Mothers' Institutional Engagement*, 97(4) SOCIAL FORCES 1785 (2019).

121. Fong, *Concealment and Constraint, supra* note 120, at 1789.

122. Fong, *Concealment and Constraint, supra* note 120, at 1795–96.

123. Fong, *Concealment and Constraint, supra* note 120, at 1804.

PART II

Care As a Smokescreen

Over the course of two years, at least 120 women living in Tennessee found themselves prosecuted and punished for the crime of fetal assault. Those who supported the legislation said that the law was about addressing the NAS epidemic and using the criminal system as a road to and provider of care. But what actually happened is quite different. In reality the law targeted and punished a particular group of women, not, in over 30 percent of the cases, because their infants were born with NAS, but simply because they used drugs while they were pregnant. And while the data is quite clear that both poor and nonpoor women engage in the conduct criminalized by the law, it appears that virtually no nonpoor women were prosecuted. As to the race of the defendants, this varied by geography. While the majority of the defendants were low-income white women, the prosecutions in Memphis, Tennessee, targeted both Black and white low-income women. Finally, as to treatment, for the vast majority of women who were prosecuted, there is no indication in their court files that treatment was a part of their criminal cases. Instead, these low-income Black and white women got precisely what the misdemeanor system regularly doles out – a whole lot of punishment and very little justice.

This Part tells that aspect of the story. Chapter 4 focuses on the questions of who was prosecuted and for what conduct and explores the role of race and class discrimination in the prosecutions. Chapter 5 turns to what happened in the cases themselves. Sadly, the data in these two chapters not only adds substantial information to the ongoing project of documenting the use of the criminal system to target poor women who use drugs while pregnant[1] but also adds additional disturbing data to the emerging story scholars are telling about the functioning of the US criminal system on the misdemeanor end.[2] More than anything though, it reveals that, all too often, the idea of care was nothing but a smokescreen that diverted attention from the harsh reality of prosecution.

NOTES

1. The data in this book makes a substantial empirical contribution to the ongoing project by advocates and scholars like Lynn Paltrow and Jeanne Flavin (Lynn M. Paltrow & Jeanne Flavin, *Arrests of and Forced Interventions on Pregnant Women in the United States, 1973–2005: Implications for Women's Legal Status and Public Health*, 38 J. Health Pols., Pol'y & L. 299 (2013)), Orisha Bowers (Orisha Bowers et al., *Tennessee's Fetal Assault Law; Understanding Its Impact On Marginalized Women*, at https://www.sisterreach.org/uploads/1/2/9/0/ 129019671/full_report.pdf), Grace Howard (Grace Elizabeth Howard, *The Criminalization of Pregnancy: Rights, Discretion, and the Law* (October 2017) (unpublished Ph.D. dissertation, Rutgers University) [https://perma.cc /8AHX-4ATW], Dorothy Roberts (Dorothy E. Roberts, *Punishing Drug Addicts Who Have Babies: Women of Color, Equality, and the Right of Privacy*, 104 Harv. L. Rev. 1419 (1991)), and Michele Goodwin (Michele Goodwin, *Fetal Protection Laws: Moral Panic and the New Constitutional Battlefront*, 102 Calif. L. Rev. 781 (2014)), and journalists like Nina Martin (Nina Martin, *Take a Valium, Lose Your Kid, Go to Jail*, ProPublica (September 23, 2015), https://www.propublica.org/article/when-the-womb-is-a-crime-scene), who have extensively documented the ways in which criminal and civil laws target and punish women who use drugs while pregnant and have traced their implications for our understanding of intersectional subordination.
2. For example, in Punishment Without Crime, Alexandra Natapoff makes arguments that the data in this book further support. For example she argues that the "the petty-offense process has quietly become a regressive features of American tax policy, [actively extracting] revenue from an ever-widening pool of mostly low-income people in order to fund the operations of private as well as public criminal justice institutions." Alexandra Natapoff, Punishment Without Crime: How Our Massive Misdemeanor System Traps the Innocent and Makes America More Unequal 10 (2018).

4 PROSECUTING POVERTY

This chapter begins the book's focus on the prosecutions themselves by asking and answering some basic questions: Who was prosecuted, who was not prosecuted, and did the legislature accomplish its purported aim to use prosecution to target mothers who gave birth to infants with NAS?

4.1 WHO AND WHERE?

During the two years that the fetal assault law was in effect, at least 120 women were prosecuted for fetal assault.[1] Prosecutions concentrated predominantly in two very different geographic regions of the state: in several counties in the northeastern, Appalachian region of the state and in Shelby County, the home of Memphis, Tennessee. To understand this information, you have to know just a little about Tennessee geography and demographics. Tennessee is long and thin, stretching from the eastern Appalachian region at the borders of North Carolina and Kentucky, through Nashville, north of Alabama, and all the way west to Memphis, which is north of Mississippi. The eastern half of Tennessee is in the largely economically distressed regions of Appalachia.[2] While the vast majority of those in the northeast are white,[3] and the areas are predominantly rural, Memphis is a majority Black city and is far more densely populated.[4]

When it comes to race, these two regions (the northeast and Shelby County) are very different. While the population of Tennessee overall is 78.6 percent white and 17.1 percent Black or African American,[5] the districts where the prosecutions took place do not reflect these statistics. Instead, the northeast is overwhelmingly white. For example, Sullivan County, Tennessee, the district in the far northeast of the state in which thirty-one prosecutions took place, was 95.1 percent white in the 2016 census. In contrast, Shelby County, where twenty-five prosecutions were brought, was 41.2 percent white and 54.1 percent Black or African American.[6]

All available evidence indicates that these prosecutions targeted, almost exclusively, low-income women. For example, in Memphis all twenty-five defendants qualified for a public defender, an appointment that cannot be made unless there is a finding by a judge that the person is too poor to afford a lawyer. Similarly, I analyzed forty-one cases, brought in the northeast of the state, in detail to determine their income. Women were categorized as low-income in this analysis if their court files contained one of three indicators: indigency determination, listed as unemployed, or listed as homeless. They were also categorized as low-income if the infant's birth record data showed $25,000 or less in household income. Finally, one additional woman was classified as low-income, despite the fact that this other information was unavailable, because the median income in the census tract where she lived was $21,380 and 41.69 percent of people in that census tract lived below the poverty level at the time. Of those forty-one cases, there were only nine for whom none of these indicators were present, which means only that the data was not available and not necessarily they were not also low-income.

As to race, not surprisingly, the data turned out to vary significantly based on geography. In the northeast, the defendants were, with one exception, white. In Shelby County, the home of Memphis, Tennessee, however, the demographics were different. Of the twenty-five women prosecuted in Memphis, ten were Black and fifteen were white.

4.2 TARGETING DRUG USE NOT NAS

Although the Tennessee fetal assault law was framed as a response to NAS, a disturbing number of prosecutions were brought against women whose infants did not have hospital records reflecting an NAS diagnosis. The initial clue that this might be true came from the criminal court files. The files each contain a description of the acts constituting the crime. Several of them do not mention either NAS or symptoms associated with the condition. To determine whether this was an oversight or evidence that in fact those particular infants were not diagnosed with NAS, I obtained detailed birth record data for every infant born and diagnosed with NAS in Tennessee during the time when the law was in effect[7] and matched those records to the names and infant dates of birth in the court files to determine whether there were women who had been prosecuted despite the fact that their infants were not diagnosed with NAS. It turned out that this happened a lot. Of the ninety-eight prosecuted women whose names I have, thirty-three women, or 34 percent of prosecutions, do not appear on the list of mothers whose infants were diagnosed with NAS.[8] I will return to some of these cases in more detail in Chapter 5, but for now it is sufficient to note that this data quite clearly suggests that that, while those who supported the law said it was about NAS, it is far fairer to say that it was both targeted at poor women and that the targeted conduct was not NAS per se but instead drug use during pregnancy.

4.3 DISCRIMINATION ON THE BASIS OF CLASS?

As stated above, the vast majority of women who were prosecuted were poor, which leads, inexorably, to the question of whether or not there was some form of discrimination, either individual or structural, that led to prosecution of poor women and non-prosecution of nonpoor women. Now the fact that poor women were prosecuted does not necessarily mean that prosecutors (or other decision-makers) intentionally declined to prosecute nonpoor women. It may be that the conduct made illegal by the fetal assault law was only engaged in by poor women. On the other hand, it may be that prosecutors, or other individuals who exercised discretion, consciously or unconsciously used that discretion to steer poor women toward prosecution and other women away.

Now as an initial matter it is important to note that there is no smoking gun here. I have no definitive proof that any particular non-poor women who engaged in prohibited conduct was steered away from the labeling and referrals that began the process leading to prosecution. But there are serious reasons to worry that this may be the case. A few things are true: first, we know that nonpoor women use the drugs that lead to an NAS diagnosis during pregnancy. We also know that the entire process that led to prosecution is filled with professionals who have discretion and that there is every reason to believe that these professionals used their discretion to steer poor women toward and nonpoor women away from prosecution. To understand how this is the case, you have to begin with a basic question: Is there evidence to suggest that nonpoor women engaged in the conduct criminalized by the Tennessee fetal assault law?

As you might recall, under the fetal assault law a woman could be prosecuted for assault, "for the illegal use of a narcotic drug ... while pregnant, if her child is born addicted to or harmed by the narcotic drug and the addiction or harm is a result of her illegal use of a narcotic drug taken while pregnant."[9] For a prosecutor who would have to prove guilt at trial, this breaks down into three basic parts (or elements). The prosecutor would need (and the judge would require) proof beyond a reasonable doubt that, during pregnancy:

(1) the woman illegally used,
(2) a narcotic drug, and
(3) that use resulted in the child being born "addicted to or harmed."

Starting with the first element, the drug use has to be illegal which would include using both prescription drugs obtained without a prescription and/or using illegal drugs. Turning to the second element, the drug must be a narcotic, as defined by Tennessee law. It is important to be clear that we are talking about the legal and not the medical definition of narcotic. The medical definition of narcotic includes opiates but does not include cocaine, amphetamines, meth-amphetamines, or marijuana. Tennessee's legal definition, however, does include cocaine and its derivatives, but not amphetamines, meth-amphetamines, or marijuana. Finally, we get to the last element, that the infant has to be "born addicted or otherwise harmed" by use of the narcotic drug. The phrase "born addicted" is one that is used quite regularly in the popular media, but it has no medical meaning. As Dr. Omar Manjwala has explained:

> Babies cannot be "born addicted." In fact, babies can't even develop addiction. Addiction is a disorder characterized by pathologically pursuing reward or relief through the use of substances. The American Society of Addiction Medicine describes it as "characterized by inability to consistently abstain, impairment in behavioral control, craving, diminished recognition of significant problems with one's behaviors and interpersonal relationships, and a dysfunctional emotional response." None of these things are possible in a baby.[10]

Given this, it is hard to see what proof might be offered to establish that part of the crime. "Harmed" is a little more understandable from a legal perspective. A newborn exhibiting symptoms of NAS could be said to be harmed by the opiate, so a judge would probably accept proof of NAS as sufficient to establish that part of the crime.

Thus, arguably what you need to prosecute is proof of pregnancy, illegal narcotic use, and harm. Returning to my question about whether there was unfair targeting of poor women who engaged in illegal conduct, the real question is whether women who were not poor gave birth to infants with NAS and that NAS was the result of the use of illegally obtained narcotics.

All this admittedly in-the-weeds information does reframe the original question a bit. There are really two question we really need to ask:

(1) Is it likely that there were a substantial number of nonpoor women who gave birth to infants exposed to illegally obtain narcotics in Tennessee during the time the law was in effect; and
(2) Is it likely that there were a substantial number of nonpoor women who gave birth to infants who were diagnosed with NAS and that NAS was due to the use of illegally obtained narcotics?

I am going to take each of these questions in turn.

The first question to look at is whether women across class use illegal opiates during pregnancy. National studies indicate that illegal drug use occurs at fairly consistent rates across class and that opiate-use disorder during pregnancy is slightly more likely among low-income

women than non-low-income women. Now of course, in theory, someone with opiate-use disorder could be using all legally prescribed drugs,
but frankly one would hope that the vast majority could not get prescriptions at that level. Let us assume that there is a strong correlation
between illegal drug use and opiate-use disorder. As to poverty, generally, when looking at whether a woman is "poor" for these purposes,
researchers look at whether or not she received Medicaid. Medicaid is
the federal health insurance program for certain low-income households. To be eligible for Medicaid you have to fall into a category of
people that Medicaid covers, and your household income has to fall
below the income cutoff your state has set for that particular category of
Medicaid recipients. "Pregnant women" is one of the categories of
people who qualify for Medicaid. States set different income cutoffs,
usually defining it as some percentage of the Federal Poverty Level. Just
to give you a sense, in 2018 the Federal Poverty Level for a household
of three was $20,780 per year.[11] To be eligible for Medicaid as
a pregnant woman you have to be below the income threshold set by
your particular state. States vary on the cutoffs, ranging from a low of
households up to 138 percent of poverty (seventeen states), up to
a high of 324 percent of poverty (in the District of Columbia). In
Tennessee, pregnant women qualify for Medicaid if their household
income is below 195 percent of poverty. According to a study conducted by George Washington University and the March of Dimes, "in
2010 about 45 percent of births were covered by Medicaid."[12] If opiate
dependence and/or illegal use of opiates at time of delivery were evenly
distributed across class, you would expect to see about 45 percent of
those births covered by Medicaid. Although there is not perfect data on
this, and there is plenty of reason, as I point out below, to suspect that
higher income women are diagnosed at lower rates because providers
are not looking for this in nonpoor women, the data we do have
indicates a slightly higher rate of those births to women covered by
Medicaid. For example, in 2009, 60 percent of women who gave birth
and were diagnosed as dependent on or using opiates at the time of
delivery received Medicaid.[13]

   If the prosecutions were focused on opiate-use disorder in pregnant
women and opiate-exposure to the fetus with no differentials in the
likelihood of prosecution, you would expect to see slightly higher rates

of poor women prosecuted (maybe 60 percent) but that still leaves 40 percent of the population who may well have engaged in this conduct who you would expect to see prosecuted too. Regardless, you certainly would not expect that virtually no nonpoor women would be prosecuted.

Turning to my second question, if you were focused predominantly on NAS (which again over 30 percent of the prosecutions were not) then you would have to look at NAS rates by class. Now it is true that the majority of infants diagnosed with NAS are low-income. For example, according to the birth record data provided by the Tennessee Department of Health, over 80 percent of the infants who were diagnosed with NAS during the time the law was in effect were low-income. Similarly, in 2019 "93% of the 1,181 infants treated for NAS is Tennessee were born to women enrolled in Medicaid."[14]

And if infants born with NAS are poor, at a rate of about 80–90 percent, and the law was targeting only cases where the infants had NAS (which remember was not the case), it would make sense that the vast majority of prosecutions would be of poor women. But throughout the study, these numbers continued to bother me. We know that women use illegal drugs at similar rates across class. We know that about 40 percent of pregnant women diagnosed with opiate-use disorder at delivery are not poor. Why, then, are the vast majority of infants diagnosed with NAS poor?

My unease about these numbers is grounded in a long history of race and socioeconomic discrimination in both drug testing and child welfare referrals in the health care setting. With very few exceptions, in order for a woman to end up prosecuted in these cases, information had to travel from the medical setting, generally through child welfare officials, and into the criminal legal system. It turns out that there is a lot of data indicating that discrimination occurs at all these points. For the purposes of this particular set of questions, the data demonstrates discrimination in both drug testing and child welfare reporting. For example, a 2010 study looked at the question of whether race is used as a factor in deciding whether to drug test newborns when detailed protocols that do not include race as a screening factor are already in place to guide the decision to test the newborn.[15] After examining the records of 2,121 mother–infant pairs admitted to the Neonatal

Intensive Care Unit at the University of Rochester Medical Center, the researchers discovered that, despite the existence of detailed protocols dictating when testing should occur, 35.1 percent of infants born to Black mothers who met the screening criteria were tested. In contrast, only 12.9 percent of infants born to white women who met the screening criteria were tested.[16] The researchers therefore concluded that "race was used as an independent criterion for screening [for illicit drugs] even at an institution in which an established, apparently objective, screening protocol that did not include race as a factor was in place."[17] So discrimination happens at the moment when medical personnel decide to look for opiate use. If they are not looking for it, clearly, they are not going to find it.

Other researchers have focused on the rate of referral of children by hospital staff to child protective agencies. A study conducted in 1990 by Chasnoff et al. as well as a 2012 study conducted by Sarah Roberts and Amani Nuru-Jeter provide compelling data on the extent of disproportionality in the rate of referrals. Chasnoff et al. sought to determine the rate of drug use among pregnant women throughout public and private health care facilities and to explore whether the rates of reporting drug test results correlated with the rates of drug use. They conducted the study shortly after Florida adopted a statewide policy mandating "the reporting [to the Department of Health] of births to mother who used drugs or alcohol during pregnancy."[18] Pursuant to state policy, a positive toxicology screen from either the mother or the child was sufficient to require such a report.[19]

During a one-month period, the researchers obtained a urine sample from "every woman who enrolled for prenatal care ... at each of the five Pinellas County Health Unit Clinics and from every woman who entered prenatal care ... at the offices of each of twelve private obstetrical practices in the county."[20] In total they obtained samples from 715 women. The results across race and class were striking. Of the 715 women, 14.8 percent tested positive for alcohol, cannabinoids (maririjuana), cocaine, or opiates. A slightly higher percentage of white women (15.4 percent) than Black women (14.1 percent) tested positive for these substances. As to socioeconomic status, which the researchers determined from the economic demographics of the zip code in which women lived, the researchers concluded that

"socioeconomic status ... did not predict a positive result on toxico-
logic testing."[21] Despite the slighty higher rate of positive toxicology
screens in white women, only 1.1 percent of white women were
reported, whereas 10.7 percent of black women were reported: "[t]
hus, a black woman was 9.6 times more likely than a white woman to be
reported for substance abuse during pregnancy."[22]

Roberts and Nuru-Jeter's study suggests similar findings. Relying
on a variety of administrative data, Roberts and Nuru-Jeter examined
data from providers in California that had implemented universal
testing of pregnant women for drug and alcohol use.[23] They sought
to determine whether drug and alcohol use varied by race and whether
there were disparities in reporting by race. They concluded that, "[d]
espite Black women having alcohol-drug use identified by prenatal
providers at similar rates to White women and entering treatment
more than expected, Black newborns were four times more likely
than White newborns to be reported to [Child Protective Services] at
delivery."[24] Moreover, the study authors also noted that, due to some
differences among the data sets that they drew on in order to reach their
findings, it is likely that African American children were reported at
even more disproportionate rates than their data suggests.[25]

Given this well-documented history of discrimination in decisions
made in the health care setting, there is good reason to suspect that
professionals across the health care, child welfare, and criminal settings
are exercising discretion in ways that are biased against poor women as
well as against women of color. In the health care system, that bias
could affect both which women and infants are tested at all and which
infants are diagnosed with NAS. As I conducted the interviews in this
study, I posed these questions, to pediatricians, neonatologists, neonatal intensive care nurses, and those in the addiction field. What
I heard did not provide a definitive answer, but it did raise significant
questions that should be the topic of more research.

Across multiple interviews, professionals I talked to expressed significant worry that when it came to looking for drug use during pregnancy generally and opiate use and NAS in particular, higher-income
women were not the focus. To understand this, you have to know a bit
more about drug-testing protocols and the diagnosis of NAS. The first
thing you need to know is that diagnosing NAS is not simple. First and

foremost, visible symptoms often do not appear until three to seven days after birth. As anyone who has ever had a child in the United States in a hospital knows, women and infants generally leave the hospital within a day or two after birth. If the medical staff has no reason to suspect drug exposure, there would be no reason to keep that infant in the hospital. In terms of drug-testing pregnant women and their infants, practice varies substantially. While some practices and hospitals drug test all pregnant women and all infants, practice varies widely. One of the people I talked to about this was Dr. Andrew Hsi. Dr. Hsi is a pediatrician in Albuquerque, New Mexico, and has been working with substance-exposed infants and their families since the late 1980s. He is widely recognized as a leader in his field. In one of our conversations, I asked him the following question: "Tell me how we go from economically distributed drug exposure among pregnant women to fact that the vast majority of the NAS diagnosis involve infants born to poor women." Here is his answer:

> Well, two parts. One is that most of the women who have commercial insurance are using prescription opiates, either accessed through prescription or accessed from non-prescription sources. And their physicians are doing a very peremptory interview at the beginning of pregnancy and not following-up at all, and not doing urine drug screens. So when the mother comes to the hospital, there's no record of potential problems and if the baby shows signs or problems, the people taking care of this baby are less likely to suspect and less likely to diagnose Neonatal Abstinence Syndrome. And then Neonatal Abstinence Syndrome is a complex of symptoms that's poorly objectively characterized. It relies a lot upon subjective assessment and if the people assessing the baby start with the presumption that the baby would not have a diagnosis like this, the mother would not be the type of person using opioids, they wouldn't either screen fluids or make the diagnosis so it would never appear on the insurance coding or any other records.

As Dr. Hsi explained, if there is no suspicion, then there is no reason to drug test or to look for the symptoms of NAS. If doctors are more likely to believe their higher-income patients when those patients deny drug use, they are likely not to drug test. And even if an infant exhibits symptoms that could lead to an NAS diagnosis, you might miss it. Recall first that the diagnosis often cannot occur until days after birth. It is also complicated and relies largely on subjective assessment, so if you do not suspect it and your patient does not meet your idea of a mother who might give birth to an infant with NAS, you could easily miss it. To know if this might be happening in Tennessee, I spoke to Dr. Craig Towers, a high-risk OBGYN at the University of Tennessee whose practice specializes in treating women with opiate-use disorder. Dr. Towers confirmed that drug-testing protocols differ based on how the patient comes to the hospital. For example, if you come to the hospital's clinic for care, the clinic's policy will govern whether you are drug-tested. But if you have a private doctor, that doctor will make the decision. I asked Dr. Towers if he thought there were women whose infants might have NAS but are not being found. His response: "I guarantee you we are losing them, and the one's we are losing the most are in the non-Medicaid population."

So ultimately, this raises a series of questions about whether systems and actors in the health care setting exercised their discretion in ways that ultimately protected nonpoor women from the NAS diagnosis that would trigger child welfare intervention and possible prosecution but failed to protect poor women from the same intervention. Given all this, it seems quite likely that one reason that poor women are the ones who end up being prosecuted is that that there are decisions being made in the health care system that are steering poor women toward prosecution and nonpoor women away.

Looking at the criminal system overall, this turns out not to be all that surprising. Although there is no comprehensive data set documenting the income levels of those in the criminal legal system, all the available evidence suggests that it is a system targeted disproportionately at the poor. For example, the Bureau of Justice Statistics does a survey of state jail and prison inmates every five to seven years and asks about their income in the month prior to arrest. In 2004, while only 11 percent of individuals in the United States lived in a household below the poverty level, at least 34 percent of individuals in state prison fell below that threshold in the month before incarceration. The information for those in jail (which includes not only some individuals who are convicted but some who are charged) is even starker. Of jail inmates, 47 percent are below the poverty level in the month before incarceration. To get more information researchers also look at the rates of appointment of counsel. This particular data is not perfect, predominantly because the standards for appointment of counsel vary significantly across the country. Despite this, indigency determinations do indicate that a judge has concluded, at least, that the person cannot afford a lawyer. Indigency appointment data is also relevant because, unlike the jail and prison data, it includes those who are charged with a crime that could result in incarceration but in which the person is not in jail or prison. " In 2004, appointed counsel represented seventy-eight percent of felony defendants in state courts in the seventy-five largest counties."[26] So all the available information we have indicates that the criminal legal system is one that focuses its attention disproportionately on those in poverty. It is no surprise then that poor women were the ones prosecuted.

4.4 DISCRIMINATION ON THE BASIS OF RACE?

This criminal legal system, of course, discriminates not only by class but by race. We have long known that that the American criminal legal system targets poor people of color in numbers that far outweigh their percentage of the population. When it comes to race in these particular prosecutions, there was significant variation by geography. While the northeast prosecutions targeted poor white women, Memphis tells a different story: 40 percent of the prosecutions in Memphis for which the team obtained records targeted poor Black women, some of them seemingly in contravention of the terms of the law itself. Perhaps one might think that in a city that is 54 percent Black, this is not dispropor- tionate at all, but when you look more closely, it is. Before going forward, it is important to note that the sample size we are talking about is very small. The team had records for twenty five women who were pros- ecuted overall in Memphis, so we should take this data for what it is worth. Nevertheless, as I have noted before, and as the studies that I talked about above remind us, drug use, both overall and during pregnancy, does not differ significantly by class or by race. As a society we use illicit drugs at quite similar rates across class and race. What does differ is who uses what drugs. The opiate crisis is concentrated among white people. In 2017, for example, 78 percent of individuals who died of an opiate-related overdose were white. In Tennessee, it was even higher, at 88 percent.[27] Many argue that this concentration of the epidemic among the white population can be traced to bias in prescribing practices. As Anjali Om argued in the Journal of Public Health, the opioid epidemic can be traced to the introduction by the American Pain Society in 1996 of the concept of pain as the fifth vital sign. This concept was quickly embraced by the medical profession. Patients were asked to rate their pain and doctors were expected to treat that pain. Adding to this was the increasing dominance of patient satisfaction surveys, surveys that could negatively impact a doctor's practice. Add to this "the pharmaceutical industry's billion dollar opioid campaign" and the result is "an exponential increase in opioid prescriptions throughout the 1990s."[28] But what is less focused on is that, just as racial bias infected drug testing and child welfare referrals, it also infected prescription rates of opiates to minorities. As Om explained, "The subjective nature of pain measurement allowed for provider biases and misperceptions of pain tolerance to influence the demographics of prescriptions. For example, many healthcare providers minimized minority ratings of pain and thus were less inclined to prescribe opioids to minorities."[29]

Fewer opiate prescriptions lead to fewer cases of opiate addiction, which in turn likely leads to fewer cases of NAS. And in fact, that is what we see in Memphis. NAS rates at the time were far lower in the west than in the east and they grew progressively as you moved from west to east.[30]

If the prosecutions were focused on NAS, then one might expect the prosecutions to concentrate in the northeast. But as was the case overall, despite the rhetoric focusing on NAS, the actual prosecutions were more about targeting drug use by pregnant women than about focusing on either opiates or NAS. Prosecutions were targeted not only at women who used opiates during their pregnancies but also in significant numbers at women who used both cocaine and methamphetamines. In Memphis, those prosecutions targeted both white and Black women, in fact adding to the consistent national history of targeting these prosecutions at the drug use of poor Black women.

Now we know who was prosecuted, where those prosecutions took place, what conduct was targeted, and what race and class had to do with it. The next chapter turns to the trajectories of the prosecutions themselves.

NOTES

1. To gather this information, the research team on this project sent written requests pursuant to the Tennessee Open Records Act to every prosecution office, police agency, and court in the State of Tennessee, TENN. CODE ANN. §§ 10–7–501 to -516 (2018). The team followed up on those requests by letter and phone on multiple occasions. Ultimately, the team gathered information documenting the existence of 121 women who were prosecuted for this crime between April 28, 2014 and June 30, 2016. As there is no central database recording prosecutions, this project was reliant on the compliance of individuals in those offices to have kept records and then provide them in response to our requests. There is no way to guarantee that this is an accurate count of the number of prosecutions. In fact, it is likely an undercount to some degree. Nevertheless, this number of prosecutions closely matches the number of cases that District Attorneys reported having brought against women for this crime (data on file with author). The first phase of data collection often resulted in limited documentation. For that reason, in the second phase of data gathering, the team sent written follow-up requests in an attempt to collect more complete court files. This effort resulted in obtaining extensive documentation regarding seventy-seven of the ninety-six prosecutions that took place in all counties other than Shelby County (the county containing Memphis, Tennessee). In Memphis, the team obtained extensive but not entirely complete information for twenty-five women who were charged. All statements regarding the contents of the files are based upon these records.

2. Appalachia is defined by the national legislation creating the Appalachian Regional Commission as "420 counties across 13 states and spans 205,000 square miles, from southern New York to northern Mississippi." *About the Appalachian Region*, APPALACHIAN REGIONAL COMMISSION, https://www.arc.gov/about-the-appalachian-region/ [https://perma.cc/5923-AVQR]. Appalachia includes "parts of Alabama, Georgia, Kentucky, Maryland, Mississippi, New York, North Carolina, Ohio, Pennsylvania, South Carolina, Tennessee, and Virginia, and all of West Virginia." *Id.* While not all of Appalachia is economically distressed, the majority of counties in Appalachian Tennessee are classified as either economically "distressed" or economically "at risk." APPALACHIAN REG'L

COMM'N, COUNTY ECONOMIC STATUS AND NUMBER OF DISTRESSED AREAS IN APPALACHIAN TENNESSEE, FISCAL YEAR 2016 (2015) [hereinafter COUNTY ECONOMIC STATUS], https://www.arc.gov/map/county-economic-status-in-appalachia-fy-2016/ [https://perma.cc/W382-4TMX]. To determine these classifications, the Commission averages, for each year and each county, the unemployment rate, per capita market income, and the poverty rate and then compares this to the national averages. *Source & Methodology: Distressed Designation and County Economic Status Classification System, FY 2007-FY 2018*, APPALACHIAN REGIONAL COMMISSION, https://www.arc.gov/distressed-designation-and-county-economic-status-classification-system/ [https://perma .cc/P8X6-Y4XY]. Counties are classified as "distressed" when they fall into the bottom 10 percent of counties by these measures. *Id.* Counties are classified as "at risk" if they fall between 10 percent and 25 percent when compared to national averages and "transitional" if they fall between 25 percent and 75 percent of national averages. *Id.* The majority of Appalachian counties in Tennessee are classified as either distressed or at risk, but some are classified as transitional. COUNTY ECONOMIC STATUS. The majority of at risk and transitional counties have census tracts within them that fall into the distressed classification. *Id.* Note that this Article pulled data from fiscal year 2016, the only full year during which the prosecutions took place.

3. For example, Sullivan County, Tennessee, the district in the far northeast of the state and in which thirty-one prosecutions took place, was 95.1 percent white in the 2016 census. *QuickFacts: Sullivan County, Tennessee; Shelby County, Tennessee; Tennessee,* U.S. CENSUS BUREAU (July 1, 2017) [hereinafter *QuickFacts: Sullivan County*], https://www.census.gov/quickfacts/fact/table/ sullivancountytennessee,shelbycountytennessee,tn/PST045217 [https:// perma.cc/9B3J-5KPV]. Shelby County, Tennessee, in the far west of the state, was 54.1 percent Black or African American. *Id.*

4. *QuickFacts: Memphis city, Tennessee; United States,* U.S. CENSUS BUREAU (July 1, 2017), https://www.census.gov/quickfacts/fact/table/memphiscityten nessee, US/PST045217 [https://perma.cc/X6FE-GZVY]. Sullivan County has a population of 379.4 persons per square mile in contrast to Shelby County, which has a population of 1,215.5 persons per square mile. *See QuickFacts: Sullivan County, supra* note 3.

5. Clearly these are not the full race statistics. Because, with the exception of one woman, all the women were either Black or white, I am focusing on those two populations.

6. *See QuickFacts: Sullivan County, supra* note 3.

7. The data on infants diagnosed with NAS during the time the law was in effect was obtained from the Tennessee Department of Health after data staff pulled and cleaned data and performed a series of matches. As they described their process "Hospital Discharge Data System (HDDS) data files were used to identify any infant that was discharged, inpatient and outpatient, between

04/28/2014 and 07/01/2016. HDDS data is statewide data reflecting all inpatient hospitalization discharges and outpatient visits for the time period. Analysis includes inpatient hospitalization with age less than one and any diagnosis of drug withdrawal syndrome of newborn (ICD-9-CM 779.5 ICD-10-CM P961, P962). Hospital Discharge Data System records may contain up to eighteen diagnoses. Infants were included if any of these diagnoses' fields were coded 779.5, P961, P962. These are discharge level data and not unique patient data. This data was sorted, and possible duplicates were eliminated from the dataset. Identifying information like first name, last name, date of birth, date of admission and address were obtained from the dataset. Birth records were pulled for all babies born during 2013, 2014, 2015 and 2016. A matching program was used to match HDDS data to the birth data. After rounds of matching, the data was exported to Excel file for further examination (visual) to ensure that there were no false matches. False matches and non matches were removed from the data set and imported into SAS for further possible matching. A few records were not matched to corresponding birth files. Using the certificate number of the matched records, the corresponding birth file information was extracted."

8. Once the data files from the Tennessee Department of Health were obtained, research staff searched those records, multiple times for the names of the ninety-eight defendants for whom we had names. Thirty-three names were not found in those records. Those names were then provided back to the data steward at the Tennessee Department of Health to confirm that they had not been overlooked by their research staff. The data steward confirmed that, based on the data analysis described in the previous footnote those thirty-three women did not give birth to infants for whom a NAS diagnosis code appeared in the hospital discharge summary during the time that the statute was in effect.

9. TENN. CODE ANN. § 39–13–107(c)(2) (2014) (expired July 1, 2016).

10. Brian Cuban, *Shattering the Myth of the Addicted Baby*, ABOVE THE LAW (March 9, 2018) https://abovethelaw.com/2018/03/shattering-the-myth-of-the-addicted-baby/ [https://perma.cc/JP3S-LBXF].

11. U.S. Department of Health and Human Services, Office of the Assistant Secretary for Planning and Evaluation, *2018 Poverty Guidelines*, https://www.acf.hhs.gov/sites/default/files/ocs/2018_hhs_poverty_guidelines.pdf [https://perma.cc/5ZBL-ABY4].

12. Phil Galewitz, *Nearly Half of U.S. Births are Covered by Medicaid, Study Finds*, KAISER HEALTH NEWS (September 3, 2013) https://khn.org/news/nearly-half-of-u-s-births-are-covered-by-medicaid-study-finds/ [https://perma.cc/Q6RU-W34K].

13. Stephen W. Patrick et al., *Neonatal Abstinence Syndrome and Associated Health Care Expenditures: United States, 2000–2009*, 307 JAMA 1934, 1937 (2012).

14. Peggy A. Compton, Caroline K. Darlington, & Sadie P. Hutson, *Revisiting the Fetal Assault Law in Tennessee: Implications and the Way Forward*, 22 POLICY, POLITICS, AND NURSING PRACTICE 93, 94 (2021).

15. Marc A. Ellsworth, Timothy P. Stevens, & Carl T. D'Angio, *Infant Race Affects Application of Clinical Guidelines When Screening for Drugs of Abuse in Newborns*, 125 PEDIATRICS 1379 (2010).

16. *Id.*

17. *Id.* at 1383. The researchers also found that "criteria indicating screening should be performed seemed to be selectively ignored . . . for infants born to white women." *Id.*

18. Ira J. Chasnoff, Harvey J. Landress, & Mark E. Barrett, *The Prevalence of Illicit-Drug and Alcohol Use During Pregnancy and Discrepancies in Mandatory Reporting in Pinellas County Florida*, 322 NEW ENG. J. MED. 1202 (1990).

19. *Id.* at 1203.

20. *Id.*

21. *Id.* at 1204.

22. *Id.*

23. Sarah C. M. Roberts & Amani Nuru-Jeter, *Universal Screening for Alcohol and Drug Use and Racial Disparities in Child Protective Services Reporting*, 39 J. BEHAV. HEALTH SERVS. & RES. 3 (2012).

24. *Id.* at 3.

25. *Id.* at 14–15 (explaining that, due to some variations in information available in the multiple data sets they used to reach their conclusions, "comparison of racial distributions of identification data (including the data from the private provider) and reporting data would be expected to show an even greater overrepresentation of Black women among those reported to CPS than among those identified through screening in prenatal care.").

26. Erica J. Hasimoto, *Class Matters*. 101 J. CRIM. L. & CRIMINOLOGY 31, 58 (2011).

27. *Opioid Overdose Deaths by Race/Ethnicity*, KAISER FAM. FOUND., https://www .kff.org/other/state-indicator/opioid-overdose-deaths-by-raceethnicity/? dataView=1&currentTimeframe=1&sortModel=%7B%22colId%22:% 22Location%22,%22sort%22:%22asc%22%7D [https://perma.cc/S5CA- R7YD].

28. Anjali Om, *The Opioid Crisis in Black and White: The Role of Race in Our Nation's Recent Drug Epidemic*, 40 J. PUB. HEALTH 614 (2018).

29. *Id.*

30. ANGELA MILLER, M. MCDONALD, & MICHAEL WARREN, Neonatal Abstinence Syndrome Surveillance Annual Report 2016, at 11–12 (2016), https://www .tn.gov/content/dam/tn/health/documents/nas/NAS_Annual_report_ 2016_FINAL.pdf [https://perma.cc/KQ27-E5G4].

5 DEEPENING POVERTY AND DEGRADING JUSTICE

[She's in jail and can't make bail]; her baby's in DCS custody; she's losing any hope of getting her baby back just by virtue of the passing of time. That's how it works. And that's why you have these ladies pleading in that court, on things where the charge, the state may not be able to make it ... at a trial.

Criminal Court Judge, East Tennessee

Maxine Reynolds[1] is a poor white woman who was prosecuted for fetal assault in rural northeast Tennessee after her umbilical cord tested positive for opiates. Ms. Reynolds was arrested, and the judge who took a first look at her case set her bail at $25,000, which meant that if she could not come up with 10 percent of that amount, she had to remain in jail while her case was pending. The charging document in her case makes clear that the Department of Children's Services (DCS) opened a case about Ms. Reynolds' infant, and it is likely that, by the time she was arrested, DCS had already taken custody of her child. Without going too deep into the details of child welfare, there are a few rules in that system that likely played a role. Once a child is in the custody of the state, there is a very limited period of time for the parents to achieve reunification. Particularly in a case like this, where the state can prove "severe abuse," a mother has very little time before the state moves to terminate parental rights. To get the child back, parents often have to comply with a variety of requirements including securing stable housing and employment and completing treatment and parenting classes. All of that is nearly impossible to do when you are in jail.

After nine days, Ms. Reynolds pled guilty and was sentenced to eleven months and twenty-nine days of incarceration. Instead of making her serve that prison sentence, though, the judge released her on probation. This is a fairly standard practice in misdemeanor sentencing. The terms of her probation were standard. She had to comply with the directions of her probation officer, not commit new crimes, and pay her court costs, which totaled just under $500. There was no mention of treatment in her case file.

About a month after being placed on probation, Ms. Reynolds was charged with an additional misdemeanor. Because she was on probation at the time, she was also charged with a violation of her probation. That meant that if she was found guilty, she could end up serving not only the balance of her eleven month and twenty-nine-day sentence from the fetal assault plea, but any additional sentence on her new misdemeanor. Now she was looking at the possibility of at least one year in jail and probably more. A warrant issued, and she was arrested. It appears that she spent thirty days in jail that time. At the time of her new arrest, Ms. Reynolds had paid $230 toward her court costs. She pled guilty to the violation of probation, and the court sentenced her to thirty days in jail, which at that point, she had already served. She got "jail credit" for those thirty days and went back on probation. The judgment on that day indicated that the case was reset for review "as to payments." She made her last payment on her final court date, and that was the end of her case.

This all sounds, perhaps, fairly standard, even fair. She was accused of a crime; she admitted she did it; she agreed to punishment and to comply with the rules of punishment; she broke the rules, and she was punished for that too. When she finally complied with all the rules and paid her bill, the case ended.

But here is the thing. Every piece of evidence I have indicates that Ms. Reynolds did not commit the crime of fetal assault. She was among about one-third of the women prosecuted for fetal assault whose infants were not diagnosed with NAS. And that fact was clear right on the face of the first charging document. So how did this likely innocent woman end up pleading guilty and facing punishment? The answer is probably the same as it is for all too many criminal defendants: the price for fighting and the pressures to plead are just too strong. And once she pled, the system ground on, making her increasingly vulnerable to new charges, new penalties, and more costs.

Basis for Charge:
On xxxx it come to the attention of the xxxx County Sheriff's Office that
the defendant Ms. xxxx gave birth to a child and the U-Card was sent off for testing
because the defendant tested positive for Oxycodone at time of intake at the hospital.
The Test results come back Positive for Oxycodone. Det. xxxxxx received this
information from DCS xxxx. Defendant stated to DCS that she did not have a script for
the Medications and was buying it off the street. Ms. xxxxx also stated that she had used
Meth once when she found out she was pregnant. Therefore with these findings
defendant is being charged with the listed charge and falls under the New Law T.C.A.
39-13-107

Figure 5.1 Maxine Reynolds charges

Let us start with charges in her case and why it should have been obvious from the beginning that she had a potential defense.

As you can see in Figure 5.1, the charges in Ms. Reynolds' case alleged that she admitted to taking opiates without a prescription and to taking methamphetamine during her pregnancy. Like so many of the cases, the charging document does not allege any diagnosis for her infant nor does it contain any allegations that the infant was harmed. As we learned in Chapter 3, in order to prevail at trial, the prosecutor must put forward (and the judge must require) proof beyond a reasonable that three separate facts (or what lawyers call "elements") are true. They would have to prove that,

(1) the woman illegally used;
(2) a narcotic drug; and
(3) that use resulted in the child being born "addicted to or harmed."

If the allegations in the petition against Ms. Reynolds are true, then it would be pretty easy to prove the first two elements. But notice that there is no allegation of harm. And remember without an NAS diagnosis harm would have been hard to prove. On its face this petition could have been dismissed. And certainly, in a judicial system focused on using the adversarial process to ensure that only the guilty are punished, a good defense attorney should have made a motion to dismiss the case because the prosecutor did not allege the element of harm. That is basic criminal procedure: if the charging document does not allege facts supporting every element of the crime, the case should be dismissed. But none of that happened. Instead, she pled, was punished, and only escaped the system when all her debt was paid.

While researching this book, I had an opportunity to show her case file to the criminal court judge in her district. In Tennessee, a criminal court judge is one rung above the judge who would have actually presided over her case. The first thing he noticed was the lack of an allegation of harm. He wondered aloud, as I had, how the state had intended to prove the case given that there were no facts about harm to the infant. But he also explained why it makes sense that she pled. The first part of our conversation focused on the $25,000 bail. For those not familiar with the criminal system, the bail system results in a price tag for release from pretrial detention. You have to put up the full amount of bail as a guarantee that you will return. Generally, though, you post bail by engaging a bonding company. You pay 10 percent and the company guarantees the rest. I showed the judge her file and asked him if that bail was high. Here is what he had to say: "The [lower court] judge set that bail ... [The judge] ... understands [the] political climate, he would be worried about a repeat, or some sort of aggravating situation that might arise from it. But $25,000 for a class A misdemeanor is very high." As the judge explained, if Ms. Reynolds wanted to fight the case, her first priority would have likely been getting the bail reduced, so she could be released and wait for trial while living in the community. She could make that bail reduction request in front of the first judge, in the lower court, but as the criminal court judge explained "in the particular county, the judge probably would not reduce bail. She would have been waiting for me to come over." But before the higher court judge could "come over" and hear that request, there had to be an indictment. To get an indictment several events would have had to take place. Ms. Reynolds would have been entitled to what is called a "preliminary hearing" on the case, where the prosecutor would have had to prove that it was more likely than not that she committed the offense. Ask any law student and you will hear that this is a very low burden of proof. For that reason, it is basically impossible for a defendant to win a preliminary hearing. Ms. Reynolds would have either waived or had that hearing in the lower court, and then the case would have had to proceed through the grand jury and have the grand jury issue an indictment. After that, the case would have gotten scheduled for a regular setting. It is only at that point that the criminal court judge could have heard an application to reduce her bail. And the process is not over yet. Regardless of whether bail was reduced or not, if the parties did not reach an agreement, the case would eventually be scheduled for trial. But remember, unless that bail is lowered or eliminated, she is going to be sitting in jail as this entire process plays out. At this point in the interview the judge pointed to a large white board on his office wall.

> That's my calendar over there. That's where I am at any given time. . . . If you take that day [in] March when she was arrested. Now it just so happens that I would have been there the following week, but that probably would not have been quick enough to get an indictment [out of the grand jury]. She would be looking at coming all the way around to sometime in May. If she decided, I'm not resolving this case. I want a jury trial. She has to wait for the indictment, I wouldn't be back for up to five weeks. That would be the first time she could ask for a reduction in bail. And then, and her baby's in DCS custody, so she's losing any hope of getting her baby back just by virtue of the passing of time. That's how it works. And that's why you have these ladies pleading in that court, on things where the charge, the state may not be able to make it, you know, at a trial. Or having an element you can't establish. All those issues [wouldn't] be ripe [until] trial.

It seems clear from the file and from the medical records that the prosecution would not have been able to convict her of fetal assault. But presumably for her, the cost of fighting was just too high. Instead, she pled and subjected herself to the misdemeanor system.

Once the plea was entered, Ms. Reynolds' case became just another misdemeanor, to be processed the way all misdemeanors are processed in the United States. While those who supported the fetal assault law purported that this was about treatment, for Ms. Reynolds, as was the case for the majority of fetal assault defendants, this was just about punishment. And punishment, is, all too often, just about debt.

The second revealing piece of Ms. Reynolds' case is what it tells us about the role of criminal debt in her prosecution. Now remember that the judge did suspend her jail sentence and allow her to go into the community on supervised probation. Technically she was going to be on probation for eleven months and twenty-nine days, but it was possible that she would not have fully paid her costs by then. Tennessee law is very clear about what should happen in these circumstances. For a defendant who finishes her sentence (jail or probation) but has not fully paid her court debt, the court can collect the debt in civil courts, using the same laws and procedures used to collect all other debt. But the court absolutely cannot extend the criminal sentence. Once the sentence is done, the criminal case is over, unpaid debt or not.[2] But that did not appear to matter to the prosecutor, defense attorney, or judge in her case. The judgment, part of which you can see in Figure 5.2, indicated that, as part of the plea agreement, "Defendant agrees to extend probation until P.I. F." which court staff told me stands for paid in full. As it turns out, every plea agreement I saw in that county had the same notation.

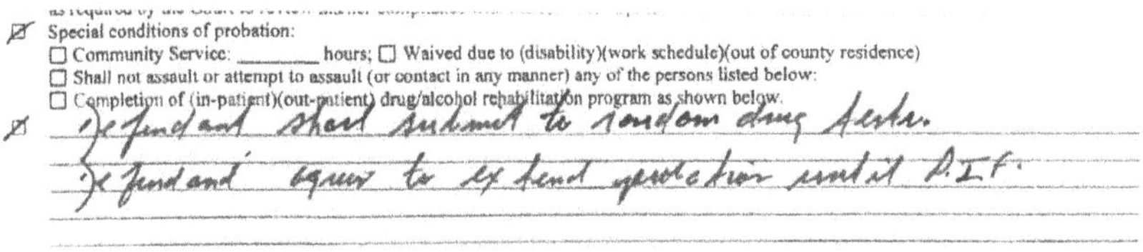
☒ Special conditions of probation:
☐ Community Service: ________ hours; ☐ Waived due to (disability)(work schedule)(out of county residence)
☐ Shall not assault or attempt to assault (or contact in any manner) any of the persons listed below:
☐ Completion of (in-patient)(out-patient) drug/alcohol rehabilitation program as shown below.
☒ Defendant shall submit to random drug tests.
Defendant agrees to extend probation until P.I.F.

Figure 5.2 Maxine Reynolds conditions of probation

Ms. Reynolds' fees for that offense, reproduced in Figure 5.3, totaled $458.50. The bill, which as we will see is quite typical, included a variety of charges for things like her public defender, fees for being supervised on probation, and fees for her arrest.

You will remember that about a month after being placed on probation, Ms. Reynolds was charged with an additional misdemeanor, and because she was on probation at the time, she was also charged with a violation of the probationary terms of her fetal assault plea. At the time of her new arrest, Ms. Reynolds had paid $230 toward her costs. After thirty days in jail, she was let back out on probation with a new court date set "as to payments." It was only after she paid that her case was dismissed.

Ms. Reynolds' case is in no way exceptional either among Tennessee's fetal assault cases or in the world of misdemeanor

Charge: ASSAULT - BODILY INJURY - 1

Fee	Pay To	Total Assessed	Total Paid	Total Due
State Litigation Tax	Department of Revenue	$29.50	$29.50	$0.00
Victim Notification Fund Tax	Department of Revenue	$3.00	$3.00	$0.00
CIC (CAPERSON)	Department of Revenue	$50.00	$50.00	$0.00
Judicial Commissioners Tax	Department of Revenue	$2.00	$2.00	$0.00
County Litigation Tax	xxxxxxx County Trustee	$29.50	$29.50	$0.00
Local County Litigation Tax	xxxxxxx County Trustee	$6.00	$6.00	$0.00
Jail Building/Crt Security Tax	xxxxxxx County Trustee	$50.00	$50.00	$0.00
Children's Center Tax	xxxxxxx County Trustee	$25.00	$25.00	$0.00
Clerk Flat Fee - CR		$64.00	$64.00	$0.00
Public Defender Fee	Public Defender's Conference	$12.50	$12.50	$0.00
Arrest Fee	xxxxx County Sheriff's Office	$40.00	$40.00	$0.00
Service Fee Data	xxxxx County Sheriff's Office	$2.00	$2.00	$0.00
Victims Assistance Assessment	xxxxx County Trustee	$42.00	$42.00	$0.00
		$3.00	$3.00	$0.00
Probation Fees	xxxxx County Trustee	$100.00	$100.00	$0.00
	Total For Charge:	$458.50	$458.50	$0.00

Figure 5.3 Maxine Reynolds cost sheet

prosecutions. In fact, it is emblematic of several key features. First, for most women, the idea of care was nothing more than a smokescreen hiding punishment, and second that punishment played out as it all too often does at the low end of the criminal system: deepening poverty and degrading justice.

5.1 CARE AS A SMOKESCREEN

We learned in the last chapter that the prosecutions for fetal assault concentrated in two geographic regions, the northeast and Shelby County, the home of Memphis, Tennessee. As it turned out, the trajectory of the cases played out very differently depending on where you were prosecuted. Twenty-five women were prosecuted in Shelby County. All these women were referred to the Shelby County Drug Court. All were presumably offered the opportunity to access drug treatment through that court. It is important to understand that drug courts generally do not actually provide treatment. Instead, they provide supervision but rely on outside providers to provide the actual addiction treatment. This is the case in Shelby County as well.

Participants are referred to area treatment providers as a part of the services provided by the court. So, just by virtue of their participation in the court, each of the twenty-five women both gained some level of access to care and were required to participate in that care as a part of her criminal case. In contrast, in the northeastern, Appalachian counties, and in the small number of prosecutions elsewhere in the state, there is no evidence that the majority of women women were offered treatment or were required to participate in treatment as part of their criminal case.

First the numbers: for the purposes of this discussion, we are focusing on what happened in seventy-seven of the ninety-eight cases that were brought in the State in all counties other than Shelby County. For twenty-one of those ninety eight cases, the documentation was not robust enough to describe what happened in the case. The remaining seventy-seven case files trace what happened in a good deal of detail. All seventy-seven women were prosecuted for fetal assault, pled guilty, received either a jail or a probationary sentence, and were, as detailed later in this chapter, assessed significant fees and fines as part of their prosecutions. Fifty of those seventy-seven files contain absolutely no notation that any form of treatment was either offered during the case or that it was required as part of the sentence. In 65 percent of the cases outside of Memphis for which we obtained sufficient documentation, despite the rhetoric of the law's supporters, prosecution had nothing to do with care.

When thinking about this data, the first thing to call your attention to is that I am not claiming that, somewhere along the way, these fifty women were not offered treatment by some system actor. What I am claiming, instead, is that there was no indication in the file that there was requirement of treatment in the criminal case. Remember that these cases generally originated in hospital settings. They generally moved from those hospital settings to child welfare and then to prosecution. It is certainly possible that somewhere along the line these women were offered treatment. If in fact a particular woman was in need of substance abuse treatment, a high-quality health care provider should certainly have made the appropriate referral, and social work staff in the hospital could have been in a good position to help a woman with any barriers to accessing that treatment.[3] In the child welfare setting, DCS may well have required that the women find care, and in fact, they were arguably required to help them get that care. Under federal law, in the vast majority of circumstances, child welfare agencies are required to make "best efforts" to reunify families. If a woman was struggling with substance abuse that was interfering with her parenting, DCS should have provided a referral to treatment as well as supportive services to make sure that the mother could actually access that treatment. Now, it is important to remember that, overall, in Tennessee, there are not nearly enough beds for pregnant women to receive inpatient care. Thus, it is not clear where either health care or child welfare professionals would have found care for all these women, but it is possible that it happened.

But none of that reflects what the legislators said about the fetal assault law. They said that the legislation creating the crime of fetal assault was necessary to get women access to treatment. But for fifty of the seventy-seven, or 65 percent of the women prosecuted outside of Memphis, there is no evidence that that happened. Instead, what their files reveal is that the cases were like Ms. Reynolds' case. They were just about punishment. As it turns out, in the majority of cases outside Memphis, prosecution did nothing more than targeted and punished poor women who used illegal drugs during pregnancy.

In thinking about these numbers, it is important to note that the category of "accessing treatment through the criminal case" was applied tremendously liberally in the data analysis. Any indication, no matter how tentative or, from a medical perspective, insufficient, was included in the category. For example, a woman who was "to be furloughed to long term treatment once arranged" and another who the file stated "may attend rehab for 6 months upon release from jail" were both included, despite the fact that there is no indication that either of these women actually accessed treatment. Women were also included if their files indicated that the judge required them to go to Alcoholics or Narcotics Anonymous meetings despite the fact that these programs are not medical treatment. For instance, a woman who was required to go to "90 meetings in 90 days" was counted in this category along with individuals who were required to go to intensive inpatient and outpatient programs. Chapter 7 turns the focus to the minority of cases in which there was an indication in the court file that treatment was suggested or mandated in the criminal case and focuses on the risks women took and the price they paid for accessing treatment through the criminal system. But the remainder of this chapter tells the majority's story, a story all too common on the low end of the criminal system.

5.2 DEEPENING POVERTY

In 2014, in the wake of the killing of Michael Brown in Ferguson, Missouri, the United States Department of Justice (DOJ) issued a series of reports. While the first focused on whether or not the police who shot Mr. Brown had violated any federal laws, the second report focused much more broadly on the operation of the policing and court systems in Ferguson. In addition to the extensive overt acts of racism uncovered in that report, the DOJ exposed the extent to which criminal system debt (restitution and a myriad of costs charged to defendants) was central to the conduct of both the police and the municipal court. As to the court, the DOJ found that,

> Ferguson has allowed its focus on revenue generation to fundamentally compromise the role of Ferguson's municipal court. The municipal court does not act as a neutral arbiter of the law or a check on unlawful police conduct. Instead, the court primarily uses its judicial authority as the means to compel the payment of fines and fees that advance the City's financial interests.[4]

While this particular report focused on one jurisdiction, what was happening in Ferguson was by no means anomalous. It is in fact a dominant feature of the American misdemeanor system. Professor Alexandra Natapoff, whose scholarship focuses on the operation of the

United States' criminal legal system, explains that "the petty-offense process is a method of taxation. It rounds up low-level offenders and charges them with fines and fees, which are then plowed back into the system to fund those very same jails, probation offices and the local governments that oversee them." Ultimately, she argues that "the petty-offense process has quietly become a regressive feature of American tax policy. It actively extracts revenue from an ever-widening pool of mostly low-income people in order to fund the operations of private as well as public criminal justice institutions."[5]

Tennessee is no exception. Tennessee law allows, and in many cases requires, courts to impose a dizzying array of costs, fines, and fees in criminal cases. To begin, criminal sentences often include both incarceration and a monetary fine. If the victim of a crime suffers monetary damage, then the court can impose restitution, ordering the defendant to pay for that harm. But, in the fetal assault cases, and in misdemeanor cases in general, the real price for the defendants comes in the form of costs and taxes. Under Tennessee law, "[a] defendant convicted of a criminal offense shall pay all the costs that have accrued in the cause."[6] These costs may include "all costs incident to the arrest and safekeeping of the defendant, before and after conviction, due and incident to the prosecution and conviction, and incident to the carrying of the judgement or sentence of the court into effect."[7] This includes costs charged by private probation companies for supervision and what advocates call "pay to stay," fees imposed for the cost of incarceration.

In addition to costs, Tennessee law imposes a wide variety of litigation taxes on criminal defendants. A substantial portion of these tax revenues (32.15 percent) go into the state's general fund, to pay for a wide variety of basic government expenses. But they are also earmarked for particular programs. Litigation taxes fund, among other programs, the Tennessee corrections institute, driver education in the public schools, policing of public housing, the state court clerk's conference, the victim of crime assistance fund, the criminal injuries compensation fund, the victims of drunk drivers compensation fund, the salaries of public defenders, the Tennessee general sessions judges' conference, the public defender program, the civil legal representation of indigents fund, the purchase, installation, maintenance, and line charges for electronic finger imaging systems, and the sex offender treatment fund.[8] Finally, Tennessee law permits counties and localities to impose their own additional litigation taxes "to be used exclusively for the purpose of jail or workhouse construction, reconstruction or upgrading, or to retire debt, including principal and interest and related expenses, on such construction, reconstruction or upgrading or for courthouse renovation."[9] In total, in fiscal year 2019, Tennessee collected over $11 million in litigation taxes.[10]

All of these fees, fines, costs, and taxes add up and increase the burden on the low-income defendants who populate Tennessee's lower courts. As Judge Don Arnold, who as of this writing presides in a lower court in Washington County Tennessee and who used to serve in the Tennessee legislature, explained during our interview:

> When I was in the legislature, I used to feel a great deal of insult. I used to get on the floor at times and say the poor people were the ones punished by our laws, our courts … Every time the DAs wanted to add a little more to the retirement, we'd pass a law and put it on as part of the court costs. That's the people that least could afford it. I never did win on that, I lost every time, but I always voted [against] it anyway.[11]

It is true that Tennessee law permits judges to suspend the payment of costs and taxes if the defendant is indigent and the judge concludes that the equities of the case require it,[12] but for the vast majority of women in this study, despite a finding by the court that they were indigent for the purposes of appointment of counsel, no such relief was granted. In fact, as is evident from Ms. Reynolds' file, the cases focused on collection.

While Ms. Reynolds' costs totaled under $500, things can get much more expensive for defendants who are deeper in the system and spend more time in jail. Take for example the case of Vanessa Thomas. At the time of her prosecution for fetal assault, Ms. Thomas was already on probation for other misdemeanor charges. She had pled guilty to those charges the year prior to her pregnancy and was in the midst of serving two consecutive sentences of eleven months and twenty-nine days each on probation. Any violation of that probation could result in the reinstatement of her almost two-year jail term. Because she was already on probation, a condition of that probation was not to commit additional crimes. In her original case, Ms. Thomas, like Ms. Reynolds, had been ordered to pay several hundred dollars in court costs, but she had not kept up with her payments. At the time of her child's birth, Ms. Thomas was then facing sanction not only for fetal assault but for two separate instances of violation of probation. This set of circumstances would significantly impact the trajectory of her case and would make the consequences of any failure to comply with court orders very steep.

Ms. Thomas gave birth to her child in January 2015. An arrest warrant was issued twelve days later, and she was arrested and taken to jail on that day. No bail was set, so, presumably, Ms. Thomas remained in jail until her case was resolved. A judge at that point made a determination that Ms. Thomas was indigent and appointed a public defender to represent her. Ms. Thomas's fetal assault case would not be resolved for nearly two more months, during which time she presumably sat in jail. Between the fetal assault charge and her ultimate plea three months after she was charged, the state filed two separate allegations of violation of probation – one for a failure to pay and one for having committed the crime of fetal assault while on probation. Though her court costs had originally been lower, by that time they were up to $1,701.75, and she had made little progress in paying them. She also found herself facing the potential of significant jail time. If her probation on the original charges was revoked, the judge could do a variety of things, including continuing probation, imposing some jail time followed by more probation, or imposing the original jail sentence of eleven months and twenty-nine days.[13] In addition, a finding of guilty of the fetal assault charge could result in another eleven month and twenty-nine day sentence for that charge, or a total of almost two years in prison.[14] So, going into court Ms. Thomas faced serious risks of incarceration.

Unsurprisingly on that day, Ms. Thomas did plead guilty, and she was sentenced to a year in prison – six months for the violation of probation and another six months for the fetal assault charge. She was apparently released early because, seven months later, there was a new violation of probation filed, alleging two violations – that she had failed to appear for her long-term treatment and that she had failed to make any progress on her court costs. She got arrested two months later, was ordered to serve 180 days in jail. and then was again placed on probation, "until compliance." Presumably, this order was focused on compliance with the order to pay costs. By 2016, Ms. Thomas's costs on the fetal assault charge, as well as the various violations of probation, totaled $4,478.25. Her cost bill, like all the cost bills in the sample, included a wide range of charges. For example, on one of the violations of probation, reproduced in Figure 5.4, for which she owed a total of $3,827.75, she owed sixteen different categories of fees.

Several items are of note in this cost sheet. First, note the number of parts of the system that are funded, at least in part, through the imposition of small fees charged to criminal defendants. Everything from the prison library to the taking of fingerprints is paid for, at least in part, by the defendants themselves. A second thing to note is the $3,600 charge for her jailing. The practice of charging defendants for costs associated

In the case of: State Of Tennessee vs xxxxxxx
Case Number:
Reference Number:

Fee	# of Fees	Due Date	Last Paid Date	Fee Amount	Total Assessed	Total Paid	Total Due
State Criminal Fee	1			$2.00	$2.00	$0.00	$2.00
State Cic $26.50	1			$26.50	$26.50	$0.00	$26.50
Attorneys Reim Tax	1			$2.75	$2.75	$0.00	$2.75
Fingerprint Tax	1			$1.00	$1.00	$0.00	$1.00
Victim Notification Fund	1			$3.00	$3.00	$0.00	$3.00
Judicial Comm.Tax	1			$2.00	$2.00	$0.00	$2.00
Officers Costs-County	1			$40.00	$40.00	$0.00	$40.00
County Litigation Tax	1			$37.50	$37.50	$0.00	$37.50
Courthouse Building Fund	1			$2.00	$2.00	$0.00	$2.00
Library Fund	1			$1.00	$1.00	$0.00	$1.00
Data Entry Gen Sess	1			$4.00	$4.00	$0.00	$4.00
Clerk Fee Gen Session	1			$62.00	$62.00	$0.00	$62.00
Jail Fees - Other	1			$3,600.00	$3,600.00	$0.00	$3,600.00
Data Entry Officer	1			$2.00	$2.00	$0.00	$2.00
Misd/Felony Tax $12.50	1			$12.50	$12.50	$0.00	$12.50
Litigation Tax	1			$29.50	$29.50	$0.00	$29.50
			Totals:		$3,827.75	$0.00	$3,827.75

Figure 5.4 Vanessa Thomas cost sheet

with their jailing is quite widespread. The data above was run and provided to me on December 29, 2016, nearly a year after the last event in Ms. Thomas's case. At that point, she had not made any payments.

And Ms. Thomas and Ms. Reynolds are by no means alone. The case files reveal the high costs imposed on indigent defendants and the iron grip of the courts in attempting force payments. Take for example, Raven Brewer, whose costs at one point totaled $4,105.50. Now, Ms. Brewer and Ms. Thomas were certainly on the high end in terms of costs. Overall, in East Tennessee, the costs in the fetal assault cases averaged $796. But that was not the case in Memphis, Tennessee. In Chapter 7, I talk more about the Memphis cases, in which women participated in the Shelby County drug court. While those women got more access to treatment opportunities than the women in the eastern, Appalachian regions of the state, they also faced higher costs, averaging $1,871.74. It is also interesting to note that the vast majority of women were not able to pay those fees. At the time I obtained the data on those cases, in February of 2019, eight months after the law was no longer in effect, the vast majority of those fees remained unpaid. At that point the unpaid balances of the women in Memphis averaged $1,853.24.

The indigency of these clients and their resulting inability to pay did not slow down the systematic pressure to pay. Remember, for example, that in every case in Ms. Reynold's district, probation, and therefore the supervisory power of the court, was extended until the defendants paid. Court dates were regularly set "as to payment," meaning that the defendant would have to appear to let the judge know what progress they were making on payment, with the obvious threat that they could be punished for their failures. Defendants were consistently rewarded with dismissal once they did. Marcy Russell's case, to give just one example, was dismissed with a notation stating that she was "paid in full." Clearly, payment is the ticket out of the system.

And failure to pay does not just keep you embroiled in the misdemeanor system. In Tennessee, like in many other states, the failure to pay can result in the loss of your driver's license. Tennessee law allows for the revocation of a driver's license if an individual has not paid all litigation taxes, court costs, and fines within one year of the judgment.[15] And, of course, driving on a suspended license is also a misdemeanor.[16] In a state that is almost entirely dependent on cars for transportation, this leads almost inevitably to poor people picking up additional criminal charges for driving on a suspended license. This cycle of conviction on tickets and charges, imposition of costs, failure to pay costs, license suspension, and subsequent charging for driving on a suspended license, is so prevalent that Natapoff estimates that, "suspended-license cases comprise as much as 30 percent of certain local dockets, in some places reaching 60 percent."[17] As she explains, "most licenses are suspended because people cannot afford to pay a traffic fine."[18] When you think about this cycle, remember that the vast majority of women prosecuted were poor and think again about Ms. Reynolds. Her probation was going to be extended until "paid in full." While you are on probation, you are at heightened risk of being pulled back into the system. Thus, prosecution not only makes you poorer, by exacting often exorbitant fees, fines and costs, but when you are too poor to pay, it makes it all the harder to escape the system.

5.3 DEGRADING JUSTICE

Prosecution is targeted at those in poverty and prosecution not only makes you poorer but it makes it that much harder to escape from the criminal system. But there is another pernicious effect of poverty in the misdemeanor system. If we think of justice in the criminal system as being able to avail oneself of fundamental constitutional guarantees that are designed to preserve rights and protect against wrongful conviction – the right to trial, the right to counsel, the right to confront witnesses and challenge the evidence against you – justice, for those in poverty, does not measure up. This is true in very particular ways for those charged with misdemeanors and low-level felonies.

Recall the allegations in Ms. Reynold's case and in particular the lack of any allegation of harm to her child and the fact that her child's medical record did not indicate an NAS diagnosis. As a Law Professor, I work in my school's clinical teaching program, teaching my students to defend clients. As such, the lack of an allegation of harm caught my eye. If there was no evidence of a central element of the charged crime, she simply should not have been punished for this crime. But as the

Criminal Court judge in that district explained, that is not how the system works. Even if Ms. Reynolds' attorney had explored this issue, the high bail, the long delays between court appearances, and the ever-advancing clock of the child welfare system, could easily have persuaded her to plead guilty even if she was not guilty.

And Ms. Reynolds was not alone. As one public defender who represented some of the women charged with fetal assault explained about these cases. "[In the fetal assault cases] it was never a clear case of here's your charge and you made bail so we can fight this thing. They're in jail and offer. You can be out of jail with your new baby, if you want to consider this offer. And often, they'll do it."[19] In this sense, Ms. Reynolds' plea was the result not of a rock-solid case against her but instead of the ever-present pressures of the misdemeanor system. And Ms. Reynolds is not alone. In fact, nationwide "97 percent of misdemeanor convictions are the result of a guilty plea."[20] And this is a central feature of the relationship between poverty and the criminal system in the United States. As Alexandra Natapoff explains in her searing indictment of criminal process on the low end of the criminal system,

> It is often said that we have two justice systems, one for the rich and one for the poor, but in practice there is no bright line. Rather, there is gradual erosion. As offenses get pettier and defendants get poorer, a host of pressures and resource constraints diminish basic commitment to rules, evidence, fairness and the presumption of innocence, slowly and quietly changing how the system does its work.[21]

Now, some in the criminal system in Tennessee would certainly disagree with this analysis at least as it pertained to the fetal assault prosecutions. In the course of researching this book, I asked Barry Staubus, the prosecutor in Sullivan County, why all the women in his district pled guilty to fetal assault. His response: "First is the strength of the case. I mean what would be the defense?"[22] Staubus went on to talk about how the prosecutions led to treatment, but that is a topic for the next chapter. Clearly, he believed that the women who were accused had no defenses at all.

But as I looked the criminal court files in these cases, the lack of an allegation of harm in cases like Ms. Reynolds' bothered me more and more. In overwhelming numbers, the women who were prosecuted did what Ms. Reynolds and the defendants in Sullivan County did: they pled guilty. The case files tell this story clearly. While a few cases were dismissed, the rest ended in a guilty plea. There were no motions filed and no hearings or trials held. They were charged, often jailed, and pled in a wide variety of circumstances that suggest that, in fact, they may well not have been guilty. There are three types of case that fall into this category: cases in which the women were prosecuted for taking drugs that were not actually criminalized by the fetal assault law; cases in which the allegation is that they took cocaine during pregnancy; and cases, like Ms. Reynolds', in which there was no allegation of harm.

I'll begin with the cases of Angel Cooper and Alice Lester. The petition in Ms. Cooper's case is reproduced in Figure 5.5.

Ms. Lester's arrest report, in Figure 5.6, makes similar allegations.

Recall from the beginning of this chapter that, in order to be found guilty of fetal assault, the woman had to have illegally used a narcotic drug during pregnancy. Tennessee has a specific definition of "narcotic" and that definition simply does not include either benzodiazepines or THC.[23] So, assuming the allegations summarized the proof that the state had, Ms.

I, the affiant named below, after being sworn, state under oath that on or about xxxxxxx
in xxxxx County, Tennessee,   xxxxxxx
committed the offense(s) of violation(s) of T.C.A.   39-13-101 Simple Assault-Attempted
I further state under oath that the essential facts constituting the offense(s), the sources of my information and the reasons why this information is believable and reliable are as follows:

On x date, xxxx gave birth to an infant at the xxxxx Medical Center. Analysis, (umbilical cord blood), indicated that at the time of delivery the infant's toxicology tested positive for Benzodiazepines indicating that the infant was exposed in utero to the un-prescribed, illegal narcotic. xxxx is charged with one count of Simple Assault (Attempted), in violation of T.C.A. 39-13-101, as she engaged in reckless conduct that placed the infant in danger of bodily harm. The toxicology report indicated that the infant had also been exposed to T.H.C. Said offense occurred in xxxxx TN.

Figure 5.5 Angel Cooper allegations

Title: INITIAL ARREST
On x, xxxx came to the police department where she was given a citation and a court date for xxxx. After reviewing all of the evidence in the case it was determined that xxx's infant child xxxxx had been exposed to a benzodiazepine during pregnancy. Ms. xxxx was not seeking any help during her pregnancy for this narcotic. Ms. xxxx was released from the police department with the citation.

Figure 5.6 Alice Lester allegations

Cooper and Ms. Lester were not guilty. But in neither case did this matter. Ms. Cooper pled guilty to attempted fetal assault and was sentenced to five months, which was suspended to probation. She missed one probation appointment and, during another appointment, tested positive for THC. To be clear, neither missing an appointment nor testing positive for THC are crimes. However, because Ms. Cooper was on probation, they were violations of the terms of her plea. The private probation company that was supervising her filed a motion to have her jail sentence reinstated. She ultimately served forty-five days in jail and was assessed $429.50 in costs. Ms. Lester also pled guilty and was sentenced to eleven months and twenty-nine days in jail, suspended to probation. We do not know as much about what happened next for her, but suffice it to say that she was now, like all the defendants on probation, at a heightened risk of additional punishment. And all this despite the fact that everything we know about their cases suggests that Ms. Cooper and Ms. Lester, like Ms. Reynolds, did not commit the crime of fetal assault.

The second category of cases in which it appeared that there was a significant possibility of a lack of guilt involved cocaine. Tennessee law is strange in this respect. From a pharmacological perspective, cocaine is not a narcotic drug. But legally, at least in Tennessee, it is defined as a narcotic. Prosecution for taking cocaine during pregnancy resulting in harm to the infant did state a crime. But recall from Chapter 2 that the evidence that cocaine exposure causes specific harm that can be clearly identified has been thoroughly questioned. The scientific data on the subject is complex, and researchers report that it is tremendously difficult to know whether any observed harm results from cocaine or a myriad of other issues in the pregnancy. Thus, in any particular case it would have been quite difficult to prove both that there was harm and that the harm was caused by the cocaine exposure. But this did not matter. It did not matter for Ms. Mason, whose case spanned well over a year and resulted in nine months in jail and costs totaling $1,914.50. And it did not matter for Ms. Richards, who was accused of taking cocaine and marijuana during her pregnancy and who pled guilty, was sentenced to probation, served fourteen days in jail during her case, and was charged a total of $3,404.50.

This leaves us, finally, with another set of cases that raise serious questions as to their legality. As I mentioned in Chapter 4, in the course of my research I obtained the birth records of all infants born in Tennessee during the time that the law was in effect who were diagnosed with NAS. My team and I then cross-checked that list with the list of women who were prosecuted to see if women had been prosecuted who did not give birth to an infant with NAS. There turned out to be a substantial number of women in this category – thirty-three out of the ninety-six women whose names we know[24] and who were prosecuted for fetal assault. To try to figure out if there were potentially illegal prosecutions, I went back and took a deeper look at these women's files. I was looking to see if there were cases in which there was a significant possibility that there was, in fact, no proof of harm to the infant. If that was the case, and if they pled guilty anyway, these pleas happened despite the fact that the state likely could not have convicted them of the crime. When I pulled the criminal files of these thirty-three women, only seven of them had their charges dismissed. I eliminated those seven on the theory that the system actually worked to bring those cases to the right result. I also eliminated ten cases that did not have sufficient information. That left sixteen women for whom there was a guilty plea, punishment, no NAS diagnosis, and sufficient information in the criminal file to analyze the charges. Five of those cases, a few of which I described above, involved allegations that the women took cocaine during their pregnancies, raising significant questions about whether the prosecution had the evidence to convict. In four cases there was an allegation of harm, even if there was no NAS diagnosis in the hospital records, so maybe there was harm there. That left me with eleven cases which broke down into two categories. Six included some allegation of harm. Given the absence of an NAS diagnosis, it is not at all clear how the prosecution would have proven that harm, but potentially they could have been able to.

But for five of these women, there was nothing to indicate harm – no allegation of harm to the infant and no NAS diagnosis. Without an NAS diagnosis, it is hard to imagine how the state would have won these cases if they had gone to trial. But instead of raising this defense and potentially avoiding punishment, these five women pled guilty and were punished. There are no indications in the files that their attorney made the state put forward proof at a preliminary hearing or explore these problems. They did not move to dismiss the petition for failing to allege facts that meet the crime. Instead, like Ms. Reynolds, and like so many charged with misdemeanors in the criminal system, they pled. All five spent time in jail. One served ninety-one days in jail before sentencing. Two were sentenced to six months' incarceration. These are not small harms and, to the extent it appears that these women were in fact not guilty, this represents a serious miscarriage of justice. For these five women, for the two who were not accused of taking narcotics during pregnancy, for the five who were accused of taking cocaine during pregnancy, and perhaps for many more, the justice system failed. These prosecutions were not exceptional, as the proponents of the fetal assault law had suggested; they were not about treatment. They were just misdemeanors, and they played out exactly as misdemeanors do throughout the United States every day in the lower courts of the American criminal legal system – targeting poverty, deepening poverty, and degrading justice.

While this story, of care being little more than a smokescreen, and of prosecuting and deepening poverty and degrading justice, is the story of the majority of cases, it is not the entire story. The case files reveal that a minority of women were in fact offered some form of treatment as a part of their criminal cases. It is to these offers, the form of care offered, and the price they paid that we turn in Part III.

NOTES

1. All defendant names used in this book are pseudonyms.
2. TENN. CODE ANN. § 40–24–105(f) ("If any fine, costs or litigation taxes assessed against the defendant in a criminal case remain in default when the defendant is released from the sentence imposed, the sentence expires or the criminal court otherwise loses jurisdiction over the defendant, the sentencing judge, clerk or district attorney general may have the amount remaining in default converted to a civil judgment pursuant to the Tennessee Rules of Civil Procedure. The judgment may be enforced as is provided in this section or in any other manner authorized by law for a civil judgment.").
3. It is worth noting that it is not at all clear that health care professionals would view themselves as the best source of a referral for treatment and other supports. Instead, some recent research by Kelley Fong indicates that in fact health care providers, as well as other professionals who are mandated to report cases to child welfare departments, view the child welfare agency as the agency in the best position to provide those referrals. Kelley Fong, *Getting*

Eyes in the Home: Child Protective Services Investigations and State Surveillance of Family Life, 85(4) Am. Soc. Rev. 610 (2020).

4. U.S. Department of Justice: Civil Rights Division, *Investigation of the Ferguson Police Department*, at 3 (2015) available at https://www.justice.gov/sites/default/files/opa/press-releases/attachments/2015/03/04/ferguson_police_de partment_report_1.pdf [https://perma.cc/ML2M-RG3Z].

5. Alexandra Natapoff, Punishment Without Crime: How Our Massive Misdemeanor System Traps the Innocent and Makes America More Unequal 10 (2018).

6. Tenn. Code Ann. § 40–25–123(a).

7. Tenn. Code Ann. § 40–25–104.

8. Tenn. Code Ann. § 67–4–606. Disposition of proceeds.

9. Tenn. Code Ann. § 67–4–601. County and municipal authority.

10. Tennessee Department of Revenue, Revenue Collections, January 2019 at 8 (link to update: https://www.tn.gov/revenue/tax-resources/statistics-and-collections/collections-summaries.html). [https://perma.cc/5MLF-TA8U].

11. Arnold transcript at 3 (on file with author).

12. Tenn. Code Ann. § 40–25–123 (b).

13. *See* Tenn. Code Ann. § 40–35–311(e)(1).

14. This potential sentence would be reduced by any days Ms. Thomas had already served, before various hearings and trials, in jail. For example, if she was sentenced to two eleven month and twenty-nine-day consecutive sentences but had already been in jail before various court proceedings for twenty-two days, she would serve the full sentence minus twenty-two days.

15. Tenn. Code Ann. § 40–24–105. Collection of fines, costs, and litigation taxes; license revocation; hardship exception; payment plans.

16. Tenn. Code Ann. § 55–50–504.

17. Natapoff, *supra* note 5, at 50.

18. Natapoff, *supra* note 5, at 50.

19. Rural Public Defender Transcript at 6 (on file with author).

20. Natapoff, *supra* note 5, at 5.

21. Natapoff, *supra* note 5, at 7.

22. Barry Staubus Transcript at 36.

23. Tenn. Code Ann. § 39–17–402(17).

24. In the course of research at times the research team received evidence indicating that prosecutions had taken place but did not obtain the names of the women some of the women who were prosecuted. For example, in Sullivan County the District Attorney informed us that ten women had been prosecuted, had completed the terms of their probation and had subsequently had their convictions expunged. As a result, no physical record of their prosecution was available to the public.

PART III

Criminalized Care

You are poor, you are pregnant, and you are struggling with substance-use disorder. If you haven't had this experience, imagine it for a moment. Although your addiction to drugs has been dominating your daily existence for quite some time, your pregnancy changes things. You, like many women in your circumstance, are newly motivated to seek care, address your addiction, and ensure that your child is healthy. The pregnancy motivates you to lead a healthier life. But you are also terrified – terrified of the stigma, terrified that DCS might take your baby, terrified that you could be hurting your baby or that you already have, and terrified because you have no idea who to trust or what to do next. You are likely, as the SisterReach study taught, to have faced extraordinary trauma in your life. Remember that in that study of women who were affected by the fetal assault law,

> [e]ighty percent of the women ... were raised in households where substance use was common. More than two-thirds of the women were unemployed at the time of the discussion and reported having had sex in exchange for money, drugs, or other basic needs over the course of their life. The stress of limited finances was compounded by a history of domestic and sexual abuse for almost all participants – highlighting the impact of adverse childhood and adult life experiences and the vulnerability of substance using women.[1]

Reproductive Justice dictates that women require, in such a moment, "the right to have children under the conditions [they] chooses and the right to parent the children [they have] in safe and healthy environments."[2] It also places the obligation on "government and society to ensure that the conditions are suitable for implementing her decisions."[3]

To put this in more concrete and immediate terms, recall the words of Dr. Nzinga Harrison, a psychiatrist whose practice focuses on the care of those who suffer from serious persistent mental illness including severe substance use disorders and whose work was highlighted in Chapter 2. As she explained,

> overwhelmingly, mothers want to take care of their babies. And so if a woman has a substance use disorder and she gets pregnant, you want to create the environment and the community that 1. She automatically knows where she can go, and 2. That when she gets there she's going to be received with compassion and open arms and following throughout her pregnancy with increased access to the resources that she does not have.[4]

That is, in the context of substance use during pregnancy, what this book has been calling care. While these women likely needed, in many cases, this robust form of care, what they got instead, if anything at all, was what this book calls *criminalized care.*

This section moves from what Part II called *care as a smokescreen* to the provision of care proximate to or inside of punishment systems, both in the fetal assault cases in particular and in the broader system in which those cases were processed. Chapter 6 begins this story, outlining a series of laws, rules, and practices, in the health care, child welfare, and criminal systems that drew information and ultimately women out of the health care system and deeper and deeper into the child welfare and criminal systems. Chapter 7 delves into the provision of care within punishment systems, describing the myriad ways in which opportunities for care are in fact located behind the doors of punishment, a reality that draws individuals in need of care deeper into those systems. Finally, Chapter 8 turns from the mechanisms drawing women into punishment systems to the degraded care women receive. Criminalized care, in this story, leads to three profound effects: care at the price of surveillance and degradation; care at the risk of severe punishment; and care decision-making that is deeply corrupted by its proximity to punishment systems.

NOTES

1. Orisha A. Bowers et al., Tennessee's Fetal Assault Law: Understanding Its Impact on Marginalized Women at 4 (2019) https://www.sisterreach.org /uploads/1/3/3/2/133261658/full_fetal_assault_rpt_1.pdf [https://perma.cc /8BKC-VYTE].
2. LORETTA J. ROSS, ET AL., *Introduction to* RADICAL REPRODUCTIVE JUSTICE: FOUNDATIONS, THEORY, PRACTICE CRITIQUE 14 (Loretta J. Ross et al. eds 2017).
3. *Id.*
4. Interview with Dr. Nzinga Harrison, Chief Medical Officer and Co-Founder Eleanor Health (June 25, 2018).

6 THE PATH IN: FROM HEALTH CARE TO CHILD WELFARE TO CRIMINAL SYSTEMS

The laws in effect prevented me from it being a care issue. It became a law, a liability issue.

Research Respondent, SisterReach Fetal Assault Study

About a year and a half into gathering the data for this book, I hired a law student to assist in data analysis. She was in law school at the time but had worked as a labor and delivery nurse at a local hospital for many years. She was, to say the least, an ideal candidate for the research team. One of the first assignments I gave her drew on her medical and practice knowledge. I asked her to go through the criminal court files for the women who were prosecuted and look specifically at the allegations contained in the charging document. Her task was to determine whether or not the public criminal allegations against the fetal assault defendants included information obtained by health care providers in the health care setting. Several days later she stopped by my office visibly upset. As it turned out nearly every file contained such information. I had read all the files already, so that fact did not surprise me. But it shook her. For years she had provided care to women during labor and delivery. She always told them she was there to help. She told them that everything they said to her was confidential. She told them that they should answer her questions because the truth was essential to their care. She was, of course, following her training, but as it turned out, she had not been telling the truth. She felt betrayed, by her training, by her colleagues, and by the system she worked within.[1] To get a sense of what she was looking at, reproduced in Figure 6.1 is a set of

I, the affiant named below, after being sworn, state under oath that on or about (date of incident) the XX   day of XXX   20   in XXXXXX

Tennessee, the Defendant   County,

39-13-101 ASSAULT   committed the offense(s) of Violation(s) of TCA section(s)

_____I further state under oath that the essential facts constituting the offense(s), the sources

of my information and the reasons why this information is believable and reliable are as follows:

ON THE ABOVE DATE xxxxxxxxxxx WAS BORN AT xxxxxxMEDICAL CENTER WITH THE DEFENDANT BEING MOTHER

OF CHILD. UPON ADMISSION TO THE HOSPITAL xxxxxxx TOLD STAFF THAT

SHE HAD BEEN TAKING SUBOXONE THAT SHE DID NOT HAVE A PRESCRIPTION. SHE DID TEST POSITIVE FOR

SUBOXONE. SHE TOLD DCS WORKER THAT SHE WAS TAKING SUBOXONE AND DID NOT HAVE A PRESCRIPTION.

THE UMBILICAL CORD CAME BACK TESTING POSITIVE FOR SUBOXONE. THE CHILD WAS TRANSPORTED TO xxxx

xxxxx HOSPITAL BECAUSE OF THE HIGH LEVELS ON ITS FINNEGAN SCORE, AND THE CHILD HAD NEONATAL

ABSTINENCE SYNDROME. SOME OF THE SYMPTOMS WAS EXCESSIVE CRYING, SWELLING, SNEEZING, NASAL

STUFFINESS, MILD TREMORS, SLEEPS LESS THAN ONE HOUR AFTER FEEDS. ON xxxx xxxxx HOSPITAL REPORTED

THAT THE FINNEGAN SCORE WAS UP TO 15.

Figure 6.1 Petition

allegations in one of the Petitions in the cases. This Petition is typical of the cases we examined.

During the course of my research, we examined all the charging and arrest documents we gathered. In that process we examined sixty-three fetal assault case files for which we had charging or arrest documentation.[2] Of those sixty-three files, fifty-seven contained detailed information clearly obtained through medical testing or in conversations between the defendant and medical personnel. This included a wide range of information, from test results, to diagnosis, to statements by the women to nurses and doctors. An additional three casefiles contained allegations concerning medical facts, but there was no clear indication of the source of that information. Only three charging documents contained information solely based on nonmedical sources, for example an admission by the defendant to DCS or investigative staff. There is nothing surprising about this. In the late 1980s, Professor Austin Sarat interviewed welfare recipients about what he described as the meaning and significance of the law in their lives. At the start of that piece, he quotes a man named Spencer, "a thirty-five-year-old man on public assistance." As Spencer describes it "the law is all over."[3] People in poor communities and in communities of color are constantly at risk of having personal information about them used against them in one way or other. In this particular instance, as one woman who was pregnant and using substances during the time the law was in effect put it, "the laws in effect prevented me from it being a care issue. It became a law, a liability issue."

Becoming, in that woman's words, a "law issue" instead of a "care issue" would, as we will see in Chapters 7 and 8, have significant negative consequences for the women involved and the care they received. This chapter, though, focuses on the law, policies, and practices that allow disclosures from the health care to the child welfare system and on the practices, within child welfare, that draw information from the child welfare into the criminal systems.

6.1 DISCLOSURES AND THE LAW

This part of the story begins in the health care setting. As my research assistant, and every other health care provider in the country, know, federal law protects the confidentiality of medical records. These privacy protections are designed to encourage honest communication between care providers and their patients. They are designed, in short, to ensure that what takes place between a medical professional and her patient keeps the focus on the "care issue." But as we will see, for the women in this story, that turns out not to be true. A variety of laws, rules, and practices come together to create a steady and open stream of communication between health care providers and the child welfare and criminal systems. The story starts, but does not end, with the rules around disclosure.

The principal federal legal protection creating patient confidentiality is the federal Health Insurance Portability and Accountability Act (HIPAA).[4] As a general rule, HIPAA protects the confidentiality of what it defines as "protected health information," which includes, among other things, precisely what was found in the charging documents in the fetal assault cases: the contents of medical records and statements made to medical personnel during the course of treatment.[5]

HIPAA, as well as state and federal law concerning child abuse, however, significantly limits these protections for individuals suspected of child abuse. HIPAA authorizes the disclosure of protected health information in two circumstances relevant to these cases. Such information can be disclosed to "[a] public health authority or other appropriate government authority authorized by law to receive reports of child abuse or neglect."[6] In addition, providers can disclose to a government authority information about an individual that the health care provider "reasonably believes to be a victim of abuse, neglect, or domestic violence."[7] Moreover, like all states, Tennessee law requires health care providers to report suspected cases of abuse or neglect.[8] This overall legislative schema carves out specific exemptions that allow health care providers to disclose both suspected cases of child abuse and to share the medical information of potential victims of abuse.

Arguably, as I will argue in Chapter 9, HIPAA exceptions alone are sufficient to ensure that appropriate cases are reported. They allow hospital staff to distinguish between a woman whose substance use disorder is being treated and one in which there is evidence of actual abuse.

Despite this, both state and federal law open the doors to reporting much further. Every state has some form of mandatory reporting law. Beyond this, in the particular circumstance of substance use and pregnancy, the Child Abuse Prevention and Treatment Act (CAPTA), imposes specific requirements as a condition of receiving federal funds.[9] In order to receive CAPTA funds, each state must submit a plan for the administration of its CAPTA program that complies with a variety of federal requirements.[10] Among other conditions, states must put in place "policies and procedures ... to address the needs of infants born with and identified as being affected by substance abuse ... including a requirement that health care providers involved in the delivery or care of such infants notify the child protective services system of the occurrence of such condition in such infants."[11]

In addition, in 2016 CAPTA was revised to include a mandate that states have a plan in place for

> the development of a plan of safe care for the infant born and identified as being affected by substance abuse or withdrawal symptoms, or a Fetal Alcohol Spectrum Disorder to ensure the safety and well-being of such infant following release from the care of health care providers, including through—
>
> (I) addressing the health and substance use disorder treatment needs of the infant and affected family or caregiver; and
> (II) the development and implementation by the State of monitoring systems regarding the implementation of such plans to determine

whether and in what manner local entities are providing, in accordance with State requirements, referrals to and delivery of appropriate services for the infant and affected family or caregiver.[12]

So a combination of HIPAA, mandatory reporting laws, and CAPTA provide the legal basis for both reporting and disclosures, creating a wide net and exposing a wide range of families to child protective services agency scrutiny and intervention. But the exposure does not stop there.

Even beyond these legal rules, it appeared quite clear from my interviews that hospital staff are often willing and eager to share information with prosecutors. For example, one prosecutor described her relationship with the local hospital, where most of the cases originate. In her words, the doctors were "phenomenal." When I asked about whether the office had ever had any problems getting information from a hospital, the prosecutor responded, "no never a problem, it would be the opposite." Similarly, when I asked Barry Staubus, the District Attorney in Sullivan County, about this he explained that "If we needed to talk to a nurse about a situation, or we needed additional records, we could get those records. If we needed to go down to a facility, and meet with people, and talk to them about it, or needed information ... I've never had any obstacles with the local hospitals at all."[13]

Clearly, from the perspective of these prosecutors, there are no barriers whatsoever to getting any information that they might need to build a criminal prosecution directly from hospital staff. In addition, as detailed in Section 6.2, these disclosures are not limited to cases where either illegal conduct or child abuse is even suspected.

6.2 "RISK PREVENTION" AS A BASIS FOR INTERVENTION: REPORTING WOMEN TAKING PRESCRIBED MAINTENANCE MEDICATIONS

Despite the state law emphasis on abuse and harm, and the emphasis in CAPTA on requiring reporting in cases of substance *abuse*, it is clear that Tennessee's child welfare net is wide and includes pulling in cases on the basis of "risk prevention," even when a woman is no longer abusing drugs and is following the advice of her doctors.

It is important, at this moment, to remember that the majority of cases of NAS arise as a predictable consequence of the use of pre-scribed maintenance medications during pregnancy. It is also import-ant to remember that the American College of Obstetrics and Gynecology endorses maintenance medication as the best practice, in terms of the health of both mothers and infants, for treatment of substance use disorder during pregnancy. Ideally, prescribed medica-tions are linked, during pregnancy, not only to ongoing prenatal care but to ongoing mental health support, all of which is, at least in theory, available inside the health care system. One way to look at a case like this is that both the mother and her infant are getting, through the health care system, the care they both need. It is true that, under CAPTA, the state is required, as a condition of federal funding, to have a plan in place to address, "the health and substance use disorder treatment needs of the infant and affected family or caregiver." What is important to notice, in this provision, is that this is a requirement for the provision of care, not a requirement for child welfare intervention. There is no reason, based on this statutory language, that this care could not be provided through the public health system. In fact, as detailed in chapter nine, in at least a few states that is what is happening. But in the world of criminalization of care, it is not surprising that care, supervision, and threat of child removal come as a package for this group of poor women.

The first time I became aware of this particular issue was during the interview of a woman named Kristen Kakanis. Ms. Kakanis was, at the time of our interview, the Director of the Mothers and Infants Sober Together, or MIST program, a well-regarded outpatient treat-ment program for pregnant and parenting women in East Tennessee. As she explained, DCS regularly refers women to her program who are prescribed Subutex for "risk prevention."[14] Travis Bishop, who supervises DCS cases of substance-exposed infants in the East Tennessee Region, confirmed that this is their policy. All infants exposed to drugs, even prescribed maintenance medications, are considered infants who should be reported to DCS. Bishop attributed the shift to including infants "exposed" to maintenance medications to the 2016 revision of CAPTA, contained in the Comprehensive Addiction and Recovery Act or CARA. Here is our conversation about suboxone (which is a maintenance medication) and DCS's policy as to which cases should be referred to the agency:

WENDY BACH: [For a referral to take place, does the exposure have] to be [to] illegal drugs? . . .

TRAVIS BISHOP: Not now. There's policy change in which would be now suboxone-use during pregnancy

WENDY BACH: Even if it's prescribed.

TRAVIS BISHOP: Yes. Doesn't mean that we'll have to take drastic measures. It just means there needs to be a plan of safe care for that mother to continue to wean, treatment, and the plan of safe care is in the statute now, I think since October 2016.

As this particular state official understands federal law, because of the federal law focusing on safe plans of care, he now has to open cases against parents even when the woman is following the recommendations of her doctor and that doctor is following the recommendations of the American College of Obstetrics and Gynecology.

Given this legal framework, perhaps some of the disclosures that took place in the fetal assault cases were legal under federal and state law. But I do not want to give the impression that I am saying that any specific disclosure made in these cases was in fact legal. It is not clear that everything here falls within the mandatory reporting and CAPTA provisions. What appears to be entirely free communication between prosecutor, police, and hospital staff is certainly questionable. As Amnesty International has clearly documented, these breaches likely violate international human rights norms.[15] In addition, as Professor Michelle Goodwin has argued, there is ample evidence to suggest that women in these circumstances are not informed of the risks they faced if they disclosed information or consented to blood testing, and the failure to inform these women of these risks likely breaches the fiduciary duties that physicians owe to their patients.[16]

Whether legal or not, these disclosures happened in the fetal assault cases and clearly regularly happen. Chapter 9 returns to the topic of disclosure rules and the legal interventions and reforms that might be appropriate to curtail this level of disclosure. But for now, all of that is, in some sense, beside the point. These disclosures happened. They are part of a long history of surveillance and reporting of the behavior of individuals in poor communities and communities of color; they are deeply associated with stereotypes surrounding drug use and pregnancy, particularly by poor women, and they are deeply tied to society's need to monitor and control the decisions of poor pregnant women.

6.3 CHILD WELFARE CASE PROCESSING

The disclosures from the health care to the child welfare setting are only part of the story. What comes next reveals a set of policies that both heightens the risk of termination of parental rights and facilitates the further transfer of information, and with that information, women themselves, out of the child welfare system and into the criminal system.

6.3.1 Drug Exposure As "Severe Abuse"

When a case is reported to child welfare, an entire regulatory system kicks in to determine how that case is going to be handled by the agency. Unsurprisingly in a legal system, words, categories, and administrative systems end up being very important.

As I started to interview service providers, child welfare staff, and judges who sit on child welfare cases involving fetal assault, drug use during pregnancy, and termination of parental rights, the term severe abuse kept coming up. Judge Sharon Green, the juvenile court judge who sits on every child welfare case in Johnson City, Tennessee, described these cases as "dependency and neglect on steroids." And service providers described severe abuse as what the agency used to move aggressively against parents and to terminate parental rights. As one service provider, who works closely with women and children affected by substance use disorder, described it, "The court ended up finding a loophole by charging everybody with severe abuse, so while it's not a criminal charge, it makes it incredibly difficult to get their children back; it makes it easy to take a child, and it makes it easy to terminate their rights."

Under Tennessee law, "severe abuse" includes the most egregious forms of abuse and neglect. It is defined as,

> abuse or neglect that is likely to cause serious bodily injury or death, ... the knowing use of force on a child that is likely to cause serious bodily injury or death ... Brutality, abuse or neglect towards a child that in the opinion of qualified experts has caused or will reasonably be expected to produce severe psychosis, severe neurotic disorder, severe depression, severe developmental delay or intellectual disability, or severe impairment of the child's ability to function adequately in the child's environment.

It also includes the most serious forms of sexual abuse. Recall here the information from Chapter 2, that current research is largely inconclusive about the long-term effects of drug exposure and that, as was the case with crack cocaine, any observed effects are hard to distinguish from other environmental conditions. Given this research, it is hard to see how in utero drug exposure could be seen as equivalent to abuse or neglect leading to serious bodily injury, death, or other severe medical conditions. But as it turns out, both the agency and the courts have decided that in utero drug exposure is severe abuse. I asked a DCS official about this, and this is what he explained:

WENDY BACH: Do drug exposed children fall in the category of severe abuse?

TRAVIS BISHOP: For the department it would only be for ... Right now, it's only neonatal abstinence syndrome (NAS) would be the only severe abuse. However, when you start seeing drugs in the system of a child [the agency is] moving to where that would be severe abuse as well.

So, for both the courts that hear termination of parental rights cases and the agency that administers the program, drug exposure is severe abuse. This matters in two really important ways. First, if the case involves severe abuse, first, the agency can move to termination of

parental rights more easily and quickly, and second, police and prosecutors will play a role in the case well before any criminal charges are
brought.

6.3.2 No Reasonable Efforts Required

In general, under federal and state law, child welfare agencies must
make reasonable efforts to either prevent removal of a child from his
or her parent or, when temporary removal is necessary, to "make it
possible for a child to safely return to the child's home."[17] This legal
provision gives parents and their attorneys important leverage. In
child welfare cases, parents are generally obligated to comply with
a whole host of requirements in order to keep their kids or get them
back from the agency. But reasonable efforts means that the parents
are not the only ones with obligations. The agency has to help as
well. And, if the agency does not help, the parent can argue that the
agency has failed and therefore parental rights cannot be
terminated.

   While this is true in the vast majority of circumstances, both federal
and state law include some exceptions to this rule, allowing termination
of parental rights without requiring the agency to try to prevent
removal and reunify children with their families. Included in this category are very serious acts – for example federal law does not require
agencies to make reasonable efforts to keep children and parents
together when the parent committed murder, manslaughter, or "a
felony assault that results in serious bodily injury to the child or another
child of the parent."[18] Beyond these clearly serious acts, federal law
does allow states some latitude in deciding what cases will and will not
require reasonable efforts. States can forgo reasonable efforts when
"the parent has subjected the child to aggravated circumstances (as
defined in State Law, which definition may include but need not be
limited to abandonment, torture, chronic abuse, and sexual abuse)."[19]
Now, like murder, the listed suggested grounds for aggravated circumstances are very serious. It is hard to imagine someone opposing
termination of parental rights if the parent actually tortured or sexually
abused a child. But notice that those are just suggestions. In Tennessee,
"severe abuse" is included in the State's definition of aggravating

circumstances, and severe abuse includes drug exposure in utero. For example, if there is a finding of drug exposure, in Tennessee, and in at least four other states,[20] the state is relieved of its obligation to provide reasonable efforts to reunify the child and parent. This is what Judge Green meant when she said that severe abuse is dependency and neglect on steroids. Judge Irwin, who is the elected Juvenile Court Judge in Knoxville, Tennessee, was also clear about what that meant in his courthouse:

> [A court hearing in drug exposure cases] used to take about five hours to try one of them. Now it takes 15 minutes [because] there's just not a whole lot of defense. If you're positive and the baby's positive or you admit to drug use during your prenatal visits, in all those cases that go up [on appeal], it's determined to be severe abuse, which is a ground for termination of parental rights.

To be fair, all this does not necessarily mean that DCS does not provide women with opportunities to access treatment and support prior to terminating parental rights. In fact there are cases where it's clear that the courts and the agency do hold off on entering a finding of severe abuse to enable the parent to get help. But what's important to understand in this case is they do not have to. It's entirely up to them. If the agency can prove drug exposure, and they want to terminate parental rights, there is little to stop them. They hold all the cards.

6.3.3 The Role of Police and Prosecutors in Case Processing

Severe abuse also matters for an entirely different reason. In Tennessee, when a case is reported to DCS, it is initially placed into one of two basic categories: "assessment" or "investigation."[21] While the classification of a case as "assessment" covers the vast majority of cases, the designation "investigation" is reserved for cases classified by the agency as severe abuse.[22]

An administrative classification of severe abuse not only allows the agency to terminate rights more quickly, but it indicates that the abuse might lead not just to child welfare intervention by DCS but also to prosecution of the parent.[23] Because the cases are considered more severe and because they might involve criminal investigation and prosecution, a severe abuse classification both affects how the case is investigated and triggers the convening of what in Tennessee is called a Child Protective Investigative Team (CPIT), in which information is shared among the team participants.[24] In terms of the impact on investigation, a DCS official explained that "every case of drug exposed child we needed to include law enforcement. We needed to have law enforcement to go out on some cases to gain evidence for prosecution. That's what you would do for any severe abuse case."[25]

After initial investigation, every severe abuse case goes to the CPIT. That team is made up of DCS officials, prosecutors, police, and various other mandated participants.[26] In some jurisdictions, individuals from the Juvenile Court, which will ultimately hear many of the cases coming out of CPIT, also attend the meetings.[27] The team makes a variety of decisions concerning the child welfare case itself.[28] In this category falls, among many other issues, decisions as to whether the child will remain in the home or be removed, any services to be offered or required, whether the agency will plan for return of the child to the home, and what the parents or guardians must do to facilitate this return.[29] In addition, the CPIT will make a recommendation to the District Attorney's office as to whether it should prosecute the parent.[30]

Barry Staubus, the District Attorney in Sullivan County, describes the CPIT in this way:

> The DCS workers present. They just essentially give you a reader's digest summary of what's going on in the case. If it was a case where it looked like there was potential for prosecution or for charges, whatever law enforcement agency was involved could throw in their piece of the puzzle. If they had interviewed the mother, or gotten medical records, that sort of thing. That's information that would be shared as well.

From one perspective, perhaps the details about how the agency processes particular cases might not seem meaningful. But I want to suggest that, when you think about the purpose of child welfare agencies, policing, and prosecution, and then combine that with a long history of criminalization of poverty, this administrative detail takes on enormous significance. Child welfare agencies' intervention is, by statute, designed to both protect children and to support families. Its function is not to police or to prosecute. Those functions are left to agencies within the criminal legal system. When, however, the agency makes a decision to classify a case as severe abuse they are, by procedure, sharing facts about the case with both police and prosecutors.

One of the things that most struck me about this was the fact that this policy remained in effect and in fact expanded even after the fetal assault law sunset. I came to this understanding during my conversation with a DCS official. We first talked about why the cases went to CPIT while the law was in effect and then transitioned to a conversation about why it remained there even after fetal assault was no longer a crime:

WENDY BACH: Why did you have to include [every case of a drug-exposed child in CPIT]?

TRAVIS BISHOP: Because it would be a case handled by officers, by detectives. If that law was in effect, we were trying to speak to the district attorney at the time to … Well, that was then how it started. We needed to have law enforcement to go out on some cases to gain the evidence for prosecution. That's what you would do for any severe abuse case …

WENDY BACH: Is this still the same process [now that the law is not in effect]?

TRAVIS BISHOP: Yes.

WENDY BACH: What's the point of having law enforcement there today?

TRAVIS BISHOP: Law enforcement today will say, 'DCS, go ahead and take the lead for the investigation. However, please contact us if you find manufacturing drugs in the home.' They've even talked about has the mother used drugs around other siblings.

Even today, when fetal assault is no longer a crime, DCS investigators are being instructed to look for evidence of other crimes and to report it to the police if they find it. And this applies to every case where an infant is diagnosed with NAS and, increasingly, in every case where there is drug exposure during pregnancy. In a world where poor families are disproportionately subject to child welfare intervention, this adds one piece to the overall criminalization of their families.

So, it is clear that a combination of laws, rules, procedures, practices, and motivations draw information and women into contact with both the child welfare and the criminal system. But another fact is also important. For those who are poor, who are stigmatized and who are, disproportionately, Black and Brown, it is not only the rules that draw them into the system. All too often, it is the presence of care opportunities inside, rather than outside of those systems, that plays a significant role. It is to that part of the story that Chapter 7 turns.

NOTES

1. Special thanks to Lindsey English, for giving me permission to share this story.
2. As noted previously, documentation of the fetal assault prosecutions were obtained as a result of records requests to courts, district attorneys, and police agencies. Different jurisdictions record and keep information differently, and the kind of documentation for any particular case varied significantly. For example, in some cases policing agencies provided investigative files and arrest reports. Courts sometimes provided documents that were filed and in other cases we received only electronic printouts documenting key events in the case. This led to significant variation in the data we were able to gather for any particular defendant.
3. Austin Sarat, *The Law Is All Over: Power, Resistance and the Legal Consciousness of the Welfare Poor*, 2 YALE J. L. & HUMAN. 343 (1990).
4. Health Insurance Portability and Accountability Act of 1966, 42 U.S.C. § 1320d (2012).
5. HIPAA extends these protections to what it defines as "protected health information." *Id.* The term "health information" is defined as "any information, including genetic information, whether oral or recorded in any form or medium, that: (1) Is created or received by a health care provider, health plan, public health authority, employer, life insurer, school or university, or health care clearinghouse; and (2) Relates to the past, present, or future physical or mental health or condition of an individual; the provision of health care to an individual; or the past, present, or future payment for the provision of health care to an individual." 45 C.F.R. § 160.103 (2017). "Protected health information" is defined as "individually identifiable health information." *Id.*
6. 45 C.F.R. § 164.512(b)(1)(ii).

7. *Id.* § 164.512(c)(1).

8. Tenn. Code Ann. § 37–1–403 (2018). Indeed, Tennessee's law is unusually broad in that it requires "*any* person" to make sure to report. *Id.* (emphasis added).

9. *Child Abuse Prevention and Treatment Act* (CAPTA) *State Grants*, Child. Bureau, Admin. for Child. & Families (May 17, 2012), https://www .acf.hhs.gov/cb/grant-funding/child-abuse-prevention-and-treatment-act-capta-state-grants [https://perma.cc/C8HV-NS89].

10. 42 U.S.C. § 5106a(b)(1) (2018). This requirement was added to CAPTA as a result of the Keeping Children and Families Safe Act of 2003, Pub. L. No. 108–36, 117 Stat. 800, 800–31 (2003).

11. § 5106a(b)(2)(B)(ii).

12. 42 USCA § 5106a.

13. Interview with Barry Staubus, District Attorney, Sullivan County, Blountville, TN (August 4, 2017).

14. Interview with Kristen Kakanis, Director, MIST, Oakridge Tennessee (October 28, 2016).

15. Amnesty Int'l, Criminalizing Pregnancy: Policing Pregnant Women Who Use Drugs in the USA, at 55 (2017), https://www.amnesty.org/en/ documents/amr51/6203/2017/en/ [https://perma.cc/RMS6-Q8HQa0].

16. Michelle Goodwin, *Fetal Protection Laws: Moral Panic and the New Constitutional Battlefront*, 102 Cal. L. Rev. 781, 820 (2014).

17. 42 U.S.C. § 671(a)(15).

18. 42 U.S.C. § 671 (a)(15)(D).

19. *Id.*

20. Child Welfare Info. Gateway, Reasonable Efforts to Preserve or Reunify Families and Achieve Permanency for Children (U.S. Dep't of Health & Human Servs., Admin for Children & Families, Children's Bureau 2020), https://www.childwelfare.gov/pubpdfs/reunify.pdf [https://perma.cc /QCX4-UTDP].

21. *See Tennessee Child Abuse Hotline FAQ*, Tenn. Dep't Child. Servs., https:// www.tn.gov/dcs/program-areas/child-safety/reporting/hotline-faq.html [https://perma.cc/FJY5-X5AC].

22. Interview with Travis Bishop, Supervisor, Tennessee Department of Children's Services, Knox Region (May 30, 2018) (transcript on file with author). In Tennessee, the courts have made clear that prenatal substance abuse may constitute severe child abuse for the purpose of termination of parental rights. *See In re* B.A.C., 317 S.W.3d 718, 725 (Tenn. Ct. App. 2009).

23. Interview with Travis Bishop, *supra* note 22. It is notable that a NAS diagnosis is still considered severe abuse even after the Tennessee statute explicitly criminalizing this conduct is no longer law. When asked about this Mr. Bishop explained that prosecutions are no longer recommended but

      that the police and DCS officials continue to collaborate, sharing, for example, evidence discovered by DCS of other drug crimes. *Id.*

24. *See* Tenn. Code Ann. § 37–1–607(b)(1) (2018).

25. Interview with Travis Bishop, *supra* note 22, at 3.

26. Tenn. Code Ann. § 37–1–607(a)(3) ("It is the intent of the general assembly that the child protective investigations be conducted by the team members in a manner that not only protects the child but that also preserves any evidence for future criminal prosecutions. It is essential, therefore, that all phases of the child protective investigation be appropriately conducted and that further investigations, as appropriate, be properly conducted and coordinated."); *Administrative Policies and Procedures: 14.6*, Tenn. Dep't Child. Servs., https://files.dcs.tn.gov/policies/chap14/14.6.pdf [https://perma.cc/G5WT-4L62].

27. Interview with Timothy Irwin, Judge, Knoxville Tennessee (June 15, 2018).

28. *See* Tenn. Code Ann. § 37–1–607(b)(2).

29. *See id.*

30. *See id.* § 37–1–607(b)(5); *see also Administrative Policies and Procedures 14.6*, *supra* note 26.

7 CRIMINALIZATION AS A ROAD TO CARE AND THE PRICE YOU PAY

Lock 'em up, clean 'em up and start over.

Cindy Jones, Drug Treatment Coordinator, Rural East Tennessee

Cindy Jones[1] has lived and worked in and around the criminal courts in a rural East Tennessee county for decades. What she told me epitomizes what happens when three phenomena – bias, reliance on punishment systems for care, and incredibly resource-poor environments – collide. Cindy has been a jail administrator, a treatment coordinator, and a probation officer, among other jobs. I originally got her name from the local public defender who is assigned to her courthouse. When I explained my project he said that he was happy to talk to me but that the person I really had to talk to was Cindy. She was his go-to person to get help for his clients and she, more than anyone else in his community, knows how to get people treatment. So my research assistant and I got in the car and drove out to meet her.

To say that the county where Cindy and this particular public defender work is under-resourced does not begin to do justice to the situation. The county is over 95 percent white and nearly a quarter of the population lives below the poverty line. The median income is $16,000 lower than the median income in the state. The closest drug court is in another county, and lots of folks do not have cars or gas money, so even if they were assigned to go there, it is not clear how they would get there. There are a few short-term detox facilities and a few faith-based longer-term programs outside the county, but Cindy told me that there are no halfway houses or counseling programs nearby, so even if you can get someone an inpatient bed, if they return home there will be no services there to support them when they return. On top of that, many of the people Cindy works with don't have insurance, so getting treatment is incredibly difficult.

When we asked about how she helps people in her community who suffer from addiction, her response was immediate: "lock 'em up, clean 'em up and start over."[2] At first my research assistant and I were a little confused about what she meant, but slowly it became clear. As she explained it, for the vast majority of her clients, poor people without health insurance, her access to treatment beds was mostly through grants that could only be accessed if a judge authorized the payment. She had access to three grants, and two of them required a judge's signature, so getting someone into court was the easiest way to get them help. If she gets a call, for example, from a person who wants to get help for someone, the first thing she asks is whether the person has committed any crimes. She made clear that she did not mean major crimes, just a little one, maybe a misdemeanor. If the person could be arrested for that crime, then she can help. Now from her perspective, a misdemeanor is not that big a deal, but as we've seen with the fetal assault charges, the consequences can be significant. Nevertheless a "little charge" allows her to get someone arrested and brought to jail. The person would detox in jail and then, eventually, once the person pled guilty, she would be able to use her resources to get that person into treatment. That's just the way it works. And if that didn't work the first time, as was likely, they could try again once the person was on probation – "lock 'em up, clean 'em up, start 'em over." In that statement, and in the confidence of the fetal assault law proponents about criminalization as a road to care, we hear three interlocking ideas that characterize the relationship between punishment and care. First, punishment systems are a road to care; second, facilities controlled by punishment systems are used as locations of care; and finally, punishment is a form of care in and of itself.

7.1 PUNISHMENT SYSTEMS AS THE ROAD TO CARE

To tell the story of the role of criminal charges and criminal system involvement in accessing care, we are going back to Sullivan County, the home of Barry Staubus and the largest number of women prosecuted for fetal assault per capita in the state. Sullivan County is slightly more resourced than the rural county where Cindy works, so there are more providers and more programs. To understand the fetal assault cases and the general relationship between prosecution, child welfare intervention, and treatment in the area, I spoke to prosecutors, defense attorneys, judges, treatment providers, and lawyers who represent parents and kids in child welfare proceedings. Everyone I spoke to agreed. For folks in poor communities, the road to treatment runs through the agencies and courts.

In the State of Tennessee, every judicial district has an elected public defender. Staff in that person's office represent the vast majority of individuals charged with a crime who the court determines to be indigent. In many of these counties, that's virtually everybody. I interviewed a group of public defenders in Sullivan County about both the fetal assault prosecutions and about the larger relationship between prosecution and treatment. Here's the conversation we had:

WENDY: So, let's say you have a client that you wanted to get into treatment. Can [that client] get a bed?

ATTORNEY: If you have money, yeah. If you don't have money, it's going to be tougher. Usually, you're going to get that bed after you've been convicted of something. We've got some outfits in the county that they used to move some people out of the jail system. In Kingsport [a city nearby] they've got this place called the Hayhouse and part of their work is they work with people that are drug addicted. But it's a small outfit. They've been around for a while and they've grown and they're part of our judiciary in a way.[3]

During this particular interview I was sitting with four other attorneys in the office. None of them disputed this statement. Barry Staubus said something similar. I asked him if it is easier to get treatment once you are inside the system. He said he thought it was, but for Staubus this was about the knowledge of people inside the system. "If you're on probation, I think it would be easier, because they have much more knowledge of the facilities, the resources, and the programs than a person that doesn't."[4]

Providers in the area (and beyond) confirmed that their treatment spots are largely taken up with people who are required to be there by either the criminal or the child welfare courts. For an example, take one highly respected program in the area. In the view of the professionals I talked to, this program provides significant support to women struggling with substance-use disorder during pregnancy. The program is a licensed substance abuse and mental health treatment facility, providing intensive outpatient services and support to their patients. The Executive Director confirmed that most of their slots are allocated to system-involved clients and that they struggled to find funding for programs for people outside those systems. Similarly, another strong program I saw includes several programs, but one of the most striking is their residential family treatment program. Technically it is two programs – an intensive outpatient program and a parallel housing program – since the State of Tennessee does not have a mechanism to license inpatient treatment programs that include a woman with her children. Nevertheless, in that program, which has seventeen slots, women can live there with their children while getting treatment. As was the case at most programs I saw, those beds go to women who are in the criminal system. As the Executive Director told me, "[t]he overwhelming majority of the pregnant women on our waiting list are incarcerated."[5] We had an extensive conversation about how they prioritize the people on the waiting list. The Executive Director would not go so far as to admit that system-involved women were given priority, but they did explain how it works. The "wait list is based on how our grants are prioritized." Several of the priority categories had to do with health: pregnancy, injecting substances, unmanaged drug use. But system involvement mattered to. What was clear from that conversation was that being system-involved, either with child welfare, a criminal case, and/or being incarcerated, was a factor that would make it more likely that they would give you a bed. As they explained, "the more problems or the more issues or the more challenges you have the higher you go"[6] on the priority list. Whatever the system, the basic fact remained true. The vast majority of the women were incarcerated prior to entering the program.

Mary Linden Salter, who runs the Tennessee Alliance of Alcohol Drug and Addiction Services and spends her days talking to treatment programs all over the state agrees.

> If you are a treatment provider and you have a drug court judge who makes you a referral and certainly if you're a pregnant woman, that's going to get moved to the top of the list a little bit differently than somebody else. What we end up having is a system where drug courts often get preference.[7]

It's tempting to think that this problem – that it is difficult to get a treatment slot if you are not system-involved – is solely a scarcity problem – that given the limited number of beds and the limited resources available, it only makes sense to take those most in need; system-involved folks are the most in need, so the limited beds go to them. There is some truth to that. But there is more. The issue is not only about scarcity, it's also about priorities.

The fetal assault law prosecutions certainly took place in a landscape in which there were almost no treatment resources available in the community for pregnant women struggling with substance use disorder. The Substance Abuse and Mental Health Services Administration hosts a national listing of available treatment resources.[8] A recent search of facilities that provide substance abuse treatment of any form in Tennessee and accept Medicaid resulted in ninety-eight programs in the state.[9] When that search was narrowed to facilities that are willing to treat pregnant women and postpartum women, only twenty-eight facilities were on the list.[10] In 2014 a similar search was run and journalists from *America Tonight* followed up with the listed facilities seeking to gain information about whether there were any open treatment beds. From the listing at that time, only "[f]ive clinics confirmed that they allow pregnant women to enroll in their residential treatment and accept Medicaid. With two of the programs completely full, there [were] fewer than fifty beds in Tennessee available to pregnant drug users."[11] Even less available are facilities that allow women to receive inpatient treatment without having to find alternative housing for their children. These facilities, which combine residential treatment with residential care for children, are few and far between. Their programs, however, are a model for how to provide care to pregnant parenting women. Understanding why is quite simple. For women who already have children and would benefit from residential treatment, offering a program in which they can both recover and parent in the same facility is essential. It allows them to get the help without having to find a place for their children to stay in the meantime, and equally importantly, it allows them to work on healthy parenting as part of their recovery. But this best-practice form of care is also tremendously hard to get. At the time that I completed research for this book, there were only thirty-one beds available statewide that offered this form of residential treatment. All those facilities were not only almost always full but also almost always had an extensive waitlist. For example, one of these facilities, which has capacity for seventeen families at a time, has, at any one time, about sixty on their waitlist.[12] So, in this world of scarce resources, the criminal and child welfare systems play an outsized role in the road to care.

But the issue is not only about scarcity of treatment beds; it is also about funding priorities. To get a sense of this, let's return to a program in Johnson City. I interviewed Judge Sharon Green, the juvenile court judge who sits on every child welfare case in Johnson City, Tennessee (one of the three of the tri-cities) and Judge Arnold, who sits in both Juvenile Court and the lower-level criminal court in the local county. According to both judges, the services that one particular organization provides offer enormous positive support to the women they serve. It is in fact the first choice of the judges in terms of effective service provision. Judge Green reports that it is by far most effective program in the area, specifically at providing the support necessary to help women keep custody of their children. What was striking about my conversation with the Executive Director of that program was their inability to find funding for programs that focused on families without child welfare or criminal involvement.

To say that this Executive Director is resourceful in securing the financial support for her program is a profound understatement. As they explained it,

> [Our organization] is unique, because we get funding from the department of health, from the department of mental health and substance abuse, from department of children's services. We hold a recovery drug court contract, and we also get an appropriation in

the governor's budget, and next week we will have a 200 plus fundraiser with people in the community to raise even additional resources above what the state will pay. So we go into situations and look at what people really need, and then we find the resources, the leverage to bring about that kind of change in their life.[13]

To put it mildly, this is an Executive Director who knows how to access the resources that exist to support the organization's clients and mission. At one point our conversation turned to the topic of whether or not they provide services to women in the community who are not involved with DCS or courts. As they explained,

There are families who have more of an internal motivat[ion] to seek out the services, and we've seen some good engagement from them as well. There's just not a lot of funding out there for it. We have a partnership with [a local hospital] and we were doing a nurturing parenting baby steps program and it was just offered to people with high [adverse childhood experiences] scores, and those families ate it up with a spoon. They were not like the nucleus of high risk, high need, but they were on the periphery, and we found some of those people just loved to have the service that came to their house, that was free, but for whatever reason, that's not really funded.[14]

They then went on to talk enthusiastically about another community-based program but again, "we can't fund it." "We've really tried to get it funded, and just haven't been able to yet." When I asked them how much of their caseload is referred to her by DCS and courts, she was clear. It's about 80 percent of the caseload. So here was the organization that was universally recommended to me as the best and most comprehensive treatment and support provider in the area and who wanted to but could not fund programs for non-system-involved women. The result: 80 percent of the caseload came through the agency or the courts.

The judges who hear Juvenile Court cases concur that DCS and courts are the road to treatment in their community. I asked Judge Green about this:

WENDY: There's no funding for people who aren't agency- and court-involved?

J GREEN: Yes.

WENDY: Is that your experience?
J GREEN: Yes. If DCS is not paying the bill for it, it doesn't happen.

Similarly Judge Irwin, who presides over child welfare cases in
Knoxville, concurred. I asked,

WENDY BACH: [Is it] easier for kids or for the folks we're talking
                     about to get access to treatment through the
                     agency of the courts than it is in the community.
                     Do you think that's true?
JUDGE T. IRWIN: Yes.[15]

It's important to be clear that I am not highlighting these facts to
make an argument that women who have a child welfare case or
a criminal case should not get treatment or even that others should
not be lower on the priority list. In a world of almost no resources, in the
world that Cindy Jones, and treatment providers, and Barry Staubus
occupy, perhaps it does make sense to prioritize the beds for people
facing criminal charges. What bothers me though is that our society
seems content to live with a baseline of so few resources, because the
result is that, all too often, you have to be in the child welfare or criminal
legal system in order to get care.

This can lead to some really disturbing results. Cindy Jones was
utterly clear. She had to get them on a "little charge" before she could
get them help. Stephen Lloyd, the Director of Journey Pure, who is an
addict and was the Medical Director for Substance Abuse in Tennessee
from 2015 to 2018, was also clear. During our interview we talked
a good deal about access to treatment, both as he accessed it, and as it is
accessed for individuals in poverty. He talked a lot about the comprehensive treatment he got as a member of the medical profession, and it
was clear he thought that everyone deserved what he got. But not
everyone gets that. For someone who is poor he had another plan:
"Even knowing what I know, if I needed somebody in treatment that
didn't have insurance I'd tell them to go to Greene County and get
caught shoplifting. They'd get into drug court and they could get them
treated."[16] He was not happy about this option, but he understood, like
the judges, like Cindy, like the defense attorneys and the prosecutors,
that, in poor communities, this is the road to care.

This reality is not lost on those who need treatment. As Mary Linden Salter explained in talking about her work on the Tennessee Redline (a hotline that refers people to treatment):

> I've had people who call the Tennessee Redline who have said, "What do I have to do? get arrested in order to get treatment?" They know that that's the way to get treatment. You shouldn't have to go to jail to get treatment. You should be able, if you're ready to get treatment, to access the system without having to go through any kind of a court situation.[17]

The moral import of all of this was not lost on Dr. Lloyd: "How in the world is this possible? Really, we're the richest country in the world. How is this possible we've got to get somebody to go to jail to get treated?"

7.2 JAILS AS TREATMENT FACILITIES

Access to treatment through the criminal legal system is not just a mechanism for prioritizing slots. It also involves using the mechanisms of punishment as, in effect, part of treatment plans. One of the most striking pieces of this story is the role jails play in treatment. As detailed in Chapter 2, this is not a new story. Dr. Carolyn Sufrin, in her book *Jailcare: Finding the Safety Net Behind Bars* provides a window into this reality.[18] Sufrin provides a rich and nuanced description of how care is provided in that setting and, as you might recall, argued that "jail is the new safety net."[19] Sufrin did her field research in San Francisco, at the women's jail where she was employed as a doctor.[20] While San Francisco is, in many ways, a world away from rural East Tennessee, Sufrin's conclusions were echoed in my interviews. Take, for example, Cindy Jones. In her practice, jail is essential because jail is where you go for detoxification. That's where you "clean 'em up." One story Cindy told made this clearer than anything else. She told us about a man in her community that suffers from severe alcoholism. He was on probation and on her caseload for many years when she was a probation officer. She told us that she kept a look out for when the whites of his eyes turned yellow. That's when she would file a probation violation – to get him arrested and put into jail – to give his liver a break. It turned out that detoxification in jail, without access to medication-assisted treatment, is standard practice in many jails throughout the area. My first glimpse into this reality came when reading a study, conducted in Tennessee, on detoxification of pregnant women and the effect on newborn health. The study, which I talk about extensively in the next chapter, looked at the outcomes for 301 women–infant pairs. Of the 301 women in the study, 108 "underwent acute detoxification involuntarily because the jail program in east Tennessee has no ability to provide opiates to prevent or perform an opiate-assisted medical withdrawal."[21]

Using jails as detoxification facilities also plays a key role in a program in Knox County, the home of Knoxville, Tennessee. Knoxville's jail has a program for inmates in which they undergo detoxification in jail and then are placed on Vivitrol. Vivitrol is an opiate-blocker and is one of the prime medications prescribed for the long-term management of substance-use disorder. It is administered monthly, as an injection. Vivitrol is favored by officials in the court and jail systems because, unlike drugs like suboxone, which is generally taken in pill form, it comes in a shot form, so it cannot be sold on the street. Commencing treatment with Vivitrol is difficult, though, because you have to be opiate-free for seven to ten[22] days. That's where the Knox County jail comes in. Individuals are fully detoxed while incarcerated and then put on Vivitrol. One official in the local criminal system explained it to be this way:

KNOX COUNTY OFFICIAL: [The prosecutor's office does] a criminal background check to determine if they're suitable candidates and then Helen Ross McNabb [a local treatment program] does a medical/psychological part of the testing to make sure that they're suitable to go into this treatment program. And if they pass both of those entrance tests, then what we do is we put them in the vivitrol program. They're administered a vivitrol shot in the Knox County

> Jail ... We leave them there a week to make sure they're not having any adverse reactions to that shot. Then they're transferred to Helen Ross McNabb and [that agency] starts the treatment portion of that Vivitrol program.

The import of this is astounding. Jails are established to hold defendants pretrial and sometimes to incarcerate defendants serving misdemeanor sentences. There is a world of constitutional strictures limiting the ability of the government to deprive someone of their liberty and hold them in a jail. But here, even if there is technical compliance with constitutional law, as a practical matter all that disappears. Criminalization of care means, in this case, that jail is no more than part of a treatment program.

In a world of criminalized care, this might make a perverse sort of sense, but it's essential to remember that detoxification in jail, all too often without any medical assistance, while staggeringly common, is not medical treatment. I talked to Dr. Stephen Lloyd about the practice of detoxification in jail. He first explained his own practice for the management of withdrawal and detoxification:

STEPHEN LLOYD: If I have somebody that comes in and needs strictly detox, use suboxone [a maintenance medication]. It's what it's indicated for. I get them stable [on suboxone], and then taper them off over a period of days, depending on their symptoms.[23]

But in most cases that's not what's happening in jail. In jail, you might get other medications to ease the symptoms of withdrawal (although that's certainly not always the case), but you probably will not be tapered. You'll just detox. As to the ethics of this practice, Dr. Lloyd was unequivocal:

STEPHEN LLOYD: What they are doing with opiate withdrawal is inhumane. You would not do it for another medical condition. It's the equivalent of withholding insulin from a diabetic, absolutely. There's no doubt or argument about that, yet they do it all the time.[24]

And jails are not just being used for detox. They can play a key role in other forms of "care." The final story Cindy told us takes us back a little closer to what started this research – the criminal system's response to women who use illegal substances during pregnancy. Cindy was clear about her court's policy for women like this. If a woman is on probation (either for fetal assault or for another crime) and came in pregnant and testing positive, the probation officer files a violation of probation, alleging a violation of the rule that they not take drugs while on probation. As Cindy describes it the judge will then "lock them up for safekeeping" for the duration of their pregnancies. As she put it, "many a baby has been saved that way." The public defender in the court confirmed this. In his words, the court would make its intentions very clear.

PUBLIC DEFENDER: [As the court puts it], "there's only one way
                         I can protect this baby, if I revoke your proba-
                         tion and you stay in jail for the next few months
                         then you won't be taking drugs in there."

So jails are detox facilities and jails are where people are put for "safe-keeping," all ostensibly in the name of providing care and "saving babies." But as Dr. Lloyd said, this is not what doctors mean when they think about care. It is inhumane. It's likely unconstitutional,[25] it ignores everything we know about best practices for treatment, and it causes enormous harm.

7.3 CARE AT A COST

As we have seen, a wide range of laws, rules, and practices lead women out of care systems and into the child welfare and criminal systems. And the systems themselves are, all too often, the place to get care. All these laws, rules, and practices work together as a whole, reinforcing and strengthening the criminalization of care. But, returning to the case study, the question then becomes, what happened in terms of care access? Did criminalized care "work" in the sense that women actually got access to care? And if it did, what do we know about the form of that care.

As we learned in Chapter 5, for the fetal assault defendants, outside of the Shelby County Drug Court, the idea that prosecution leads to care was, more often than not, a smokescreen hiding a system focused primarily on punishment and debt collection. The women, the vast majority of whom were indigent, often faced months of incarceration and were saddled with significant debt, and for the majority of defendants, their case files contained no indication that treatment was offered at all. But it is the case that a minority of the defendants did in fact get referred to care as part of their criminal cases. It is to that story that this chapter turns next.

In the fetal assault cases, the relationship between treatment and punishment varied significantly based on geography. The majority of case files outside of Shelby County contain no notation at all indicating that treatment was offered or required as a part of their criminal case. When, in the minority of cases outside Shelby County, notations of treatment access appeared, it seemed almost haphazard. A woman might have been required to get a drug and alcohol assessment or might have been offered an inpatient bed after some period of incarceration, but overall, even in these cases, the focus was on plea agreements, probation, and debt collection. In contrast, the twenty-five women prosecuted in Memphis, the largest urban area in the state, appear to all have been offered a spot in the Shelby County drug court, offering what at least some believe to be a successful model merging care with prosecution. As detailed in Chapter 3, problem-solving courts, like the Shelby County Drug Court, are supported by extensive public and private funds and embrace rather than reject the court's role in solving social problems. These courts are generally structured around intensive judicial supervision, have a detailed system of dolling out both rewards and punishments, have extensive case management teams, and are often closely allied with treatment providers, But as we will see, even this "best" form of criminalized care involved serious risks.

Before turning to those risks, it is important to note that, for both sets of women (those prosecuted in East Tennessee and those prosecuted in Shelby County), the files themselves reveal very little about the content of treatment itself. We can know that, at least in the view of whomever was taking notes, treatment was offered, and we can know a lot about what happened to the woman in the criminal case, but we know little to nothing about the content of the treatment.

Nevertheless, the files do shed light on what happened in court, both to the women who successfully completed whatever treatment was assigned by the court and to the women who, in the court's view, did not. In both regions, the stories of those who completed are often a harder story to tell from the criminal case files because, in least in some of these cases, the records of their prosecutions no longer exist. This is likely due to the right, in limited circumstances, to have records destroyed (or expunged) if a case is dismissed after completion of a required program.[26] So for example, in Shelby County twelve of the twenty-five women who were prosecuted for fetal assault no longer have public records, indicating that they completed the drug court program and had their records expunged.[27] Nikki Brown, who testified in the legislature that she was thankful for the program, is one of those women. And Ms. Brown was not alone. Some of the women who spoke to the SisterReach researchers indicated that the longer-term residential and outpatient treatment services available through the Shelby County Drug Court were beneficial.[28] Similarly, in Sullivan County, the District Attorney informed me that the public records of ten women's cases were expunged because they successfully completed the requirements of probation. Some of those women may have successfully completed treatment. So, to the extent that the women succeeded and potentially therefore did not face punishment, that may well be a positive outcome. But we do not know what happened. Some may have been jailed along the way to completion and others may still have paid a price in loss of children to DCS. But all faced the risk that, had they failed, punishment was the default. To get a sense of the risks women faced in accessing treatment inside this system we can look to the files of women who appear to have gotten offers of treatment but for whom that treatment did not lead to dismissal of their charges and destruction of the court files. This takes us to the Shelby County Drug Court. As we learned in Chapter 1, this is the court that many believe was the driving force behind the fetal assault law and was the model that supporters of that law referred to when suggesting that the fetal assault law would lead to care.

Twenty-five women were prosecuted in Shelby County for fetal assault during the just over two years that the law was in effect. Twenty-one of those women were accepted into the Shelby County Drug Court program and attempted to complete it. Twelve of those women appear to have successfully completed drug court. For three of these women the files exist but their cases end in dismissal, an entry that indicates successful completion. For the remaining nine I obtained their names and evidence of their prosecution early in their cases, but by the time I pulled public records more than a year later, the public records no longer existed, indicating that they had successfully completed the program and had had their records destroyed. Nine other women tried to participate but did not complete the program.

The Shelby Court case files contain a full listing of every event in the case. What is immediately striking is the number of court appearances. These appearances are often described as a form of "judicial probation."[29] It is through this frequent contact that the court, supported by a team of case managers, counselors, and lawyers, personally oversees the defendants' cases, offering encouragement as well as sanctions. This all sounds fairly reasonable, but in practice it can have some very harsh consequences.

To get a sense of the risks women faced when accessing treatment through the drug court, take a look at the case of Lennon Mason, a low-income white woman prosecuted for fetal assault in Memphis. Ms. Mason gave birth to a daughter in 2015. Both Ms. Mason and her child tested positive for cocaine at birth. She was referred to treatment as a part of her DCS case, but the Petition alleges that she "failed to meet her goals" and was dismissed from the program that DCS suggested. Ms. Mason was charged with fetal assault, arrested, and then, like all the Shelby County defendants, held without bail until her first appearance before Judge Dwyer, the judge in charge of the Shelby County Drug Court.

Ms. Mason had several court appearances during the first months of her case. Finally, twenty-two days after her arrest, she pled guilty and was sentenced to nine months' incarceration. Although it is not the focus here, it is important to remember that, given the dearth of solid scientific evidence that cocaine exposure causes harm, it may well have been very difficult for the state to convict Ms. Mason of this crime. Nevertheless, Ms. Mason, like the vast majority of the women charged with fetal assault, pled guilty.

It was only after that plea that this sentence was suspended to enable to her to participate in the court's drug treatment program. Upon agreeing to that participation, she was released from jail. Between that day in late 2015 and mid-2016, when she ultimately failed to complete drug court and was sentenced, she went before the court *fifty-three times*, all but one of which was a labeled in her file as "Drug Treatment Program." Along the way, she missed a few court dates. Each time that happened a warrant issued for her arrest, and she was, once again, jailed until her next court appearance. All told, Ms. Mason spent an additional fifty days, or nearly two months, in jail. Her appearances before the court were presumably standard drug court appearances, in which she met with team members (drug court counselors, attorneys, and the Judge) to monitor her progress in treatment. That treatment itself was likely provided by the Cocaine and Alcohol Awareness Program, the treatment program most closely aligned to the Shelby County Drug Court. Ultimately, after she missed court the second time, Ms. Mason's participation in drug court was terminated. At that point she was sent to jail to serve the remainder of her nine-month jail sentence. She was also required to pay costs which, by the end of her case, totaled $1,914.50.

Take a moment and think about this set of facts. This low-income woman, who if we believe the court, was struggling with substance-use disorder, was required to be in court fifty-three times over the course of about nine months – somewhere between once and twice a week. If she missed a court appearance she was arrested and jailed, either separating her from her child or making it all the more difficult for her to be reunited with that child. Ultimately, she spent two of the nine months, or just under a quarter of her "treatment," incarcerated. And when that failed, she just went to jail and came out owing the court nearly $2,000.

The other women who participated in but did not succeed in drug court faced similar consequences. Like Ms. Mason, they all pled guilty at the start of their cases and agreed to a sentence they would serve if they did not succeed. They also, like her, served time in jail during their case – an average of thirty-seven days in jail prior to the final imposition of the sentence. Three of them ultimately served sentences from six months to a full year in jail. Five others were transferred to an additional year of regular probation. In total their costs averaged $2,491. Notably, it was clear that these women could not afford to pay those costs. At the time I pulled their files, generally more than a year after their cases were over, they owed an average of $2,461 to the court. To be clear that means that, on average, the women were able to pay only $31 toward their costs in a year.

This data reinforces much of the literature on problem-solving courts. They are intensive and require a good deal of their participants. They use jail as a sanction, often referred to in the literature as shock incarceration, and impose punishments that are often harsher than the punishments a defendant might have received in a more standard court. While the opportunities for treatment are often present, the sanctions for failure are harsh. And for the women who do not complete the program, punishment prevails.

These costs – in jailing and fees, in punishment and family separation – are the price defendants pay for accessing care inside a criminal system. As it turns out, this price is not a fluke. In fact, it's baked into the model. Judge Don Arnold, a judge in Washington County, Tennessee, runs a recovery court. During our interview he patiently answered my questions about the structure of recovery courts, and in particular the way that punishment is related to treatment. I was particularly curious about whether individuals were at risk of higher punishments if they agreed to go to recovery court. The answer was an unequivocal yes. As he explained,

> At the time they are brought into court, they plead guilty to the offense, and usually we set a high sentence … When I take their plea, I take their plea of guilty, and I explain to them ahead of time, when you plead guilty, I'm going to sentence you now … If they don't successfully complete the recovery court, I'll put them in jail the day they're brought back. They'll serve their full time.[30]

Judge Arnold was clear. "The sentence is less if you're not in recovery court than it would be if you go to recovery court." The program is structured, intentionally, to exact a high price from the defendant who fails. Care at a cost is baked in. This means that a defendant who agrees to go to recovery court is taking a huge risk. If they pled guilty in regular court they would serve one, shorter sentence, but if they fail recovery court the sentence will be longer. And Judge Arnold is not doing anything unusual here. This practice, of setting harsher sentences for an individual in a problem-solving court than they would get for the same charge in a regular court, is fairly standard.[31]

Even in the best of circumstances, when the court is organized to conform to best practices around problem-solving courts, the price of care is high. If you succeed then perhaps, like Ms. Brown, you might be "grateful for the program." But if you fail you face harsh consequences: you pay, in incarceration, in fines, in separation from your family and community and in many other ways that incarceration and conviction can make life tremendously difficult. Criminalized care, it turns out, comes at a high cost. But that is not all. As we will learn in the following chapter, criminalization is not only costly, but it can, at times, corrupt the form of care itself.

NOTES

1. This name is a pseudonym assigned on the request of the interviewee.
2. Interview with Cindy Jones (pseudonym), Drug Treatment Coordinator, Rural East Tennessee (July 6, 2017).
3. Interview with Assistant Public Defenders, in Kingsport, TN (August 7, 2017).
4. Interview with Barry Staubus, District Attorney, Second Judicial District, in Kingsport, TN (August 7, 2017).
5. Interview with Executive Director of a Treatment Facility (August 9, 2018).
6. *Id.*
7. Video Interview with Mary Linden Salter, Executive Director of the Tennessee Alliance of Alcohol Drug and Addiction Services (July 3, 2017).
8. *Behavioral Health Treatment Services Locator*, Substance Abuse & Mental Health Services Admin., https://findtreatment.samhsa.gov/ [https://perma.cc/48ZM-UYA2].
9. *Locator Map*, Substance Abuse & Mental Health Services Admin., https://findtreatment.samhsa.gov/locator [https://perma.cc/VDL8-SEAQ].
10. *Id.*
11. Sanya Dosani, *Should Pregnant Women Addicted to Drugs Face Criminal Charges?* AL JAZEERA AM. (March 31, 2015, 4:00 PM), https://america.aljazeera.com/watch/shows/america-tonight/articles/2014/9/4/should-pregnant-womenaddictedtodrugsfacecriminalcharges.html [https://perma.cc/4EVR-RCT9].
12. *See supra* note 5.
13. Interview with Executive Director, Treatment Program in East Tennessee (July 26, 2018).

14. *Id.*
15. Interview with Judge Timothy Irwin, Juvenile Court Judge, Knox County, in Knoxville, TN (June 15, 2018).
16. Interview with Stephen Lloyd, Director of Journey Pure, in Murfreesboro, TN (August 9, 2019).
17. Video Interview with Mary Linden Salter, Executive Director of the Tennessee Alliance of Alcohol Drug and Addiction Services (July 3, 2017).
18. *See* Carolyn Sufrin, Jailcare: Finding the Safety Net for Women Behind Bars (2017).
19. *Id.* at 5.
20. *Id.* at 15.
21. Craig V. Towers, Jennifer Bell, Mark D. Hennessy, Callie Heitzman, Barbara Smith, & Katie Chattin, *Detoxification from Opiate Drugs During Pregnancy*, September 2016 American Journal of Obstetrics and Gynecology 374, 374 (2016).
22. Food and Drug Administration, *Highlights of Prescribing Information* (1984), https://www.accessdata.fda.gov/drugsatfda_docs/label/2010/021897s015lbl .pdf [https://perma.cc/6RKN-87SA].
23. Interview with Stephen Lloyd, Director of Journey Pure, in Murfreesboro, TN (August 9, 2019).
24. *Id.*
25. Jailing pregnant women solely as a way to care for the fetus likely violates the constitution. Just like any other person in the United States, a pregnant woman has the right to be free from unwarranted detention and confinement and the right to reproductive decision-making. *See* April L. Cherry, *The Detention, Confinement, and Incarceration of Pregnant Women for the Benefit of Fetal Health*, 16 Colum. J. Gender & L. 147, 150 (2007). The Supreme Court has held that the state must present "an identified and articulable threat to an individual or the community" for the detention to be deemed constitutional. U.S. v. Salerno, 481 U.S. 739, 751 (1987). Further, the state must show by clear and convincing evidence that detention is necessary to protect a third party. *Id.* However, under *Roe*, the fetus is not a legal person, and therefore cannot legally be considered a third party. Roe v. Wade, 410 U.S. 113, 158 (1973). Thus, the state does not have a compelling interest in jailing pregnant women, and they are not able to demonstrate that confinement is the least restrictive alternative way to protect the states' interest. City of Bourne v. Flores, 521 U.S. 507, 515– 16 (1997).
26. Tenn. Code Ann. § 37–1–153 (2019). This provision allows the expungement or destruction of the public records of dismissals, cases resolved diversionary plans and, in limited circumstances convictions. The result, for the purposes of this research, is that the public records of these prosecutions were not available.

27. Although these records were ultimately expunged, my awareness of their existence resulted from the timing of when data was accessed for this project. I accessed data about the Memphis cases twice, once at the time when these cases were still pending, and therefore when the records were available, and again later when they no longer appeared in the court management system. This indicates that these women likely completed their cases, moved to expunge their records, and were given this relief.

28. Orisha Bowers et al., *Tennessee's Fetal Assault Law: Understanding Its Impact On Marginalized Women*, https://www.sisterreach.org/uploads/1/2/9/0/129019671/full_report.pdf [https://perma.cc/8BKC-VYTE].

29. REBECCA TIGER, JUDGING ADDICTS: DRUG COURTS AND COERCION IN THE JUSTICE SYSTEM 13 (2012).

30. Interview with Judge Don Arnold, Johnson City General Sessions Court Judge, in Jonesborough, TN (July 26, 2018).

31. Josh Bowers, *Contraindicated Drug Courts*, PUBLIC L. & LEGAL THEORY, Working Paper no. 180, 9 (2007) (citing a study of NYC drug courts clearly indicating more punishment than traditional court dispositions, even when including graduates).

8 CORRUPTING CARE

Inevitably, when we criminalize care, we affect far more than just the road to any particular program or support. Chapters 6 and 7 focused on those roads, describing how rules, practices, and bias draw women and families out of care systems into punishment systems and how the locations of care inside punishment systems draws them further in. In this chapter, the focus turns from the road to care to the end of that road, to the care itself. It asks and, in the context of this study, answers, a fundamental question: What happens to care itself when care is criminalized? As we learned in Chapter 3, care for those who we stigmatize, for those who we deem worthy of surveillance and punishment, for those who we are willing to label "criminal," is all too often substantively different than the care we provide for everyone else. Drawing the lens back for a moment, away from fetal assault and treatment for substance-use disorder, to other forms of care, we can see this phenomenon in something as basic as support for housing or health care.[1] In the realm of housing, we support low-income families through programs like Section 8, and we support wealthy families through programs like the Home Mortgage Interest Deduction. Both Section 8 and the Home Mortgage Interest Deduction are economic supports for housing, but they are received by very different groups. The Home Mortgage Interest Deduction benefits individuals at the top of the income scale and Section 8 benefits those at the bottom. In the realm of health care, we support poor families through Medicaid and support wealthier families by subsidizing private health insurance through the tax system. Again, both are economic support for a particular basic need – in this case health care – but they are structured quite differently.

While we provide support for basic needs in all these programs, the structure of those supports are often radically different across class and race. In the realm of housing, a support like the Home Mortgage Interest Deduction is easily obtainable and comes with no surveillance, scrutiny, or risk. In contrast, housing subsidies for low-income households are characterized by a high level of surveillance and a high risk of punishment.[2] One need only recall Priscilla Ocen's study, described in Chapter 3 and entitled *The New Racially Restrictive Covenant*, to remember the substantial risk of surveillance and punishment families face by taking Section 8. Similarly, in the health care realm, Khiara Bridges' work has demonstrated[3] that women seeking prenatal care through Medicaid are subject to extensive intrusions on their privacy as a condition of support, whereas the middle- and upper-class individuals whose health care is subsidized through the tax code face no such risks. So, although we provide care, as a society, to individuals across the class and race spectrum, the form of care differs. Care offered to those we stigmatize (and all too often criminalize) looks, feels, and is different than the care we offered to others.

Moving a bit closer to the context of this study, Allison McKim's *Addicted to Rehab* provides a window into how drug treatment programs are affected by the proximity to and use of punishment systems. Here too, we find strong evidence that the form of care (in this case not housing or health care but addiction treatment) can differ significantly based *who* is receiving care. As was the case in housing and health care, here the care offered to those we stigmatize, those in the criminal system, is radically different from the care offered to those who are not criminalized.

McKim's study, which I discussed in Chapter 3, looked deeply at the structural differences between two treatment programs – Women's Treatment Services (WTS), a program "funded by the state's criminal justice system"[4] and Gladstone Lodge, a program with "no relationship to the criminal justice system."[5] She found that the structure of treatment in these two programs differed significantly. In short, "Women at the Lodge were customers, from higher class backgrounds, and were not criminalized. In contrast, WTS was fundamentally more punitive. The threat of prison backed the program's power, and this showed in its therapeutic and disciplinary methods."[6]

These differences in how we provide care are rooted in racism, stigma, and entrenched notions of who deserves support, who should be surveilled, and who should be reformed. They are deeply enmeshed in the institutions of our society and are embedded in the connections between systems of care and systems of punishment that I have been describing.

In researching this book, I began exploring the question of how this entanglement affected not only the risk of accessing care but the substance of care for criminal defendants and parents in the child welfare system. Relying on my own research as well as the research conducted by SisterReach, it became clear that care was affected in several ways. First, treatment providers, like those who we learned about in Chapter 7, whose clients are referred predominantly from the child welfare and criminal systems, inevitably find themselves accountable not just to their patients but to actors in those systems who have the power to punish their patients. These connections inevitably undermine the trust essential to the provision of health care. Second, and related to the first, as a result of these risks women engaged strategically, taking the risk of punishment into consideration as they decided what information to share with their health care providers. The effect of this, of course, is that health care providers may not have the information they need to provide the best care for their patients. Third, care decisions themselves, about what medications individuals should take when trying to stabilize and in particular when pregnant, were deeply affected by a phenomena Stephen Lloyd labeled "practicing medicine without a license." This chapter lays out these findings in detail.

8.1 LOYAL TO WHOM?

One of the most significant implications of being in treatment while you have an open child welfare or criminal case is the effect of that case on the conduct of your treatment provider. Every provider I interviewed described themselves as, in effect, accountable not just to their patients but to the agencies on which they depend for referrals and to which they must report. Although both compliance with the program and accessibility of medical records is nominally in the hands of the woman, in practice, as we learned in Chapter 6, this could not be further from the truth.

Treatment professionals are regularly in communication with both child welfare and criminal system staff. Those agencies require both compliance with treatment by the patients and reporting from the treatment provider as a condition of the participation. These collaborations, between child welfare and criminal system actors and treatment providers, are ongoing and are often essential to the existence of the programs themselves.

This has many important implications. First, treatment providers depend on the child welfare system and courts for the vast majority of their referrals. This is not a Tennessee aberration. Nationwide, "criminal justice institutions are the largest single source of referrals to rehab."[7] As a result, having a strong relationship with those institutions is essential to their ability to continue operating. But providers also have ethical obligations to their patients and real safety concerns to take into consideration. All of this leads not only to difficult daily decisions by providers but also inevitably to diminished trust between mothers and their treatment providers.

A couple of interviews made this very clear. Kristen Kakanis from the MIST program, who we met in Chapter 7, described her relationship with DCS as "their biggest source of referrals" and "a good relationship."[8] As to the relationship between voluntariness and child welfare, here's what she said:

KRISTEN KAKANIS: We are a voluntary program ... I tell the women that too because they do get stuck in that mindset of DCS is telling me that I have to do it, then I always explain to them they might be telling you that, but we're not them. Yes, we work with them, but we are not them. We are a program, and we are voluntary. You make the choice to do this program. They might be telling you to, but it's still ultimately ... It's your choice whether or not to participate with us.

WENDY BACH: How do they hear that? Do you think they hear it?

KRISTEN KAKANIS: I think they still hear it as they need to do it.

WENDY BACH: They do, don't they?

KRISTEN KAKANIS: Well, yeah.[9]

While the women's HIPAA protected information is nominally protected in these settings, in actuality these protections are compromised. Another conversation with a provider in Knoxville, who provides comprehensive treatment to pregnant and parenting mothers and their children, gives you a sense of just how far this can go. This particular provider works as a part of the partnership between UT Hospital and the child welfare agency. The vast majority of her clients have open child welfare cases and some of them might have open criminal cases as well. Every woman in the program signs a general authorization allowing the provider to share information about her progress with every member of the team. Given the general nature of this release, the content of those disclosures is entirely up to the provider. The staff member I talked to explained that her programs send weekly reports to every partner on the team.

WENDY BACH: When you say partners, who are you talking about?

CARLY MADDOX: Probation Officers, guardian-ad-litems, attorneys, UT high risk [child welfare].[10]

From the providers' perspective, this level of information sharing and collaboration makes sense. All parties in the collaboration feel comfortable that no information will be held back and that they will all know what is happening in the particular woman's case. The problem, though, from the woman's perspective, is at least twofold. Lack of confidentiality in and of itself is harmful both to her dignity and to her willingness to be honest with her care providers. But beyond that, the people on the "team" provided represent an enormous threat. Probation officers can file a motion to violate her probation for a positive toxicology screen and have her sent off to jail. Guardians-ad-litem, who are appointed to protect the best interest of the child, can bring a motion to restrict or terminate parental rights; the child welfare agency can make a similar motion. And recall that each of these women are easily classified as having committed "severe abuse," so once the professionals decide that termination of parental rights should happen, there's very little to stand in their way. So yes, these women were receiving care, but it was care that came with enormous risk.

8.2 STRATEGIC ENGAGEMENT

The risks that women face when accessing care inside the system are no secret. Poor women are aware that drug use during pregnancy can lead to child welfare intervention. In addition, while the fetal assault law is no longer in place, taking that one possible criminal charge off the table, child welfare intervention leads to home inspections, rendering the family vulnerable to attempts by child welfare officials to detect and transmit information about other criminal activity in the family. In the face of these real risks, women struggle to make choices that will enable them to both have a healthy pregnancy and protect their families. The women interviewed by SisterReach reported that this fear impacted their engagement with prenatal care. As the researchers reported,

> we learned that some women elected to delay or forgo seeking prenatal care during their pregnancy. The choice to forgo prenatal care was not taken lightly by participants. Many felt guilty about jeopardizing the health of their children but were able to justify their actions because they felt it increased the chances of them maintaining their parental rights.[11]

Mary Linden Salter, who runs the Tennessee Association of Alcohol, Drug and other Addiction Services, made a similar observation:

> There are so many women who might know that they're pregnant, but they're not accessing any kind of services until very late in their pregnancy because again, they're trying to stay off the radar. You still have a very limited ability to intervene with these women because they're trying not to be known to the system.[12]

Additional research confirms that women in these circumstances are aware of the risks they face and that that awareness effects how they engage in care. For example, a 2015 study conducted by Rebecca Stone, based on interviews with thirty pregnant women who used alcohol or drugs during pregnancy, found that,

> Punitive policies have indeed had some chilling effect on women's help-seeking behavior by discouraging women from accessing prenatal care or leading them to skip appointments, and by motivating

women who did attend appointments to withhold medically relevant information about their substance use. Some women were honest with medical professionals but then experienced poor treatment, making them less likely to be honest again in the future.[13]

Even when women did engage in care, they could experience both shame and stigma. As one woman reported to SisterReach,

> I feel more ashamed about not getting prenatal care than I do about doing drugs. I didn't do drugs the whole time. I tried to space it out. That doesn't make it ok. But not going and not knowing what's wrong and what's good or what's going on through pregnancy of your baby because of a fear of a law is not healthy in my opinion for babies.[14]

When they did engage in care, they encountered stigma which affected the quality of their relationships with their care providers, and that could, in turn, deprive medical providers of information essential to their health care. As SisterReach found,

> For some women the kinds of care received would be limited by the depth and accuracy of information shared during the visit. As an example, we heard from one respondent using methadone or buprenorphine (brand name: Subutex) – drugs used to treat addiction to opioids – during pregnancy that she delayed revealing her attempts to detox via use of these medications during prenatal care.[15]

In this way, the close relationship among and active flow of information between care providers and child welfare and criminal system actors degraded trust and resulted in strategic engagement. But that was not the only way that the content and nature of care was affected.

8.3 COMPROMISING CARE

I first heard the phrase *Practicing Medicine Without a License* from Dr. Stephen Lloyd, who we met in Chapter 2. He was the doctor who, in Chapter 7, recommended committing a misdemeanor as a road to accessing treatment inside a problem-solving court. Dr. Lloyd was not an addiction medicine specialist early in his career. His road to that specialty led through his own serious struggles with an opiate addiction.

To address his own addiction, he received inpatient detoxification, ninety days of what he called "high quality treatment at a world-class facility" and five years of follow-up. He paid out of pocket (to the tune of $60,000) for that treatment, and he ultimately agreed to lifetime supervision and random drug screening, as a way to keep himself accountable. This experience, and the information he learned, changed his career. He started focusing, on the side at first, on treating addiction. By 2017, he had become the Director of Substance Abuse Services for the State of Tennessee. When I interviewed him, he had recently left that position and was working as the Medical Director at Journey Pure, an addiction treatment facility in Tennessee that offers a full range of addiction treatment services. Dr. Lloyd has been a powerful voice for high-quality addiction treatment both in the state and beyond and has, for decades, also run a practice treating pregnant women with substance-use disorder. We had an extensive conversation, during our interview, about the role of judges and child welfare officials in influencing treatment decisions, and on this topic he was unequivocal:

> DCS, even before the fetal assault law, was flexing muscle that they did not have. They would tell women things that were going to happen, as a result of their pregnancy, with no authority whatsoever ... First of all, women who are, it doesn't matter if you're pregnant or not, [maintenance assisted treatment] is a viable treatment. If you can't do the things that I did and go to treatment like I have, or come somewhere like here [referring to Journey Pure, the facility he was running at the time of our interview], what the hell do you expect people to do? They don't just quit. It is viable treatment. You're having people tell you can't be on this. They're practicing medicine without a license.

In Dr. Lloyd's view, what really should be a health care decision made by a woman and her doctor is being corrupted by its placement inside the child welfare system. That's corruption of care. The balance of this chapter takes a deep look at two medical decisions that patients struggling with substance misuse face and the ways in which criminalization, stigma, and proximity to punishment systems can negatively affect the outcome of those decisions and the care they receive.

8.4 CORRUPTING DECISIONS

When an individual is struggling with substance-use disorder and wants to stabilize, one of the key questions they will face is whether to take maintenance medications. This decision is complicated for anyone and is even more complicated when the person is pregnant. Ideally, this is a decision an individual should make in consultation with his or her doctors. But as we will see, policies and practices in the child welfare and criminal systems are impacting these decisions, resulting in what this chapter terms corruption of care. The next section delves deeply into two medical issues involving maintenance medications that are the subject of conversation not only between care providers and their patients but also among professionals in the child welfare and criminal systems. What we will see is that the opinions of individuals in the child welfare and criminal systems, as well as the policies and practices of those institutions, play a large role in the decisions patients make. What becomes clear here is that it is the systems themselves, as well as the professionals inside them, that are practicing medicine without a license. The first example focuses on opiate addiction outside of pregnancy and the second focuses on the particular decisions pregnant women face.

8.4.1 Choosing Your Maintenance Medication

In Chapter 7 we learned about a program in the Knox County Jail in which defendants are given Vivitrol, a form of maintenance medication. Those defendants are kept in jail for the week to ten days it takes to fully detox and are placed on Vivitrol once that process is complete. As I argued in the last chapter, the use of jailing for this purpose paints a picture of just how far we have traveled down the road to using the mechanisms of the criminal system as a part of our care system. In addition, it became clear that this arrangement, to favor Vivitrol over other treatments, and to use the jails as part of the protocol, was influenced by the preferences of nonmedical professionals in the local criminal and child welfare systems.

I first began to learn about this issue in conversations about a local juvenile court judge. That judge oversees all the child welfare cases in this particular county. The judge's position on medication and substance use was a topic of conversation in many of my interviews with treatment providers in his area. He is well known for his preference for Vivitrol over maintenance drugs like Suboxone or Methadone. Unlike Suboxone or Methadone, Vivitrol blocks your opiate-receptors, so you do not get high when you take it. But the thing that judges likes most about Vivitrol is the way it's administered. Suboxone is administered in pill form, while Vivitrol is administered through a monthly shot. From a criminal or child welfare control perspective, it's much easier to monitor a person who is receiving a shot than one who is taking pills. Vivitrol is also better, from that perspective, because, unlike Suboxone pills, it cannot be illegally sold.

From a medical perspective, Vivitrol is an approved medication for treating substance misuse. It is one of many potential treatments, each of which has risks and benefits. Individual patients, working with their treatment professionals, might choose several different potential courses of treatment for a variety of reasons. What interested me, though, was the effect of this particular judge on the use of Vivitrol. The first time I heard about his perspective was from a nurse who worked in a local neonatal intensive care unit. She told me a story about a patient she knew who had a child welfare case in front of that judge. "This judge, his approach is unless you're on Vivitrol, forget it. That's his personal opinion. He just says he has not seen anything work but Vivitrol. So, he has the ability to use his personal opinion. I can't use my personal opinion in my job, but he can." The Executive Director of an outpatient treatment provider said the same thing: "That judge is not a medical doctor, number one. So, saying that you have to [go] off the opiates and be on Vivitrol because you can get your kid back. That's a medical decision, isn't it? So, I think they're operating outside their purview, that's just not what they're there for."[16] After hearing about his practice from multiple sources, I had a chance to talk to the judge himself. He understands the critique of his practices in the community, but he said that, from his perspective, he has to evaluate the quality of the treatment in making his decisions about child safety:

> If someone is getting treatment, there are different ways to get treatment and you can assign different levels of trust to the different

levels of treatment ... You have Suboxone and Subutex. The problem with those two is they're readily available on the street and everybody knows that. It's very difficult to trust what's going on when you get Subutex and Suboxone, so we want to see a prescription; we want to see a counseled, wise choice of treatment, and we want to see a step-down because you're supposed to step down on those drugs. You're not supposed to be on them forever. Then you move to Vivitrol, which is my personal favorite form of assisted treatment because it doesn't get you high. It's more accountable. If you get that shot each month and you're tested and you're not seeing opiates in your bloodstream, I know for sure. I love the Vivitrol. I kind of discovered it. I heard about it from a guy in Chicago and brought the reps in here and talked to all our judges and now its commonplace.[17]

Several things are important here. First, just in this one exchange, the judge is clearly expressing at least one medical opinion – "you're not supposed to be on them forever." Second, he likes Vivitrol not only for medical reasons – "it doesn't get you high" – but for the way in which it makes it easier for him hold the parties accountable. With Vivitrol, he can "know for sure." So, his preference is clear. Is he, as Dr. Lloyd might suggest, "practicing medicine without a license?" He would say no, but recall that this judge has the power to terminate the parental rights of a woman in front of him. If he thinks Vivitrol is right and is more comfortable returning children to women if they are on Vivitrol, that's an enormous thumb on the scale of this particular treatment decision.

The use of Vivitrol in this one court is tied to a larger story about this particular drug and its relationship to drug courts. According to an in-depth report in ProPublica in 2017, Vivitrol's manufacturer, Alkermes, was having trouble developing a market for the drug, largely because of resistance in the addiction medicine community and concerns about the high price and "the company's decision to go to Russia to conduct the clinical trials required by the FDA."[18] In response, the company began marketing the drug directly to drug courts, a strategy that turned out to be tremendously effective. In 2014 the company donated $50,000 to the National Association of Drug Court Professionals. By 2017 ProPublica reported that "more than 450 public initiatives in 39 states [were] making use of Vivitrol," including a court in Ohio called the "vivitrol drug court." So, this local judge was part of a much larger trend in which judges were marketed to and were favoring the use of this particular medication.

In this example, it is clear that a judge is putting his finger on the scale, influencing what should be decisions made solely by patients in consultation with their health care providers. Judges are not the only ones affecting treatment decisions, however. For pregnant women with substance-use disorder, child welfare policies play a similar role.

8.4.2 Detoxification during Pregnancy

For a pregnant woman with substance-use disorder the conversation about treating her addiction is complicated. Even under the best circumstances, she has difficult decisions to make. Making them well involves working closely with her doctors to make the best decision for her own health, for the health of her child, and for the long-term health of her family. This section delves deeply into these decisions. It demonstrates that two related forces – judges with strong opinions and the power to enforce them and child welfare policies – deeply impact the decisions women make. In effect, judges and policies are pushing women toward detoxification during pregnancy despite a serious lack of data about the health risks of detoxification for women, children, and families.

As we learned in Chapter 2, the standard of care, as endorsed by the American Association of Obstetricians and Gynecologists (ACOG), clearly dictates that the safest course of action, for both mother and child, is to begin and maintain a course of medication-assisted treatment during her pregnancy. Generally, a woman who is treated according to these guidelines will be given Methadone or Buprenorphine. These medications "prevent opioid withdrawal symptoms and [are] shown to prevent complications of nonmedical opioid use by reducing relapse risk and its associated consequences. [They] also [improve] adherence to prenatal care and addiction treatment programs."[19]

Adhering to this treatment protocol involves, at least initially, working with a doctor to help the pregnant woman transition to an effective dose of this medication. It then requires ongoing follow-up, ideally as an integrated part of prenatal care, to ensure that the treatment remains effective throughout the pregnancy.

There is, however, a downside to following this protocol: the use of maintenance medication is also associated with NAS. While an infant exposed to maintenance medication will not necessarily develop NAS, it is certainly a possibility. For this reason, there is significant interest in the question of whether a woman can safely undergo detoxification during pregnancy. Knowing the answer to this involves weighing the short- and long-term risks of various decisions on the health of both the mother and the infant. While ACOG has articulated a standard of care, there is also interest among researchers in figuring out whether there is a safe path involving detoxification. But, as we will see, there is also enormous concern in the research community about this option. In East Tennessee, this conversation starts with Dr. Craig Towers, a Professor in the Division of Maternal-Fetal Medicine at the University of Tennessee.

In 2016, Dr. Towers and a colleague published a paper in the American Journal of Obstetrics and Gynecology concluding that detoxification during pregnancy is not harmful to infants. Dr. Towers runs a practice in which he assists pregnant women who wish to detoxify during pregnancy. His practice involves not only the provision of traditional OBGYN care but includes a behavioral health component.

Dr. Towers' study is well known in local circles. The study was based on an examination of the records of 301 infants born to women who detoxed during pregnancy. Of the 301 women, 108 "underwent acute detoxification involuntarily because the jail program in east Tennessee has no ability to provide opiates to prevent or perform an opiate-assisted medical withdrawal." An additional 100 women under-went rapid, 5 to 8-day inpatient detoxification, and the remaining 93 were detoxed more slowly, over 8 to 16 weeks, in an outpatient setting. The study contains information about the extent to which women had access to ongoing behavioral health interventions, the rates of NAS among the infants, and the rates of relapse among the mothers. Dr. Towers and his colleagues examined the medical records of these patients for "pregnancy complications including fetal demise and preterm labor" and concluded that, in all 301 cases, there were no "adverse fetal outcomes related to detoxification identified."

Dr. Towers' research has been subject to significant critique in the academic literature. The critique focuses on three general issues – the quality of the data, the interpretation of the data, and the failure to focus on the effects on mothers. The research question Dr. Towers and his colleagues posed focused on the risk of harm to the fetus from detoxification during pregnancy. On that issue, critics point out that the data that Dr. Towers and his colleagues relied on did not include any monitoring for fetal stress. This lack of this data, as they see it, fundamentally undermines the conclusion that there were no adverse fetal outcomes. As they explain, "acute opiate withdrawal is a known physiological stress, causing a prolonged surge in corticosteroids. Corticosteroid excess signals poor environmental conditions from mother to fetus, causing rapid modification of neurotransmitter systems and transcriptional machinery and triggering permanent modifications of behavior, brain morphology, and neuroendocrine function." Stating it more bluntly, his critics make a sharp point: "[t]hat the fetus can survive withdrawal does not mean that it survives unharmed."[20]

In addition, Dr. Mishka Terplan, the lead author of the critique, drew my attention to the authors' conclusion that, in all 301 cases, there were no "adverse fetal outcomes related to detoxification identified." While this is in fact the article's stated conclusion, it is important to note that the researchers did report two intrauterine fetal demises among women who detoxed during the first trimester of their pregnancies. The paper does not explain how the researchers concluded that these adverse outcomes were not related to detoxification.

The third critique has to do with the implications that can be drawn from the study about the appropriateness of detoxification. To understand this set of issues, recall that the ACOG standard maintains that the current standard of care is to recommend maintenance medications. To know if that standard is inappropriate, you have to look at the health outcomes in a larger way. You have to ask: How does it affect the child, how does it affect the mother, and how does it affect the family unit as a whole? The conclusion of the Towers' study focuses only on the first question, but it contains disturbing data on the others. Recall

that there were four different groups of women who underwent detoxification in the study. The first group was incarcerated; the second
underwent rapid detoxification (five to eight days) and engaged in
intensive behavioral health services after birth; the third underwent
rapid detoxification without behavioral health, and the fourth underwent a longer detoxification protocol and also engaged in intensive
behavioral health after detoxification. The rate of relapse during
pregnancy[21] varied based by group, with a low of 22.5 percent for
the group that received the slow taper with behavioral health to a high
of 74 percent for the group who did the rapid taper and received no
behavioral health services. The study authors did not follow the longer-
term outcomes for the children or the mothers, so we have no data on
the relapse rates of these mothers after birth, a time at which the mother
is highly vulnerable to relapse.[22]

There is no question that relapse during pregnancy is extremely
dangerous for both mother and child. During pregnancy, relapse can
lead to disengagement with prenatal care, polysubstance use, HIV
transmission, and more complications for the infant. For the mother,
relapse is also extremely dangerous. Relapse is strongly associated with
higher rates of overdose deaths. For these reasons, the current guidance
from the American College of Obstetrics and Gynecology has issued
the following guidance:

> For pregnant women with an opioid use disorder, opioid agonist
> pharmacotherapy is the recommended therapy and is preferable to
> medically supervised withdrawal because withdrawal is associated
> with high relapse rates, ranging from 59% to more than 90%, and
> poorer outcomes. Relapse poses grave risks, including communic-
> able disease transmission, accidental overdose because of loss of
> tolerance, obstetric complications, and lack of prenatal care. If
> a woman does not accept treatment with an opioid agonist, or
> treatment is unavailable, medically supervised withdrawal can be
> considered under the care of a physician experienced in perinatal
> addiction treatment and with informed consent; however, to be
> successful, it often requires prolonged inpatient care and intensive
> outpatient behavioral health follow up.[23]

Finally, if a woman relapses either during her pregnancy or after,
she is far less likely to be able to retain custody of her child, an outcome

that can bring profound harm to both the mother and the child. So, understanding whether detoxification should be part of the standard of care raises complicated and difficult issues.

Dr. Mishka Terplan is one of Dr. Towers' strongest critics. I got a chance to talk to him extensively about these issues. He described the academic literature around detoxification and pregnancy as methodologically weak. First, because the literature tends to exclude data for women who did not complete the detoxification protocol, it may well underestimate the risk of relapse. In addition, as he explained,

> A second problem with the literature is that it tends to stop collecting data at the time of delivery. We know the postpartum period is a time of increased vulnerability for all people, but in particular for people with addiction. It's a time of recurrence, relapse, overdose, and overdose death. People who've been taken off a life-saving medication during pregnancy, I'm concerned about their well-being in the postpartum period, and we don't have any data about that. I think that that's very critical to include those data in future studies.[24]

For this reason, Dr. Terplan and colleagues around the country were, at the time of our interview, just beginning a multisite study evaluating the outcomes, for both mother and child, of detoxification versus maintenance during pregnancy.

Now, in our conversation, Dr. Towers made clear that he does not tell women that they must detox during pregnancy.

> The one clear message that I want to come out with whoever I talk to, not once have I ever said that I recommend a woman be told she should detox ... Never. I have just said, "I recommend that she be given the option with informed consent." ... Here's the risks of staying on the opiates and here's the risks to getting off the opiates ... You make up your mind.

Having said that though, it appears that Dr. Towers himself does not offer maintenance medications. The US Department of Health and Human Services maintains a list of practitioners who are authorized to prescribe maintenance medications and who have agreed to release their practice information publicly. Dr. Towers does not appear on this list.[25] Dr. Towers may tell his patients they have a choice, but it appears that if they want him to be their doctor, the only choice is detoxification. Now, offering one treatment but not another may be common, but the concern for people like Dr. Terplan, is that he does not believe we have the full information a woman might need to make an informed decision about how to proceed.

To understand more about how questions like this play out in medical practices in the areas most hard-hit by the opiate epidemic, I talked to Dr. Cathleen Suto, an OBGYN at Dayspring Health in Jellico, Tennessee. Jellico is a very small town in Eastern Tennessee. It has a population of 2,400 and a median income of just under $22,000. Nearly 34 percent of the population lives under the federal poverty level.[26] Dr. Suto is the only OBGYN in her community. The local hospital – which existed at the time of our interview but has since closed – did not have a neonatal intensive care unit.

Dr. Suto has an interesting history. She went to medical school on a full scholarship from the Air Force and started her practice in Florida on an Air Force Base. After her commitment there was done, she says that she "felt called to serve the poor and started looking for opportunities to do that."[27] That's when she found Dayspring Health in Jellico. She moved there just over ten years ago and has been there ever since. She quickly realized that, due to the high levels of substance-use disorder in the community she was, by default, caring for women who her field label as high risk. Over time, she has developed a practice that enables her to care for these women. The evolution of her thinking and practice regarding detoxification during pregnancy sheds light on the complexity of decision-making in this context. Below is the conversation we had:

DR. SUTO: I started off, I would say, probably five or six years ago. I was very opposed to MAT, very opposed to Dayspring offering MAT, opposed to patients being on MAT, all of it.

WENDY BACH: Why?

DR. SUTO: I was very opposed to it. Just mainly because of concerns for diversion, and how I've seen MAT done by other clinics ... I really was, like what a lot of people say, it's just substituting one addiction for another . . . I really liked the idea of detox, of getting people off. The other problem with MAT is that, of course, the babies still withdraw . . .

Anyways. I thought, wouldn't this be a beautiful solution to detox the moms? If it worked, it would be great. But I also like to practice evidence-based medicine. Evidence-based medicine tells us that long-term success, the best rates for that are with MAT. I really try to think about [that]. I live in the community. I'm raising my child in this community. I'm invested in the community being successful. What I see long-term . . . Maybe I could detox a few moms and they could have a baby who didn't have NAS and didn't get transferred to [the University of Tennessee Medical Center]. But, in the long run, I don't know that that mom is going to be successful. Really, my ultimate goal is to have families that mom's able to keep her baby, is able to raise her baby, doesn't have her mom or grandmother raising all of her kids, and is able to do that in a successful way.

I don't think that detox is dangerous. I think detox is a legitimate option. The difficulty is that it's not a long-term solution. It's a short-term solution to have a baby that doesn't have NAS. That would be great. I would love for my babies not to all have NAS . . .

Detox would be a great answer. The problem is that my patients were not successful at doing it. I felt like I wasn't giving them the best care when I'm telling them that they have to come off . . .

WENDY BACH: Why weren't they successful?

DR. SUTO: They were relapsing. They just didn't make it through the taper. They would get to a certain point and feel really pill sick, and they couldn't finish it. I guess they were ashamed, and they

wouldn't come back for their prenatal care, and they
would just end up either showing up at the time of
delivery with whatever on board or go somewhere
else ...

I felt like I was doing more good by treating them
with maintenance therapy and having them come in
for their prenatal care and hopefully hoping that
some of the behavioral health that they're learning
at the [intensive outpatient treatment we offer] is
sinking in at some level.[28]

Now, to be clear, I am a lawyer and a law professor, and I certainly
would not presume to take a position on what is right here either for any
particular woman or for any particular healthcare provider. But what
I have learned is that this health care decision is complicated, hard, and
case-specific. Perhaps more importantly, there are still extremely
important research questions that need to be studied before the field
comes to any conclusions about the overall safety of detoxification. If
anything is clear at all, it is that a woman forced to make this choice
needs good information from her doctors and, even with this good
information, she faces a difficult set of choices. But as we will see,
policies being implemented outside the health care system are impacting these decisions.

8.4.3 Favoring Detoxification

In East Tennessee, Dr. Towers' work has had an enormous impact on
how various professionals outside of the medical field view the question
of whether a woman should detoxify during pregnancy. He character-
izes his own work as, "working to stop the opioid crisis in the womb."[29]
His work has received extensive local and national press coverage.
CNN characterized his work as "setting a new standard of care for
the field."[30] A local television station reported that "[a] treatment
option pioneered at the University of Tennessee Medical Center is
gaining national acceptance to help drug-addicted pregnant
women."[31] And Nashville public radio reported two facts: the decline
in NAS cases in 2018 and the fact of Dr. Towers' practice and

concluded, with no articulated basis, that Dr. Towers' work was responsible for the decline.[32]

Certainly, good press is one thing and an actual effect on policy is another, but that is precisely what is happening in both the child welfare system and the courts. Dr. Towers was, at the time of our interview, part of a team working in East Tennessee, with the Department of Child Services, to address the effect of the opiate crisis on infants, and women with open DCS cases in the region were receiving care in his practice.[33] This is in fact the "team" that Carly Maddox, who I talked about earlier in this chapter, was reporting to and that included not only child welfare officials but guardians-ad-litem and probation staff.

Beyond this collaboration, in Tennessee, as we saw in Chapter 6, it is DCS policy to open a child welfare case in every circumstance in which an infant is diagnosed with NAS. This policy was confirmed for me in an interview with Travis Bishop, who at the time of our interview led the DCS team in East Tennessee on infants affected by drug use during pregnancy. In the view of the agency, NAS is by definition a harm to the infant, so a referral and investigation is appropriate. And as detailed in Chapter 6, once the referral is made, the agency has the power to remove the child, set the terms under which reunification can occur and terminate parental rights. So, a woman can certainly choose, with her doctor, to follow the standard of care set out by the American College of Obstetricians and Gynecologists and take maintenance medications, but the risk to her family if she makes this choice is enormous. Karen Pershing, who runs the Metropolitan Drug Coalition in Knoxville and who has had countless conversations with women in these circumstances related it this way:

> So I say, if they need to re-initiate MAT post-delivery, let them do it. Put them back on it. But at least they don't have to have a baby with NAS, and have all these systems coming at them ... Because I tell you, we deal with these women. If you have an NAS baby, you got DCS taking them to court. You've got all these people coming at you, and they're trying to get their lives together and get in treatment and all that. They're having to keep 14,000 appointments with this caseworker and that caseworker, and this and that. They're completely overwhelmed ... I'm not saying there's not some people who are really trying to help them but it's just here

you are, a new mom, and now you've got all this stuff and your head's still in a fog. If you're early in treatment, you can't process all of that ... Personally, if I have a substance use disorder and I'm worried about somebody taking my baby and all that, yeah, I want to ween because I don't want all those people in my life.[34]

Dr. Towers is also highly respected by local judges who sit in drug court. Judge Duane Slone sits in a criminal court in in East Tennessee. He runs a very highly regarded drug court. Judge Slone developed his drug court practice largely in response to the presence of women in jail in his community who were pregnant and suffering from substance use disorder. He has been a very important figure in the drug court movement in the area and nationally. I interviewed him very early on, and he was the first person to talk to me about Dr. Towers' work.

Dr Craig Towers at UT Medical Center just published [a study] showing you take the woman, if we can get them early enough in pregnancy, and the Department of Health is getting ready to publish some stats supporting this as well, that if you can get them below 5 mg at delivery, there's no NAS. The child will not be in the hospital for any period of time suffering that way. If it's going down gradually, it's hard to know the in-utero trauma, but it's just like with a person. If it's going down gradually, it's not the shock to the system when the child is in-utero. The amazing work there. But ideally, I like Dr. Tower's study or what he's putting out there. Let's get them really good treatment. I say [to the women in my court] here's what we got. We don't just, you're not just using Subutex. Tell your OB-GYN this. You're getting really good mental health care. You're getting addiction treatment. You're getting drug screened at least once per week. You're on a GPS monitor. Not many of them are that way. I want your OB-GYN to know this. Talk to your OB-GYN about maybe if it's right for you to begin titrating off because the standard of care has been to raise them up to a level and keep them on it. Again, that's between you and your OB-GYN, but you might consider that.[35]

Although Judge Slone, at least in his explanation of his practice, makes clear that the decision about whether to detoxify during pregnancy is between a woman and her doctor, there is no question, particularly in the context of his recovery court, that his opinion will hold a tremendous amount of weight. After all, it is the judge that will ultimately decide whether a particular defendant succeeds or fails in drug court. As we saw in the last chapter, defendants, who often plead guilty at the outset and know that failure means imposition of an often-hefty sentence, clearly understand the importance of staying in the judge's good graces. So, it is clear that the decision about whether to detoxify can be strongly influenced by the consequences of those decisions in the child welfare and criminal systems, potentially compromising the quality of that decision and the quality of care the woman and her infant receive. In that way, criminalization corrupts care.

In the end then, we have a system where criminalized care, the care that we reserve for those who are poor and those who are stigmatized, functions in a myriad of ways. It is a slightly nicer sounding smoke-screen, behind which we find only punishment. It is a means by which some who seek care are surveilled and pulled ever deeper into punishment systems, and it is, as we have seen in this chapter, a way in which the form of care not only comes at high risk and high cost but is itself is corrupted by its proximity to punishment. The final section of this book turns from describing prosecuting poverty and criminalizing care to charting a path to a different and better form of care.

NOTES

1. Wendy A. Bach, *Poor Support/Rich Support: (Re)Viewing the U.S. Social Welfare State*, 20 FLORIDA TAX REV. 495 (May 17, 2017).
2. *Id.*
3. KHIARA M. BRIDGES, THE POVERTY OF PRIVACY RIGHTS (2017).
4. ALLISON McKIM, ADDICTED TO REHAB: RACE, GENDER AND DRUGS IN THE ERA OF MASS INCARCERATION 1 (2017).
5. *Id.* at 2.
6. *Id.* at 13.
7. *Id.* at 10.
8. Interview with Kristen Kakanis, Mother and Infants Sober Together, Program Director in Oakridge, TN (October 28, 2016).
9. *Id.*
10. Interview with Carly Maddox (pseudonym), Drug Treatment Program, East Tennessee (June 11, 2018).

11. Orisha Bowers et al., *Tennessee's Fetal Assault Law: Understanding Its Impact On Marginalized Women* 21, *available at* https://www.sisterreach.org/uploads/1/2/9/0/129019671/full_report.pdf [http://perma.cc/8BKCV-VYTE].

12. Video Interview with Mary Linden Salter, Executive Director of the Tennessee Alliance of Alcohol Drug and Addiction Services (July 3, 2017).

13. Rebecca Stone, *Pregnant Women and Substance Use: Fear, Stigma, and Barriers to Care*, HEALTH & JUSTICE (February 12, 2015) DOI: 10.1186/s40352-015-0015-5, https://www.ncbi.nlm.nih.gov/pmc/articles/PMC5151516/ [https://perma.cc/G9Y8-AAJW]. *See also* Josh Gupta-Kagan, *Toward a Public Health Legal Structure for Child Welfare*, 92 NEB. L. REV. 897, 932 ("Critics have also worried that the possibility of mandatory reporting 'probably deters many families from seeking help' and disrupts families' participation in treatment. Treatment disruptions are particularly evident with mental health care; one study reported that 24% of clients stopped treatment after a report by their treatment provider and that the rate was 31% when the clients themselves were the alleged maltreater, and another reported a decrease in clients' disclosures of abuse following enactment of mandatory reporting statutes.") (citations omitted).

14. Bowers et al., *supra* note 11.

15. Bowers et al., *supra* note 11, at 22.

16. Interview with Executive Director of a treatment facility in Knoxville, TN (June 6, 2018).

17. Interview with judge (June 15, 2018).

18. *See* Alec MacGillis, *The Last Shot,* PROPUBLICA (June 27, 2017), https://www.propublica.org/article/vivitrol-opiate-crisis-and-criminal-justice [https://perma.cc/UC7U-NWYD].

19. AM. COLL. OBSTETRICIANS & GYNECOLOGISTS, COMM. ON OBSTETRIC PRAC., ACOG COMMITTEE OPINION NO. 711: OPIOID USE AND OPIOID USE DISORDER IN PREGNANCY 6 (2017), https://www.acog.org/Clinical-Guidance-and-Publications/Committee-Opinions/Committee-on-Obstetric-Practice/Opioid-Use-and-Opioid-Use-Disorder-in-Pregnancy [https://perma.cc/MY9V-MPH3].

20. *See* John J. McCarthy & Mishka Terplan, *Detoxification from Opiates During Pregnancy: Stressing the Fetal Brain*, 215 AM. J. OBSTETRICS & GYNECOLOGY 670, 670 (2016).

21. Relapse was defined in the study as "a positive drug screen on admission, an admission by the patient at the time of delivery that she had relapsed, or a positive neonatal meconium test."

22. Interview with Dr. Nicole Yorke, Assistant Professor, Family and Community Medicine, University of New Mexico School of Medicine in Albuquerque, NM (May 30, 2019).

23. AM. C. OBSTETRICIANS & GYNECOLOGISTS, COMM. ON OBSTETRIC PRAC., ACOG COMMITTEE OPINION NO. 711: OPIOID USE AND OPIOID USE DISORDER IN PREGNANCY 6 (2017), https://www.acog.org/Clinical-Guidance-and-Publications/Committee-Opinions/Committee-on-Obstetric-Practice/Opioid-Use-and-Opioid-Use-Disorder-in-Pregnancy [https://perma.cc/MY9V-MPH3].

24. Telephone Interview with Dr. Mishka Terplan, MD MPH FACOG DFASAM, Medical Director, Friends Research Institute Adjunct Faculty and Substance Use Warmline Clinician, National Clinician Consultation Center, University of California, San Francisco (May 17, 2019).

25. In order to prescribe burprehenorphine, a practitioner must receive authorization. SAMSHA keeps a list of all those who have received this waiver and who have agreed to publically share their information. That list is accessible online. At the time of this writing, June 24, 2021, Dr. Towers did not appear on that list. https://www.samhsa.gov/medication-assisted-treatment/practitioner-program-data/treatment-practitioner-locator [https://perma.cc/AG49-TL3Q].

26. *Jellico City, Tennessee*, U.S. CENSUS BUREAU, https://data.census.gov/cedsci/profile?g=1600000US4738020 [https://perma.cc/YX8U-G2AF].

27. Interview with Dr. Cathleen Suto, Medical Doctor, Dayspring Health in Jellico, TN (May 22, 2018).

28. *Id.*

29. *Craig V. Towers, MD, FACOG*, UNIV. OF TENN. MED. CTR., https://www.utmedicalcenter.org/doctors/craig-v-towers-md-facog/ [https://perma.cc/B4TW-CYT2].

30. Wayne Drash, *Stopping the Opioid Crisis in the Womb*, CNN HEALTH (May 5, 2017, 1:32 PM), https://www.cnn.com/2017/05/05/health/opioid-detox-during-pregnancy/index.html [https://perma.cc/2ZT9-9FNZ].

31. Kendall Morris, *UT Doctor Leads New Pregnancy Detox Research*, 10 NEWS (July 26, 2017, 11:35 PM), https://www.wbir.com/article/news/local/ut-doctor-leads-new-pregnancy-detox-research/459812440 [https://perma.cc/4JKE-LHNR].

32. Blake Farmer, *Tennessee Sees Drop in Drug-Dependent Births After Helping Pregnant Women Detox*, NASHVILLE PUB. RADIO (December 18, 2016), https://wpln.org/post/tennessee-sees-drop-in-drug-dependent-births-after-helping-pregnant-women-detox/ [https://perma.cc/S9YP-3JWT].

33. Phone Interview with Dr. Craig Towers, Professor, Division of Maternal-Fetal Medicine, Department of Obstetrics and Gynecology, The University of Tennessee Graduate School of Medicine (May 30, 2018).

34. Interview with Karen Pershing, Executive Director, Metro Drug Coalition, in Knoxville, TN (May 25, 2018).

35. Interview with Judge O. Duane Sloane, Circuit Court Judge in Dandridge, TN (November 18, 2016).

PART IV

Rejecting Criminalization and Reconceptualizing the Relationship between Punishment and Care

Between 2014 and 2016 in the State of Tennessee at least 120 predominantly poor women, some Black but mostly white, were prosecuted for the "crime" of fetal assault. Like all those subject to today's misdemeanor system, there was little procedural justice to be had. No trials, no motions, no evidence, just guilty pleas, jail time, fines, accusations of failure to comply, and more of the same cycle. A few of these mothers appear to have gotten some access to treatment through the criminal case, but mostly that was not the case. Instead they were shamed and they were punished. This was justified largely in the name of punishing mothers and saving their babies. But in addition, those who supported the law asserted that it was done in the name of a purported relationship between prosecution and care. We were told that, with the stick of the criminal legal system, these "bad mothers" would have a chance to be reformed, to become "good mothers." We were told that if we brought them into the criminal system, judges and prosecutors would draw treatment resources into courts. We were even told that prosecution and court involvement was a form of treatment in and of itself. If it worked, that was only good, but if it did not, well, the mothers got what they deserved. This book has set out to explore the implications of these assertions. It has looked to one set of prosecutions and the systems in which those prosecutions were embedded as emblematic of large trends in the relationship between care and punishment. Through this examination the book attempts to shed some light on a series of questions: Who are the targets of criminalized care and why? Was it true that prosecution was a road to care? If so what are the risks and what is the price of that care? Beyond the questions that the individual cases helped answer, there were also larger theoretical and systematic questions: When we criminalize care, what does it mean for care itself? What is the role of law and rules in criminalizing care and, relatedly, how do legal systems work in the context of criminalized care?

The answers to those questions are largely found in Parts II and III of this book. The final chapter moves from problem to solution, focusing first on the power of bias, the strength of the conditions that gave rise to criminalized care, and the resulting limitations of reform. Second it describes some reforms that might mitigate the harms described in this book despite those limitations. Third it highlights moments in which systems actors can wield law, even within the conditions of criminalized care, to mitigate the risks and harms of criminalized care. Finally, the Part concludes by recentering and calling for the far more extensive changes required to provide a robust form of reproductive justice and care.

9 A PATH FORWARD

The harms described in this book are born of structurally instituted bias, neoliberal disinvestment in social support, and the building of an enormous carceral system. When individuals like Stephen Lloyd recommend that a person seeking treatment commit a misdemeanor to get access to drug court; when Cindy Jones reports her own child to the police in order to get him access to what little drug treatment exists in her own community; and when Nikki Brown is grateful for the drug court that gave her access to the support she needed, they are all three making choices within a set of systems defined by structural subordination. They are choosing in a context in which, all too often, care is more easily accessible proximate to or inside punishment systems, with all the risks and harms associated with that criminalization of care. Moreover, these structural realities are, as this book has argued, deeply intertwined with intersectional forms of bias. Criminalized care is, at best, the form of care we offer to women like those prosecuted for fetal assault – poor, Black, Brown, white, and deeply stigmatized. At worst, criminalized care actually offers no care at all, acting as a smokescreen to divert attention from systems that focus exclusively on punishment. At best, it offers a deeply corrupted and risk-filled form of care.

Importantly, criminalized care is quite explicitly not for everyone. It is for the women who were targeted in the story told in this book, whose choices society stigmatizes, whose bodies society surveilles and controls, and whose opportunities are constrained by the structural socioeconomic, gendered, and racial realities that surround their lives. It is also part of a larger system of criminalized care that is born of intentional resource-deprivation and is reserved for and targeted at members of poor, subordinated communities, regardless of gender. To change that reality is ultimately a political project best realized through mobilization. Having said that, however, there is some use in articulating both the goals and limits of incremental reform, and some steps that might move us closer to those goals. This chapter sets down a framework for evaluating reforms and proposes some possible reforms in the three systems that have been the focus of this book – health care, child welfare, and criminal legal. It then concludes with a different vision of care.

As we learned in Chapter 3, reproductive justice is steeped in intersectionality theory and demands three interlocked human rights: "the right *not to have children* using safe birth control, abortion, or abstinence; the right *to have children* under the conditions we choose; and the *right to parent the children we have* in safe and healthy environments."[1] Crucially, the framework is based not only on the right "to make personal decisions about one's life" but also "the obligations of government and society to ensure that the conditions are suitable for implementing one's decisions."[2] The vision, offered by reproductive justice, demands the creation of a set of supports delinked from punishment, accessible in communities, and structured in a way that protects the privacy and respects the decision-making of those it serves.

What this book has demonstrated is that, for the women prosecuted for fetal assault and for the communities subject to the systems described in this book, we are, as a society, far from realizing that vision. Nevertheless, we can move forward incrementally toward that end.

9.1 A FRAMEWORK FOR REFORM: BUILDING WALLS, SHRINKING PUNISHMENT, AND GROWING CARE

The distance between radical restructuring and incremental reform is often wide. Proposing and enacting reform can, at times, have mixed effects. Modest reform might help some folks in the short term, but many others might pay the price, in the short and the long term, for that reform. In the contexts described in this book, proposals for reform are dangerous when their effect is to shift more resources into punitive institutions that are, as a whole, causing harm. This is a central message of abolitionist movements that, in the context of the criminal legal system, argue that "not one more dollar" should be given to carceral systems. It is similarly a central message of those who have aptly renamed the child welfare system the family policing or family regulation system and who are calling for significantly shrinking the mission and reach of that system.[3] Reform that ignores these calls inevitably does more harm than good. For example, although the fetal assault law proponents seem to have believed that creating a crime would create care, the reality, as we have learned, is that it created mostly a lot of punishment and a little bit of corrupted care. Similarly, funding more drug courts puts more and more resources, and more and more care, into punishment systems. It may get some people some access, but it diverts attention from the scale of punishment and can also corrupt the form of care received. Similarly, widening the definition of what constitutes abuse or neglect for the purpose of giving families access to support is similarly dangerous. And finally, creating and expanding collaboration between health care, child welfare, and criminal legal institutions in the name of coordination and efficiency creates the same risks and harms. Two tests of any proposed reform in this context, then, are whether the proposal serves to separate care from punishment and whether it avoids transferring any additional resources to punishment institutions, be they in the child welfare or the criminal legal systems.[4] While helpful, testing reform proposals against these measures only goes so far. Reform, once achieved, can be posited as sufficient, thereby blocking the way toward more fundamental change. Mindful of this, while I propose significant reforms that could address the harms of criminalizing care at the margins, I in no way mean to suggest that these reforms alone are enough to address these problems. Far larger change is required. Nevertheless, the following sections of this chapter move through the three systems highlighted in this book – health care, child welfare, and criminal legal – and propose reforms that are designed both to meet these tests and to reduce harm at the margins. The chapter, and the book, then concludes by returning to the need to transfer significant resources out of punishment systems and into high quality care systems.

9.1.1 Health Care: Curtailing the Flow of Personal Information Out of Care and Support Settings

As discussed in detail in Chapter 6, the prosecutions highlighted in this book relied, to a remarkable extent, on information gathered in the health care setting. Blood test results, statements to care providers, clinical observations, and diagnoses, as well as extensive lab reports, were all present in the court files. In addition, prosecutors indicated that health care providers freely provided information concerning their patients, and care providers reported having open lines of communication with child welfare and probation staff. Presumptively confidential health information found its way into public records and into the hands of those who sought not to provide care, but to prosecute and punish.

I summarized the general rules concerning the privacy of medical information in detail in Chapter 6, but to recall them briefly, confidentiality of "protected health information" relevant to these particular circumstances is governed by two federal laws: the Health Information Portability and Accountability Act, or HIPAA,[5] and another federal law called the Child Abuse Prevention and Treatment Act, or CAPTA. Under HIPAA, providers can disclose to a government authority information about an individual that the health care provider "reasonably believes to be a victim of abuse, neglect, or domestic violence."[6] So HIPAA does seem to provide a sufficient, and necessary, exception to the overall confidentiality of health information. In addition, every state has rules around who must report cases of suspected abuse and neglect. But in the area of substance use and infants, CAPTA also weighs in. In order to receive federal funding, the state must have in place, "policies and procedures ... to address the needs of infants born with and identified as being affected by substance abuse ... including a requirement that health care providers involved in the delivery or care of such infants notify the child protective services system of the occurrence of such condition in such infants."[7] In 2016, the Comprehensive Addiction and Recovery Act, or CARA, was passed by Congress, revising and broadening the CAPTA provision above.

Originally, it read a little differently. It required notification in cases involving *illegal* substance use, but CARA revised this, expanding the requirement to include any infant "affected by substance abuse." I talked about this before, in Chapter 6, when I introduced Travis Bishop, the person who supervises child welfare cases of substance-exposed newborns in East Tennessee. He is the person who explained that DCS opens a case even when the medication the infant was exposed to in-utero was prescribed. As he explained, this was a policy change. The department used to limit the opening of a case to situations where the report concerned illegal drugs. But because of CARA, DCS changed this policy.

It is worth noting that, even in the absence of legal reform, while these laws do allow for – and at times require – reporting, they are absolutely not a green light for providers to freely share the results of tests, the contents of medical records, or the statements of their patients with child welfare officials, police, or prosecutors. Understanding this involves looking more closely at the relationship between federal and state law. It is true that HIPAA authorizes disclosure of protected health information to "a public health authority or other appropriate government authority authorized by law to receive reports of child abuse or neglect,"[8] but state law, CAPTA, and CARA limit the scope of required disclosures.

For example Tennessee, which has a very broad reporting statute, requires that,

> any person who has knowledge of or is called upon to render aid to any child who is suffering from or has sustained any wound, injury, disability, or physical or mental condition shall report such harm immediately if the harm is of such a nature as to reasonably indicate that it has been caused by brutality, abuse or neglect or that, on the basis of available information, reasonably appears to have been caused by brutality, abuse or neglect.[9]

The report has to include, to the extent available, "the name, address, telephone number and age of the child, the name, address, and telephone number of the person responsible for the care of the child, and the facts requiring the report." CAPTA and CARA do go further, requiring a report in instances in which an infant is "affected by substance abuse." These requirements do allow disclosures, but in the context of the general HIPAA rule protecting health information, these requirements counsel that these disclosures be limited only to those absolutely necessary to comply with the law. To put it another way, even though HIPAA allows for disclosure, it only covers disclosures needed to comply with mandatory reporting requirements. Absent an additional exception, this provision significantly limits the content of the protected health information that can be disclosed under this exception.

HIPAA also provides exceptions for disclosures to courts and administrative agencies, pursuant to lawful orders and to law enforcement agencies, but again these are strictly limited. In the case of courts and administrative agencies, records cannot be disclosed without a judicially authorized subpoena or other court order. The subpoena or other order must be specific as to precisely what records should be disclosed.[10] In the case of disclosures for "law enforcement purposes," again there are restrictions. For example, in most cases there must be some form of legal process like a subpoena to authorize the disclosure and to define the scope of the request.[11]

The data in this book has revealed disturbing laxness in the way that health care providers conduct themselves in these circumstances. There is every reason to fear that this case study is emblematic of larger trends in health care for poor people in the USA. The women's data here was shared so easily and so extensively that it is hard believe that this is not common practice. Certainly, litigation brought on behalf of patients whose information is illegally disclosed might be fruitful, but the health care field also needs to take a serious look at whether there is, in fact, systemic noncompliance with these rules in the health care sector and in particular in the part of that sector that serves low-income communities. Serious inquiry is also warranted about whether these practices violate medical ethics principles.[12]

Reforms that might curtail the free flow of information and disincentive disclosures range from those that require no change in law to those that require significant changes. Below are three suggestions. The first requires a change in practice and the second and third suggest broader and likely more effective reforms.

9.1.1.1 *Rigorously Enforcing Confidentiality and Privacy*
Protections

Even within existing law, a focus on best practices regarding confidentiality is warranted. For a model of best practices around confidentiality, reporting, and disclosure, a group of practitioners in New Mexico provide a strong example. Understanding their practices involves a bit of a backstory. By 1987 Dr. Andy Hsi, a Professor of Pediatrics at the University of New Mexico, had completed his training in pediatrics at the University of New Mexico and was in charge of the newborn nursery at that university. The statistics from that period sound eerily familiar: as Dr. Hsi explained, "probably about six to ten percent of the babies [in that nursery] had NOWS (neonatal opiate withdrawal syndrome)."[13] In one of our conversations he explained his reaction to those infants: "I'm looking at these kids and one in ten to one in twelve had drug exposure and we're telling them, well listen go ahead and find a doctor and good luck."[14]

For Dr. Hsi, that answer – go home and good luck – was unacceptable. He believed that those families needed more care and support and that medical practice, as he had been trained in it, was not responsive to their needs. The practice he and his colleagues built in response has existed and grown through upsurges in use of alcohol, heroin, crack cocaine, methamphetamine, and opiates. In our first conversation he talked about what he learned as he worked with colleagues to design that practice. During the late 1980s and 1990s they were focused on the question of whether "interventions [could] be created that would reduce the impact of exposure and improve the long-term development outcome of kids."[15] He learned two crucial things. First, "the ability of the family to engage with services for the baby after delivery seemed to have a sense of impact not only on the ... family, but also in biophysical parameters of the baby. We could see the baby's weight and head circumference starting small and then catching up in the normal range and staying there."[16] Second, it seemed that, "environmental factors around the baby were a lot more significant than the actual drug exposure."[17] And the mother's ability to "maintain a consistent environment" was important. What ultimately resulted was what Dr. Hsi describes as a "model of care for high-risk families."[18]

Today, Dr. Hsi is the Director of the Institute for Resilience, Health and Justice at the University of New Mexico. I originally met Dr. Hsi at an academic conference. At that point I had been conducting interviews for this book for over a year. I had met Stephen Lloyd, who told me that for some in Tennessee the best road to care was by committing a crime. I had met Cindy Jones who regularly advised families to get their loved ones arrested in order to get into care. And I had met Judge Arnold, who believes strongly in drug court but in the end admitted that he wasn't sure if you needed the coercion that comes along with it. The criminal legal system was, for him, for the person who Dr. Lloyd might advise to commit a crime, and for the families that Cindy Jones advises, the only way to help people access the treatment they needed. But Dr. Hsi and his colleagues are doing something quite different.

The practice that Dr. Hsi and his colleagues created and is in operation today has multiple overlapping components. The model consists of three separate but interlocking programs: The Milagro program, for pregnant women struggling with substance-use disorder, the Focus Medical Clinic, a family care practice, and the Focus Early Intervention Program, which provides comprehensive, multidisciplinary in-home services for families who receive care at the practice. Their practice is impressive and serves as a model for providing high quality care to struggling families. But what I want to focus on here are two specific decisions made by Dr. Hsi and his colleagues: first how they have made decisions about navigating federal and state laws around reporting as it relates to communication between medical practitioners and the child welfare agency, and second how Dr. Hsi has worked with his state to craft a better response to CARA.

To understand the program's practices around communication with child welfare agencies, you first have to recall the difference between reporting abuse and neglect cases to child welfare and disclosing medical information. Practitioners often have to disclose some presumptively confidential information in a circumstance in which there is actual abuse or neglect, but that is again not a green light to disclose additional confidential records or information. As we will see below, New Mexico has made some reforms that limit mandatory report in the cases of substance exposure during pregnancy, but this does not mean that there is never a circumstance when the practitioners at FOCUS find themselves in a position where they have to report abuse or neglect. Like every care provider I spoke to, they took that responsibility seriously, but mandatory report has nothing to do with the broader parameters of disclosure of confidential information, an issue that arises with regular frequency when a program is providing services to a family with an open child welfare or court case.

Every medical, psychology, and social work professional I spoke to in researching this book regularly interacted with child welfare officials, regularly provided care to women who had open child welfare cases, and regularly fielded requests for information about those women. There was, however, a striking contrast in the ways in which they responded to those requests. The vast majority of providers understood their basic legal obligations to keep information confidential, but in the majority of cases, all participants with open child welfare cases signed a consent form at the start of the program allowing their care providers to disclose information. Although signing was "voluntary," there was no real choice. Women needed, at a minimum, to be able to prove to the child welfare agency that they were complying, and child welfare officials expected care providers to disclose extensive information about the client's progress. How providers navigated these consents and requests, however, differed in important ways. In general, providers had patients sign a general consent form and made determinations along the way, without any further conversation with the parents about how much information to disclose in response to any particular request. Recall for example Kristen Kakanis' "great relationship" with DCS. Similarly, in many of the practice settings I saw, treatment center staff thought of themselves as members of a broad team of providers working on the case. These teams regularly included not only other care providers but also child welfare and probation staff. These teams met regularly to share information on the client's progress.

The practice at FOCUS was quite different. With regard to specific requests to disclose (as opposed to reports of abuse or neglect), all requests for information are handled personally by Karen Longenecker, the Clinical Services Coordinator. Her process begins with taking a very careful look at the consent form that child welfare has provided. While many providers appear to be comfortable with a general release, FOCUS does not accept them. As Ms. Longenecker explained, "I will call [the child welfare] worker back and I will say, 'this piece of paper does not give me any idea as to what this patient has consented for me to release' … 'what is it you want? What's the information you are looking for.'?"[19] In addition, she will engage the family before proceeding. "I'm going to call the family and say, 'I got this. What are you comfortable with me sharing? What was your understanding when you signed this?'"[20] In addition, FOCUS staff regularly receive requests from their patients to communicate information to child welfare officials. Again, this request flows directly through Ms. Longenecker and involves a specific consent form and a specific conversation. Finally, in the vast majority of circumstances the client is present when the information is shared.[21]

While the differences in practice here may seem technical, in terms of client autonomy and trust, they are likely quite significant. In the first example, at several Tennessee programs, after signing a general consent, there appeared to be no process in place to inform a woman about what information was shared, nor to seek her specific consent for particular disclosures. In contrast, at FOCUS, the procedures mandated ongoing communication between the woman and her care providers about specific disclosures. While I was not able to interview women to see how much of a difference that was making to them, it seems very likely that that level of communication enhanced trust.

9.1.1.2 Complying with CARA While Keeping Care Inside Health Care Systems

Going a bit further, some state level reforms specific to substance use and pregnancy could ameliorate some harms. To understand this, we can again look at what is happening in New Mexico with regard to substance exposure during pregnancy. In short, working within the confines of CARA and preexisting state mandatory reporting rules and informed by the belief that prenatal exposure alone does not signal abuse or neglect, New Mexico has devised a way both to comply with the legislation without engaging child welfare agencies in care and to build the capacity of health care systems to provide necessary care. Here's how it works:

For an infant "born with and identified as being affected by substance abuse or withdrawal symptoms resulting from prenatal drug exposure, or a Fetal Alcohol Spectrum Disorder,"[22] New Mexico legislation is tremendously detailed both about what cannot happen and what must. First, while CARA does require that the child welfare agency be "notified" of this occurrence, that does not mean that that agency must investigate. In New Mexico, not only does the legislation make clear that exposure does "not constitute a finding of abuse or neglect" but it also forbids a report of abuse or neglect solely on that finding, stating specifically that a "volunteer, contractor or staff of a hospital or freestanding birthing center shall not make a report based solely on that finding."[23] This provision in no way bars a report to child welfare if there are other indications of abuse or neglect. Instead, it simply requires that no report be made if the only evidence is the substance exposure or withdrawal itself. But the presence of substance exposure or withdrawal, as we have seen, might indicate a need for increased support and care. The New Mexico legislation retains the burden of providing that care within the health care system by mandating that the hospital or birthing center itself create a plan of safe care.[24] As Dr. Hsi explained, "The plan of safe care ... is agreed upon by the mother and is communicated not to CYFD [New Mexico's child welfare agency] but to the care coordinator in the insurance company who then continues to coordinate care for the mother and baby after discharge from the hospital."[25] For Dr. Hsi, this was explicitly about pulling cases and care out of punishment systems. For him, CARA became a way to "actually create a service system for women through the State of New Mexico and their babies to connect them to home visiting and early intervention and continue to be here for the health of the mother as opposed to creating some punitive mechanism that tries to place babies under law enforcement protection."[26] Now certainly, because of CARA, the report and plan of safe care are not voluntary in the sense that reproductive justice calls for, and there is plenty of reason to worry that women will continue to face discrimination and inappropriate referrals to child welfare despite the New Mexico reforms. There's also every reason to think that, even if these systems actually maintain confidentiality to the maximum extent possible, women will still be aware of the history of referrals and will be slow to trust. Nevertheless, the state has taken steps to pull care out of child welfare and place it into health care systems where it belongs. Further and broader reforms along these lines are a step in the right direction.

9.1.1.3 Repealing or Significantly Curtailing Mandatory Report

To be even more effective, we likely need to go further, repealing the federal statutes that mandate communication between health care and child welfare officials in the context of substance use and pregnancy and repealing state mandatory reporting laws. In the specific context of substance use and pregnancy, we can start by doing away with the provisions in CAPTA and CARA that lay additional mandates on the state concerning substance exposure during pregnancy. As I have argued extensively in this book, there is no reason to think that substance exposure alone, whether the substance is legal or illegal, is a particularly good proxy, on its own, for the potential or existence of child abuse or neglect. Certainly as Dr. Terplan suggests, neither a positive drug screen nor an NAS diagnosis reveals anything about the presence of abuse or neglect. In addition, the allowance in HIPAA for disclosure of protected health information when the provider "reasonably believes to be a victim of abuse [or] neglect" provides more than adequate protection. For a woman receiving high quality treatment, she and her children are in fact receiving the support they need. For a woman who could be referred to and provided with such treatment inside healthcare and social welfare systems, again there is no reason for referral. Absent an indication of actual abuse or neglect in the family, there is simply no reason to force individuals to report that family.

Going beyond substance use and pregnancy, it makes sense to consider repealing mandatory reporting laws. The existence of mandatory reporting leads some women to evade care; it turns health care providers into investigators, and it incentivizes women who do engage in care to act strategically, hiding information from their doctors that could lead to punishment. Even beyond that, it sends a clear message to health care providers that they have no role in caring for families more holistically. As Professor Josh Gupta-Kagan argues, "mandatory reporting laws direct the people best suited to address a situation that they cannot and should not address it but should simply call it in."[27] If services and support are what is needed, there is no reason that health care systems cannot provide those referrals and that support. To be clear, repealing mandatory report laws would not bar reports. Healthcare providers would retain, under HIPAA, the ability to report. Instead, repealing mandatory report would simply place the discretion in the hands of those professionals – healthcare providers, educators, social welfare staff, and others – to use their discretion and to, whenever possible, provide support for families outside the punitive institutions of the state.

But even as I call for repeal or revision of mandatory report laws, other research suggests that this, in and of itself, is insufficient. Touching on this set of questions, in *Getting Eyes in the Home* Professor Kelley Fong presents findings based on her interviews of professionals who have a duty to report child abuse and neglect. While many scholars have focused on the effect of mandatory report laws as the driver of reports from helping professionals, Fong's data suggest otherwise. She finds that, in an age in which assistance is often located within or accessed through coercive authorities, reporting professionals

> do not primarily channel families to CPS to address imminent child safety concerns or to fulfill legal mandates. Instead, aspiring to help families facing adversity but unable to intervene as they would like, reporting professionals summon CPS to address families' multifaceted needs. In particular, they are drawn to CPS's coupling of care and coercion, as the agency's goal of supporting families stands alongside its power to separate them. The dual capacities of surveillance – as a means of identifying needs for support as well as controlling marginalized populations – frame CPS as a sort of all-purpose agency and a promising option to respond to family adversity.[28]

Crucially, while Fong found that "reporting professionals leveraged CPS in an effort to realize their rehabilitative aspirations for families"[29] this was more likely to be the case for professionals in underfunded agencies that serve marginalized families than in agencies serving more privileged families.[30] So while repealing mandatory report might have some limited effect, Fong suggests that presenting the solution as choosing between eliminating or keeping mandatory reporting does not fully address the issue. Instead she suggests, echoing suggestions that are explored in more depth later in this chapter, that, "[w]e might instead ask how to protect children while also promoting help-seeking and engagement . . . For poor families, additional income reduces CPS reports. Labor market protections, a strong social safety net, and supportive community services for mental illness and substance abuse could protect children without involving the child welfare system."[31] So, while repealing mandatory reporting laws might have some effect, real solutions lie in reducing stigma and building support outside of coercive and punitive agencies.

9.1.2 Child Welfare: Reforming Child Welfare Rules Regarding Drug Use during Pregnancy and Beyond

For a similar set of reasons, we need to take a hard look at the how child welfare systems respond to drug use by pregnant women families with open child welfare cases. One of the most striking pieces of policy making at the center of these cases is the decision, in Tennessee, to classify drug exposure as "severe abuse" subject to procedures that draw police and prosecution into the case of every woman who gives birth to a drug-exposed infant. In this context, it is important to note that, while the criminal law classifying this conduct as fetal assault is no longer in effect, the classification of drug exposure as severe abuse remains.[32] That decision is, in effect, a determination that women who use drugs while pregnant are analogous to those who commit sexual abuse and those whose actions result in the death or near-death of children. The significant lack of data on the long-term harms of drug exposure when contrasted with the enormous harms associated with sexual and severe physical abuse certainly calls this analogy into question.[33]

But beyond this, the designation raises questions about whether the asserted purpose of the child welfare system, like the health care system, is being distorted. Although one can certainly question (as I do above) whether the child welfare system is the appropriate one to respond, it is clear that the child welfare system and the criminal system have different purposes. Child welfare systems are in place primarily to protect children and are required, in all but a few circumstances, to make reasonable efforts to maintain a child in the home.[34] In the vast majority of circumstances they must provide services to mothers to

help them achieve reunification.[35] The stated goal is not punishment. It
is support. But when the system conceptualizes a case, from the very
start, as one in which criminal intervention is appropriate, we are
already talking about punishment. On the micro level, one way to
address the harms described in this book is to repeal this state-level
policy both in Tennessee and in the other states with similar policies.[36]

9.1.3 Criminal Legal System: Meeting Proposals That Overemphasize the Role of the Criminal Legal System As Sources of Care with Skepticism

In the context of Tennessee's fetal assault law, the relationship between
punishment and care was striking. The law was framed as a road to and
a form of care. As I argued at the start of this book, that is a very strange
justification for a criminal statute. It is one thing to provide care to
people who commit acts we all believe should be crimes, as a part of
rehabilitation, but it's entirely different to say that the care in the
criminal system is so good, so valuable, that we are willing to criminalize previously non-criminal conduct. I have argued, particularly in
Chapters 4 and 5, that much of this was a smokescreen. If you evaluate
the purpose of the law by its actual effect rather than by the words of
some of its proponents, this was mostly about punishing poor women
for using drugs while pregnant, not about providing them with care.
But what I want to focus on now is not whether the promise of care was
real but instead how it made sense in the first place. As we have learned,
the criminal system and the child welfare system do provide a road to
care, not because they should, at least in the first instance, but because
we have built our systems to work that way. We collectively seem to
believe, that for these particular, highly stigmatized women, care
should be linked to threat and punishment. We apparently believe
this so strongly that we do not provide easy access to care in the
community, and we do have structures that make it easier to access
care once you come into a punitive system. But when pressed, virtually
every professional interviewed for this book agreed that this was no way
to build either a punishment system or a care system. It is just the way it
is. But that is simply not good enough, and this story counsels, at least,
that we should be skeptical of any proposals that assume that care has to

be linked to punishment or that links access to care to involvement in punitive systems. Care should be available, in the first instance, on a voluntary basis, in the community. And it should be available in a form that is responsive to the needs of patients and clients, that protects their privacy and that is respectful of their own conceptions of what they and their families need.

This recommendation, to be very cautious of proposals that look to the criminal system as a road to or form of care, has particular implications for the ever-growing problem-solving court movement discussed in Chapter 3. It is certainly true that the vast majority of fetal assault prosecutions did not take place in problem-solving courts and that this book touched only tangentially on the issues and practices of problem-solving courts. But it is also true that the idea of those courts, and the support given to the fetal assault law by those associated with the Shelby County Drug Court, played a significant role in the hearings that led to its creation. It was, by and large, the idea that prosecution and punishment is a form of treatment that dominated. This book certainly adds data to a series of existing critiques of problem-solving courts that are laid out in Chapter 3. It contains evidence, for example, of the net-widening function of those courts and, in the Memphis cases, of the severity of punishment for those who "fail."

Beyond this, the book also argues that proximity to punishment systems and legal rules that draw cases into punishment systems, be they child welfare or criminal legal, can significantly and often negatively impact the content and quality care decisions. Recall for example Karen Pershing, the Executive Director of the Metropolitan Drug Coalition who noted that, while in an ideal world a pregnant woman struggling with substance-use disorder might be best off following the advice of the American College of Obstetrics and Gynecology and going on maintenance medications, the risk of child welfare intervention because of the presence of maintenance medications might lead her instead to choose detoxification. Think at the same time about the requirement, in CARA, that even those taking prescribed maintenance medications during pregnancy be reported to child welfare. Think about the Juvenile Court judge whose preference for Vivitrol was well known throughout the community and the criminal court judge who was deeply impressed by Dr. Towers' research on the benefits of detoxification. This book has focused on one locale and one set of medical decisions, but there is ample reason to believe that there are far broader issues as to how locating care within problem-solving courts corrupts the form of care provided. For these reasons, deep skepticism of any proposal that suggests that care inside criminal systems is inherently more worthy of investment than care outside those systems is warranted.

9.1.4 Rethinking Collaboration Structures

Finally, many of the problems associated with the criminalization of care stem from the seemingly benevolent idea of collaboration. In Knoxville, the "team" set up to work on a woman's case involved not only OBGYN and addiction medicine specialists but also child welfare and probation staff. Similarly, when an infant was reported to DCS the case was categorized as one involving "severe abuse," which meant that the case was referred to a child protective investigative team, a team that included prosecutors and police and that could lead not only to prosecution of the woman but to investigation of members of her family for other crimes. These kinds of collaborations, while framed as benevolent and efficient, lead directly to the kinds of harms described in this book. If we are to separate care from punishment and to invest resources more significantly into care and support, we need to wall off those programs from punishment systems. Just as we need to be deeply skeptical of calls to utilize child welfare and criminal systems as our first response to need, so too do we need to be skeptical of systems that rely on collaboration between care providers and those who can and do punish.

9.2 REJECTING STIGMA, REJECTING CONSTRAINT, AND REACHING FOR CARE

The reforms suggested above, if enacted, might take us closer to the goals I articulated at the start of this chapter: separating punishment systems from care systems, avoiding reforms that transfer additional resources to punishment systems, and avoiding collaboration between punishment and care systems. But to truly address the challenges at the heart of the lives of the women and communities in this book, we must do much, much more. We need, in addition, a wholesale shrinking of the criminal legal and child welfare systems, a significant transfer of resources toward family and community support that respects those who receive that support, and widescale reform of the relationship between legal institutions and families.

From a universal support perspective, scholars like Maxine Eichner[37] and Clare Huntington[38] argue persuasively that law and legal institutions have an obligation to make it possible for families to thrive and that the United States fails dramatically at this task. They not only prove these points but call for the institution of a wide range of reforms and supports. Establishing universal health care, establishing access to high quality affordable childcare, significantly strengthening the safety net, building safe communities and safe schools, and creating jobs that allow families to support themselves and care for their families would all go a long way to strengthening families.

We also need a concerted focus on poverty itself. Recall, for example, the conclusion of Dr. Hallam Hurt, who led a twenty-five-year longitudinal study of infants exposed in-utero to crack cocaine and concluded that "Poverty is a more powerful influence on the outcome of inner-city children than gestational exposure to cocaine."[39] As the American Academy of Pediatrics has concluded, "poverty and related social determinants of health can lead to adverse health outcomes in childhood and across the life course, negatively affecting physical health, socioemotional development, and educational achievement."[40] If we want to address children's health, we need to address poverty.

Moving back to the specific question of pregnant women with substance-use disorder, we should remember the words of Dr. Nzinga Harrison, who argued that, "if what we are trying to prevent is harm to the baby, then we have to start with a solution that keeps the baby attached to mom, because detaching babies from moms also causes harm." Dr. Harrison further suggested that we need to create an environment in which a pregnant woman struggling with substance-use disorder "automatically knows where she can go, and one in which, when she gets there she's going to be received with compassion and open arms and followed throughout her pregnancy with increased access to the resources that she does not have."[41] Investing in such a system is essential.

But as I argued at the start of this chapter, we cannot get anywhere near these goals without recognizing and addressing the structurally instituted forms of intersectional bias that justify and operationalize criminalized care. If this book reveals anything, it demonstrates that intersectional forms of bias are structurally embedded in the systems that have been built in American society and in the decisions those with power make. Rules and practices of the kind discussed here reinforce and systematize the implementation of biased ideas. Professionals – even, and perhaps especially, when they are attempting to help – are acting within the constraints of those systems and those ideas. Moreover, the failure of those professionals to challenge the status quo reinforces the systems as they currently operate.

Ultimately, we cannot eliminate either those structures or those harms without naming and then seeking to eliminate intersectionally rooted structural bias. It is my hope that this book contributes in some small way to that project by revealing the structural mechanisms of criminalized care and revealing the logics, shared by professionals in the systems, that produce and reinforce those structures. But naming subordination – in all its individual and structural forms – is not enough. We need to name privilege too.

To this end, one final thought: although I hope that the readers of this book are diverse in every way imaginable, I suspect that most of you hold significant privilege along at least one axis of identity. As such, you have, perhaps, never been subjected to criminalized forms of care. And you likely have access to precisely the form of support that families and communities need, and that privilege in America provides – good jobs, economic security, a safety net in times of crisis, health care, education, and physical safety – to name just a few. As I write this chapter, the rights not to have children and to choose the conditions under which we have children are under some of the most aggressive attacks in recent history. Yet it has also always been true that economic privilege provides protection even there. Privilege means that mistakes are forgiven, that health care needs are met with health care, and that the first response to a crisis is one rooted in care instead of punishment. It means that privacy rights are robustly protected and decisions are respected. All of that has certainly been true in my own life, as well as in the lives of those closest to me. So perhaps the best way to end this book is to suggest that we consider what it would mean to build a society in which those privileges are no longer the privileges of the few but the rights of all. Build that society, and criminalized care would have no place.

NOTES

1. LORETTA J. ROSS, ET AL., *Introduction* to RADICAL REPRODUCTIVE JUSTICE: FOUNDATIONS, THEORY, PRACTICE, CRITIQUE, at 14 (Loretta J. Ross et al. eds., 2017).

2. *Id.*

3. These important ideas were thoroughly explored in a recent symposium entitled *Strengthened Bonds: Abolishing the Child Welfare System and Re-Envisioning Child Well-Being* hosted by the Columbia Law Review. The recordings of that proceeding and the papers published as a result of that symposium are available at https://cjrl.columbia.edu/ [https://perma.cc /E7GT-XGXZ].

4. The issue of what reforms undermine as opposed to move toward radical positive reform is a central question of abolitionist theory and practice. For example, Dan Berger, Mariame Kaba, and David Stein, all activists and theorists with decades of experience in the prison abolition movement, argue that fighting for "non-reformist reforms" is central to the abolition movement. They define those reforms as "those measures that reduce the power of an oppressive system while illuminating the system's inability to solve the crisis it creates." Dan Berger, Mariame Kaba, and David Stein, *What Abolitionists Do*, JACOBIN (August 24, 2017), available at https://www .jacobinmag.com/2017/08/prison-abolition-reform-mass-incarceration [https://perma.cc/S48H-6NA5].

5. HIPAA extends these protections to what it defines as "protected health information." *Id.* The term "health information" is defined as any informa-tion, including genetic information, whether oral or recorded in any form or medium, that: (1) Is created or received by a health care provider, health plan, public health authority, employer, life insurer, school or university, or health care clearinghouse; and (2) Relates to the past, present, or future physical or mental health or condition of an individual; the provision of health care to an individual; or the past, present, or future payment for the provision of health care to an individual. 45 C.F.R. § 160.103 (2017).

6. 24 C.F. R § 164.512(c)(1).

7. § 5106a(b)(2)(B)(ii).

8. 45 C.F.R. § 164.512.
9. TENN. CODE ANN. § 37–1–403.
10. 45 C.F.R. § 164.512 (e).
11. 45 C.F.R. § 164.512 (f). It is important to note that there are some additional exceptions that could be relevant here. For example, subpart (f)(3) allows some disclosures for records pertaining to crime victims and (f)(1)(ii)(C) allows for disclosure pursuant to "an authorized investigative demand." As to the first, as I have argued throughout this book, it is profoundly unproductive to criminalize this conduct. As to the "authorized investigative demand" while one might interpret this provision to include informal demands by the police, given the enormous emphasis in the regulation on formal requests that limit the scope of the inquiry, a court may well find that that interpretation is inappropriate.
12. For important work along these lines, *see, e.g.*, George J. Barry & Diane L. Redleaf, *Medical Ethics Concerns in Physical Child Abuse Investigations: A Critical Perspective*, FAM. DEF. CTR. (March 14, 2014), https://www.familydefensecenter .net/wp-content/uploads/2016/04/ Medical-Ethics-Concerns-in-Physical-Child-Abuse-Investigations-corrected-reposted.pdf [https://perma.cc/N4Z8-B89Q].
13. Telephone interview with Dr. Andy Hsi, Professor, Department of Pediatrics, University of New Mexico School of Medicine (February 12, 2019).
14. *Id.*
15. *Id.*
16. *Id.*
17. *Id.*
18. *Id.*
19. Interview with Karen Longenecker, Clinical Services Coordinator, Focus Program, University of New Mexico in Albuquerque, NM (May 29, 2019).
20. *Id.*
21. *Id.*
22. 42 U.S.C. § 5106a(b)(2)(B)(ii).
23. N.M. STAT. ANN. § 32A-4-3(G).
24. *Id.*
25. Telephone interview with Dr. Andy Hsi, Professor, Department of Pediatrics, University of New Mexico School of Medicine (February 12, 2019).
26. *Id.*
27. Josh Gupta-Kagan, *Toward a Public Health Legal Structure for Child Welfare*, 92 NEB. L.R. 897, 933 (2014).
28. Kelley Fong, *Getting Eyes in the Home: Child Protective Services Investigations and State Surveillance of Family Life*, 85(4) AMERICAN SOCIOLOGICAL REV. 610, 611 (2020).
29. *Id.*, at 620.

30. *Id.*, at 626.
31. Kelley Fong, *Concealment and Constraint: Child Protective Services Fears and Poor Mothers' Institutional Engagement*, 97(4) SOCIAL FORCES 1785, 1806 (2019).
32. *See* In re B.A.C., 317 S.W.3d 718, 725 (Tenn. Ct. App. 2009).
33. *See* Emmalee S. Bandstra et al., *Prenatal Drug Exposure: Infant and Toddler Outcomes*, 29 J. ADDICTIVE DISEASES 246, 249 (2010).
34. *See* TENN. CODE ANN. § 37–1–166(a) (2018).
35. *See* TENN. CODE ANN. § 37–1–166(c)(3).
36. CHILD WELFARE INFO. GATEWAY, REASONABLE EFFORTS TO PRESERVE OR REUNIFY FAMILIES AND ACHIEVE PERMANENCY FOR CHILDREN (U.S. Dep't of Health & Human Servs., Admin for Children & Families, Children's Bureau 2020), https://www.childwelfare.gov/pubpdfs/reunify.pdf [https://perma.cc /QCX4-UTDP].
37. MAXINE EICHNER, THE FREE MARKET FAMILY: HOW AMERICA CRUSHED THE AMERICAN DREAM (AND HOW IT CAN BE RESTORED) (2021).
38. CLARE HUNTINGTON, FAILURE TO FLOURISH: HOW LAW UNDERMINES FAMILY RELATIONSHIPS (2014).
39. Susan FitzGerald, *'Crack Baby' Study Ends with Unexpected but Clear Result*, PHILA. INQUIRER (June 21, 2017), http://www.philly.com/philly/health/ 20130721__Crack_baby__study_ends_with_unexpected_but_clear_result .html?arc404=true [https://perma.cc/98NN-BDQV].
40. *Council on Community Pediatrics, Poverty and Child Health in the United States*, 137(4) PEDIATRICS April 2016. Available at https://pediatrics .aappublications.org/content/137/4/e20160339 [https://perma.cc/SW43- JKY9].
41. Interview with Dr. Nzinga Harrison, Chief Medical Officer and Cofounder Eleanor Health (June 25, 2018).

INDEX

For EU product safety concerns, contact us at Calle de José Abascal, 56–1°,
28003 Madrid, Spain or eugpsr@cambridge.org.

www.ingramcontent.com/pod-product-compliance
Ingram Content Group UK Ltd.
Pitfield, Milton Keynes, MK11 3LW, UK
UKHW020353140625

459647UK00020B/2437